Technological Innovation, Multinational Corporations and New International Competitiveness

Studies in Global Competition
Edited by John Cantwell, University of Reading, UK

Volume 1
Japanese Firms in Europe
Edited by Frédérique Sachwald

Volume 2
Technological Innovation, Multinational Corporations and New International Competitiveness: The Case of Intermediate Countries
Edited by José Molero

This book is part of a series. The publishers will accept continuation orders which may be cancelled at any time and which provide for automatic billing and shipping of each title in the series upon publication. Please write for details.

Technological Innovation, Multinational Corporations and New International Competitiveness

The Case of Intermediate Countries

Edited by
José Molero
Universidad Complutense,
Madrid

LONDON AND NEW YORK

First published 1995 by Harwood Academic Publishers

Published 2013 by Routledge
2 Park Square, Milton Park, Abingdon, Oxfordshire OX14 4RN
711 Third Avenue, New York, NY, 10017, USA

First issued in paperback 2016

Routledge is an imprint of the Taylor & Francis Group, an informa business

---

British Library Cataloguing in Publication Data

Technological Innovation, Multinational
Corporations and New International
Competitiveness: The Case of Intermediate
Countries. – (Studies in Global
Competition; Vol. 2)
I. Molero, José II. Series
338.88

ISBN 13: 978-1-138-98377-9 (pbk)
ISBN 13: 978-3-7186-5685-1 (hbk)

Contents

Part II. Experiences from Europe and Latin America

Introduction to the series

This book series collects together high-quality research monographs written from various perspectives. The study of global competition is increasingly at the centre of an 'academic crossroads' at which different research programmes and methods of investigation are now meeting. In particular, global competition has become a focus of attention for researchers working in five areas: international business, business strategy, technological change, geographical or locational analysis, and European intergration. Most of these researchers have backgrounds in economics, geography or business strategy. The series will include books undertaken from these backgrounds on the global economy as a whole, corporate reorganization, national and corporate competitiveness, and the role of the city-regions.

John Cantwell

Contributors

JOSE ANTONIO ALONSO is a Doctor in Economics and professor of Applied Economics at the Complutense University of Madrid. His research areas are concentrated in international economics with special attention devoted to the export behaviours and internationalisation process of the firm. He has been a consultant for the Ministry of Trade and Tourism and AECI (Spanish Agency for International Cooperation) and other governmental agencies. Among his books the main ones are those written with Vicente Donoso. *Características y estrategias de la empresa exportadora española*, Madrid, 1985 and *Competitividad de la empresa exportadora española*, Madrid, 1994.

MIKEL BUESA is a Doctor in economics and Professor of Applied Economics at the Complutense University of Madrid. His research areas are concentrated in industrial development, with special attention devoted to the topic of internationalization and technological change. He has been a consultant for several Spanish Public institutions and of the Commission of the European and Latin American reviews. Among his books the main ones are those written with José Molero: *El Estado y el cambio tecnológico en la industrialización tardía. Un análisis del caso español* (1984), *Estructura Industrial de España* (1988) and *Patrones del cambio tecnológico y política industrial* (1992).

JOHN CANTWELL is Professor on International Economics at the University of Reading. He has been a Visiting Professor Of Economics at the University of Rome "La Sapienza", the University of the Social Sciences, Toulouse and Rutgers University, New Jersey. His main research areas are the economics of technological change and international production. He has especially worked on international aspects of technological change, and recently directed an Economic and Social Research Council funded project into the historical structure of innovative activity in the UK, Europe and the USA since 1890. He is also a former President of the European International Business Association.

MONTSERRAT CASADO is a Doctor in Economics. Since 1989 she has been a lecturer in International Economy at the Faculty of Economics of the Complutense University of Madrid. She has worked on the strategies of multinational corporations in Spain. Her main research areas are the internationalisation process of Spanish firms and technological flows between developed countries.

FRANÇOIS CHESNAIS, born in 1934 in Montreal, Canada. Educated in England and France. Permanent staff member of the Directorate for Science, Technology and Industry at the OECD in Paris from 1967 to 1992 with particular responsibilities for the planning and coordination of projects in the area of multinational enterprises, trade in high technology and international competitiveness. Overall editor of the final background report of the OECD Technology/Economy Programme (TEP). *Technology and the Economy: The Key Relationships*. PARIS, 1992. Now professor of International Trade and Investment at the Department of Economics and Management at Paris XIII University. Coauthor with C. Serfati of two books in French on the French military industry and arms trade, and author in English of a number of studies and articles on the role of multinational enterprises in the world economy.

DANIEL CHUDNOVSKY who holds a D. Phil. from Oxford University is Director of the Centro de Investigaciones para la Transformación (CENIT) in Buenos Aires and Professor of Development Economics at the University of Buenos Aires. His previous work experience includes several years as an Economic Affairs Officer in the Technology Division of UNCTAD and as Director of the Center for International Economics in Buenos Aires. He has also served as consultant to UNIDO, UNCTC, CEPAL, UNDP, IDB, EOCD Development Centre and the IDRC. Professor Chudnovsky has written extensively on trade, foreign investment and technology issues.

JORGE KATZ was born in Buenos Aires, Argentina in 1940. He received a First Degree in Economics at the University of Buenos Aires and completed his Doctorate at Balliol College,

Oxford in 1967 with a dissertation entitled "Production Functions, Foreign Investment and Growth" which was published by North Holland Publishing Company in 1969. He has been Professor in Industrial Economics at the University of Buenos Aires for the last two decades and is presently Regional Adviser on Industrial and Technical Development at ECLAC Santiago, Chile. He also teaches a Graduate Course on Technology and Innovation at the University of Chile. He has published extensively both on the subject of Technology and Industrial Restructuring in Latin America and also on Issues related to the Structure and Behavior of the Health Sector of Latin American Countries.

FRANCO MALERBA is Associate Professor of economics at Bocconi University, Milán. After completing his post-graduate studies at Yale University, he has been teaching at the University of Brescia and at Bocconi University. He has been working in the field of the economics of innovation and technological change and he is the author of several books and articles. In particular, he has studied the semiconductor industry (The semiconductor business. The economics of rapid growth and decline, London, Pinter Publishers, 1985), learning processes within firms, the Italian national system of innovation. He is Associate Editor of the Journal of Evolutionary Economics and Industrial and Corporate Change.

JOSÉ MOLERO is a Doctor in Economics. He is Professor of Applied Economics at the Complutense University of Madrid and teaches Industrial Economy and Economy of Technical Change. He is the Director of the Research Institute for Industry and Finance and has been a consultant for many Spanish public bodies as well as for the Commission of the European Communities. His research areas include the economic analysis of technical change, the dynamics of industrialization processes and the internationalization of the economy. He is the author of numerous articles for European and Latin American reviews. Among his books the main ones are those written with Mikel Buesa: *El Estado y el cambio tecnológico en la industrialización tardía. Un análisis del caso español* (1984), *Estructura Industrial de España* (1988) and *Patrones del cambio tecnológico y política industrial* (1992).

LUIGI ORSENIGO is Associate Professor of Economic Policy at Bocconi University Milan. He took postgraduate studies at the Science Policy Research Unit, University of Sussex and afterwards he spent most of his academic career at Bocconi University. His work concerns the biotechnology industry (The Emergence of

Biotechnology. Institutions and markets in industrial innovation, London, Pinter Publishers, 1989), the empirical investigation of the patterns of innovative activities and evolutionary models of industrial dynamics. He is Associate Editor of Industrial and Corporate Change.

PARI PATEL is a Research Fellow at the ESRC funded Centre for Science, Technology, Energy and Environment Policy at the Science Policy Research Unit (SPRU), University of Sussex. He is an economist with 10 years' experience in technology policy issues. His main research interests are the measurement of technology at the firm, sectoral and national level.

KEITH PAVITT is Professor of Science and Technology Policy at Sussex University in England. He studied engineering, industrial management and economics at Cambridge (UK) and Harvard (USA), and then worked at the Organisation for Economic Co-operation and Development (OECD) in Paris. During his 20 years at the Science Policy Research Unit, he has published widely on the management of technology, and science and technology policy. His central research interests are the nature and measurement of technology, and of the reasons why countries, companies and sectors differ in their rates and directions of technical change.

Professor Pavitt advises numerous national and international bodies on policies for technical change. He has been a Visiting Lecturer at Princeton University, Visiting Professor at the Universities of Aalborg, Limière-Lyon 2, Nice, Padua, Paris-Dauphine, Reading and Strasbourg (Louis Pasteur); and Visiting Scholar at Stanford University. He is a main editor of *Research Policy.*

VITOR CORADO SIMOES is Assistant Professor at ISEG (Instituto Superior de Economía e Gestao), Technical University of Lisboa. He has been Presidente of EIBA (European International Business Association) and Portuguese delegate to the E.C. Committee on Innovation and Technology Transfer. He is currently a member of the CIS (Community Innovation Survey Steering Committee). His main research interests focus on technology transfer, innovation policy and international investment. He has published several articles on these topics, and has worked as a consultant to the E.C. Commission, UNIDO and UNCTC.

Acknowledgements

A book like this has a very long list of people and institutions behind it. In order to be brief – but not ungrateful – I wish to start with my two best colleagues and friends, Mikel Buesa and Montserrat Casado. It is quite impossible to separate their contributions from my own work throughout the last six years of researching on MNCs and competitiveness in the Spanish economy. Many other colleagues of our department have stimulated our work with criticisms and suggestions. To all of them our gratitude.

A second important place belongs to the groups which collaborated with us in the research on foreign firms investing in Spain: the FAST team of Berlin, directed by Michael Wortman and Professor Van Dijck from the University of Tilburg.

In all the stages we had the support of national and international institutions among which I want to mention the outstanding help we got from the Stiftung Volkswagenwerk, the Erasmus Programme and the IMADE (Madrid Development Institute). Additionally I have to remember the aid of my University in organizing the Summer Course at El Escorial in August 1993; six of the then chapters of the book were presented there as discussion papers.

I cannot forget the contributions of my colleagues from UK, France, Italy, Portugal, Argentina and Chile. Behind most of them there are strong links of research collaboration and personal friendship.

In the European context, a central place is occupied by our communication with the SPRU at the University of Sussex, due to a great extent to the incentives and teaching received from Keith Pavitt over the past years. More recently, our contacts have been reinforced by the collaboration with the University of Reading, where we have found a permanent help from John Cantwell, especially for the preparation of this book.

Similar cases are the relationships we have with the Bocconi University of Milan, thanks to Luigi Orsenigo; the ISEG of the Technical University of Lisbon, in which Vitor C. Simoes is a crucial figure, and, more recently, with the Paris-Nord University through the magnanimous collaboration of François Chesnais. Let me say now that all this network can not be understood without the wise advice of Dudley Seers in the time he created the "European Periphery Group" in the seventies. This was one of the many projects coming from his enthusiastic activity in the Institute of Development Studies at the University of Sussex.

Our collaboration with Latin American colleagues is very long-standing. A clear example is the common work done with the ECLA on many occasions, always with the support of Jorge Katz, Osvaldo Sunkel and Anibal Pinto. The collaboration with many other regional institutions is represented here by the CENIT of Argentina. Daniel Chudnovsky is a marvellous example of what we have learned from all of them. The memories and teachings of Raul Prebish, and Fernando Fajnzilber are alive among all of us.

Last but not least, I want to express my gratitude to Barry Readman for his help and patience with my poor English. The mistakes you are going to find respond only to my clumsiness in learning from his teaching.

Introduction

1. NEW PERSPECTIVES ON COMPETITIVENESS

It is a truism to assert nowadays that economic efficiency and its reflection in competitiveness is ruled by elements which differ amply from those prevailing in the international economy until very recently. The changes, openly manifested since the crisis of the seventies, have substantially modified most aspects of the social life and the economic operation as well. In fact, we have witnessed profound transformations ranging from the most general aspects down to very microeconomic characteristics of the firm's structure.

As in previous times of change, especially the interwar period, the substitution of the old rules and mechanisms by the new ones is taking a longer period than many analysts foresaw. After two decades of very rapid shifts we still have a by no means negligible part of the economy in a sort of "middle of the road" situation, where old and new parameters coexist. This uneven process causes high uncertainty and shows us a panorama which is very difficult to understand in its totality.

Nevertheless, it is possible to approach this new situation as a new "techno-economic paradigm (TEP)". A TEP refers not only to a new range of products and systems but also to most of all the dynamics of the relative cost structure of all possible inputs to production. Each new TEP has to have a particular input or set of inputs, which may be described as "key factors" and which fulfil the following conditions (Freeman & Perez, 1988, p. 48).

1) Clearly perceived low and rapidly falling relative costs

(. . .). Only major and persistent changes have the power to transform decision rules and "common sense" procedures for engineers and managers.

2) Apparently almost unlimited availability of supply over a long period.
3) Clear potential for the use or incorporation of the new key factor or factors in many products and processes throughout the economic system.

This is not the place to make an in depth exposition of the complex set of elements included in the comparison of new and old TEPS. For that purpose other works can be consulted (Freeman & Perez, 1988; Freeman & Oldham, 1991). However we are going to comment briefly on some parts which are crucial for the understanding of the present book.

With a central role played by the economic analysis of innovation, the literature about the recent economic changes emphasizes perhaps that the major external evidence has to do with the enormous importance of factors related to human knowledge. From that general idea several aspects can be derived.

First we must highlight the firm's use of technology. On the one hand, there is an increasing use of different production technologies. It is a consequence of both a greater availability of technologies coming from science and technology development in most sectors (technological *opportunities*) and a greater possibility of controlling their fruits (*appropriability*). Practically the same reflexion can be made for organizing technologies.

On the other hand, the role of firms as active agents in technology creation has been growing in recent times, confirming what was lucidly foreseen by Schumpeter. Both macro-statistics and microeconomic studies prove this higher activity and the consequent greater importance of firms within national systems of innovation.

This process is partly an answer of the firms to contextual changes. Certainly the more uncertain the economy is accumulating and the more accelerated the obsolescence is the greater is the need for acceding to knowledge inputs. They serve to have higher possibilities of foreseeing the changes and facing them. Unlike the rigidity of most real assets, human knowledge appears as flexible and versatile. Thus the competition is situated in a framework broader than a simple non- price competition.

As the sciences and technologies are growing faster and increasing in their complexity, there is a greater possibility of combining many different sources of innovation for an wider variety of applications. This process reinforces the importance of the elements more tacitly linked to the organization and the persons involved. Here we find the impossibility of just "importing" knowledge from outside the firm to solve the new demands. This process highlights even more strongly the importance of different forms of learning for productive organizations. In this direction recent literature emphasises that even explicit R & D activities serve the goal of increasing the learning capacities inherent to the firms (Cohen & Levinthal, 1989).

There have been multiple attempts to classify the economic branches according to their technological content. Most of them emphasize the critical function of "high tech" sectors in the new economic dynamism. Without denying that point today there is a growing awareness about the importance of incorporating a larger notion. Within it the technological capability of a firm or sector has to be studied together with its structural relationships with other firms, sectors, institutions and infrastructures. Thus, faced with a limited version of "high tech", we can find out a more systemic one (Chesnais, 1991a).

The process of national economies opening their doors to international competition is not new. It has been coming out since the 1950's, whatever the analytical approach adopted. Therefore what is really new is the extent and depth of the opening and its relationships with the growth in the internationalization of the economy.

The first point in turn refers to three complementary factors. First, the incorporation of liberal economic approaches by many countries which previously pursued protectionist policies. It has been the case of many developing countries that for decades have had strong incentives to develop national industries in a pattern of import-substituting strategies (Katz, 1993; Fajnzylber, 1990).

A second major element in this liberal wave is closely linked to the economic transition of most of the former communist countries and their integration into international competition.

Finally, the industrialized nations are also practising more liberal policies regarding international competition. It is a consequence of the success of the liberal ideology after the international crisis of the seventies. In many cases, these policies have been legitimated and reinforced by the requirements of economic integration processes. The European Union is a paradigmatic example although similar experiences can be seen today in the renewed integration trends of Latin America.

As has been said, liberalization is closely related to the acceleration of an economy's internationalization and a renewed role played by Multinational Corporations (MNCS). Certainly the second half of the 1980's has seen a very fast growth of foreign direct investments (FDI) which had the following basic features.

First of all, the group of developed countries continues being the principal agent of outflows with around 97% of total outputs in the period 1986–90. More important is the fact those countries have considerably increased their share in total inflows. While in the first half of the decade they received 75% of world FDI, in the second their share grew up to 83%, according to IMF data. A large part of this phenomenon refers to the new dynamism of the USA as a receiving country.

The real position of less developed countries (LDCS) has to be understood by considering two additional factors. The first has to do with the growth of the FDI they received. In the first five years the average annual rate of incoming FDI was 4%, while in the following five it was 22%. The decline in total share is due to the faster growth shown by developed countries' inflows which grew 24% per year between 1985 and 1990. The second factor is that a major part of that inflow belongs to a reduced number of countries; ten of them account for about 50% of total LDCS receipts.

Another significant characteristic is the fast increasing of service- related activities. To the share of more classic services like finances or tourism, we have to add other branches of a firm's services which include a wide series of activities such as advertising, leasing, consultancy , etc.

A high proportion of new FDI corresponds to mergers and takeovers. Behind it we find other complex transformations related to the restructuring of activities both inside each country and at an international level. In many cases the results lead to higher levels of concentration. That process has had special peculiarities in many LDCS because it was associated with their reorientation within the international economy (Chudnovsky, 1994; Katz, 1993; Lall, 1987).

Perhaps the element which has produced most differences of

opinion is the new pattern of technological behaviour the MNCS have been developing in recent years. In previous times the technological activity of MNCS had a crucial impact on the international economy basically through their activity in technology transfer (Vaitsos, 1977; Katz, 1976). therefore the novelty lies in other factors, principally in the growing number of firms establishing R&D departments as well as other less formalized activities in countries different from their headquarters'. The internationalization of R&D is thus a key question and one very frequently quoted as a cause of the globalization of the economy.

The "globalization" topic arises from a cluster of empirical data which show how in many branches and areas of activity, there is a small number of relevant firms operating and there are no national boundaries to competition. So in sectors like finances, telecommunications, aerospace, semiconductors, etc., there exists real world-wide competition among a reduced number of firms. That competition comprises all the firm's aspects from personnel training to technology creation (Porter, 1990; OCDE, 1992; Chesnais, 1991a; Buckley, 1993; Dunning, 1993).

However, later debates and more precise empirical evidence are now showing this is in many ways exaggerated, at least in its most radical version. It is not a matter of denying the increasing level of internationalization the world economy is undergoing, but to insist that "national" factors are still significant for most multinational corporations. What can be true for all fields of economic activity is much more evident for the specific area of technology creation. Different authors have commented on that point in recent works (Patel & Pavitt, 1991; Cantwell, 1993a; Casson, 1991).

Most of the significant factors related to oligopolistic competition have been already put forward. There is only an additional qualitative element I want to underline. The new framework established by the economic crisis and its direct consequences on increasing uncertainty and costs — especially those related to technological developments — forced drastic organization shifts on many firms, mostly if they operate at the international level. One principal trajectory of these changes refers to modifying some of the classic elements usually taken into account when they have to decide between the market and internal economic transactions (Williamson, 1985).

The new phenomenon of networks and strategic agreement proliferation is a direct consequence of such response (Michalet,

1991; Mytelka, 1991). a strategic agreement gives a higher degree of flexibility between the two classic rationalities: the "market-liberal transaction" and the "internal-hierarchical organization". nevertheless, there is a clear loss of independence and a risk of one part being taken over by its partner at the end of the process.

Summing up we can arrive at a final picture where FDI requirements are today absolutely different from what they were years ago. Geographical changes registered by international statistics are only a superficial reflection of the new economic and technological conditions comprising the new pattern of internationalization. Multinational corporations are now looking for other explicit and tacit inputs, which are more knowledge intensive. As far as their organization is concerned, they are searching for other models which contradict very fundamentally the traditional dichotomy of internal-external decision-making strategies.

The responses of the economic analysis to the above changes have been slow and incomplete. Of course there is nothing similar to a perfect theory of the new international competitiveness, rather there are different partial advances within several theoretical fields. Let us refer briefly to some of those most directly related to our research.

The industrial economy in its classic expression had many difficulties even for analysing the market structures at an international level. It was born with the aim of being a scientific support for implementing policies which can reorganize market competition when it detaches itself from the ideal efficient structure. Thus it implicitly assumed the national scenario for the empirical research and theoretical reflexion. Of course, part of this analysis — concentration, entry barriers, etc. — can be used if we extend the empirical field to the world economy. The problem is the difficulties in obtaining statistically valid information increase extraordinarily and in many cases hinder the study.

Recent contributions coming from the economy of technical change have been more significant. Although it has contacts with industrial economy tradition, many of the new contributions form part of what has been called the evolutionary theory of innovation, which directly lead us to Schumpeter. In the last decade different authors (Nelson & Winter, 1982; Rosenberg, 1975; Freeman, 1982; Pavitt, 1984; Dosi, 1984) have produced important works, all of them realizing the central role of innovation both for micro and macro dynamics. far from previous and still prestigious approaches, which focused on technical change as an exogenous determinant, the new approach emphasizes the endogenous character of innovation.

The richness of the reality has made it possible to abandon an analysis of which the central aim was to find out the determinant elements of the market structure that stimulate or retard the creation and diffusion of innovations (Kamien & Schwart, 1982; Scherer, 1980). The accumulation of empirical research showed it was a wrong perspective because it ignored two crucial facts. First, in a dynamic world market structures are to a great extent the consequence of technological innovation, so static relationships are of little interest.

Secondly, instead of a sole way of innovating, real economy brings us a large variety of experiences. We have to explain diversity rather than determinism. Hence a new school has been established which starts from a better understanding of the features of technology. So the central objective of this theory is to explain the real innovative process using a method where taxonomy and comparison occupy central places (Pavitt, 1984; Orsenigo, 1989). the fundamental role of technology change in the economic dynamic has contributed to the increasing influence of this very stimulating renewal on many other theoretical areas.

Economic growth analysis is one of these areas receiving that impact. In fact, in recent years, the theory itself made interesting efforts to bring itself nearer to the real changing world through the introduction of non-classic assumptions, such as external economies, market imperfections and scale economies (Lucas, 1988; Romer, 1990). In a more applied version, there have been important efforts to answer the very central question of why rates of growth differ. The response is found to be closely related to technical change, especially if it is not identified with R&D (Fagerberg, 1988).

A very similar trajectory can be seen in international trade theory. Here, starting from attempts to solve the well known Leontieff paradox about USA trade specialization, there have been many contributions that in one way or another incorporated the technological factor (Wells, 1969; Vernon, 1966; Posner, 1961; Huffbauer, 1986). More recently a flow of renovation came from the innovation theory. It provides new proof of the close relationship there is between technological change and international trade (Dosi, Pavitt & Soete, 1990).

Also the theory of multinational corporations is nowadays influenced by advances in technical progress understanding. Through the accumulation of research work about MNCS' behaviour in technical innovation the literature is enlarging its considerations on MNCS' role in the creation of technological capabilities and their international diffusion. The basic features of the technology – for instance, its being a specific knowledge and embodied in social organizations – has been used to develop a new understanding of technological competition (Cantwell, 1993). Additional considerations have been made trying to incorporate to that approach the connexion among firms and between them and some socio-economic structures. Thus, technological competitiveness is explained as a structural competition in which micro, meso and macro economic elements take place (Chesnais, 1991b; Porter, 1990, Patel & Pavitt, 1991).

Interestingly all this renewal is pushing the debate to an area which recovers the interest in industrial policy, after many years of abandonment in favour of the liberal philosophy (Krugman, 1993; Porter, 1990). that debate is even looking back to contributions from development studies about which their creators had very critical positions (Hirschman, 1980). In many countries the concept of economic structure was used during decades to look for a more adapted approach to their realities. After the transformations which occurred throughout the seventies and eighties they laid aside their search for originality. Nowadays, perhaps coming again form the North, we have to rescue our "obsolete" perspective about industrial policy.

WHY INTERMEDIATE COUNTRIES?

Having seen a general revision of the international preoccupations which surround this book, it is time to say a word about why a specific group of countries formed with South European economies and some of the most industrialized of Latin America.

From an analytical point of view the reason for studying a group of countries lies in some structural differences we realize exist between them and all the leading economies. Three arguments can summarize these differences.

The first has to do with entrepreneurial organization. The basic point is these countries do not have a significant number of large international companies. Thus most theories about multinational corporations are not so useful to explain their international position. That is the case, for instance, of models based on vertical integration or complex structures related to firm's advantages. On the contrary, we need other approaches which could see internationalization much more as a gradual process based on the accumulative experience of the firm.

A second argument is their industrial structure is more dependent on traditional sectors. So, the way in which technical progress takes place is qualitatively different from the cases of more advanced countries. Instead of more explicit and ready to codify elements (e.g. patents) we have to pay more attention to factors like capital good production and importation or new commercialization practices.

Finally, their technological levels give a greater importance to assimilation in comparison with other innovative tasks. This obliges us to start from another analytical perspective in studying technical change and competitiveness.

Other sorts of reasons can be added to justify our selection. When in the seventies our research group started its work on Spanish economic internationalization, we dealt with a quite closed nation. In the midst of a very profound economic crisis it tried to find a new course in the international economy. Many of us (Molero, 1986; Donoso, Molero, Munoz, Serrano, 1980) always thought we had to complement our priority orientation towards Europe; we were thinking of Latin America economies. The reason was not only our cultural linkages, — incidentally, more and more concrete as important "economic" elements about internationalization possibilities — there were as well two other real factors to consider.

The first has to do with the crucial role played by Latin American countries in the first wave of Spanish outward internationalization. Even today this region is very significant for the international expansion of Spanish firms (Molero, 1993).

The second argument is based upon the existence of an interesting parallelism between the Spanish industrialization process and others developed in several industrialized countries of Latin America. This is based, on the one hand, on the degrees of industrialization which, in spite of real differences, can be reasonably compared. On the other hand, the industrial policy established in Spain until the middle of the seventies was very similar to the import substitution developed in Latin America (Buesa & Molero, 1988). Thus, many present problems can be analyzed in the light of these historical similarities, as we have done in other works (Molero, 1986; Donoso, Molero, Munoz, Serrano, 1980). With regard to European nations our coincidences are particularly clear with Southern countries. From a general point of view, the degree of development is more comparable to Italy and Portugal than to the central or Northern countries. However there are other arguments which refer to structural similarities.

Years ago we made two different comparative studies for the Spanish economy, respectively about Portugal and EEC countries. They followed the methodology of Productive System Differentiation. We basically studied the similarities and differences existing in the weighted value added sectorial distribution. Our results showed that, among European economies and without concealing their differences, Portugal and Italy had the two most similar structures (Molero & Buesa; Buesa & Molero, 1988).

More recently other international comparisons of international Revealed Technological Advantages have shown the Spanish industry sectoral pattern has important similarities with the Italian case (Patel & Pavitt, 1991a). Unfortunately we have not any similar comparison with Portugal. The statistics used for this analysis USA Patent Office – do not provide enough data for the comparison. Nonetheless, in another general comparative study (Molero & Bastos, 1991) we commented on the similarity of the two Iberian countries evolutions after their entry into the EEC.

In comparative studies nothing is perfectly equal and we can work with practically any group of countries. However we have shown scientific justifications for proceeding the way we did. Moreover there are other reasons I want to make explicit. In the present moment of difficulties in the construction of Europe, it is increasingly realized that the structural differences among economies are the basis of the problems to converge as the Maastricht agreement foresaw. For different reasons, Mediterranean countries have many common problems to discuss together, particularly if the new enlargement of the European Union is to the North. Hence, to know something else about their common pattern and of course about their many differences in the new competitive world seems to be a worthwhile undertaking.

From another point of view it is a permanent factor that Spain wishes to improve the relationships between Latin America and the European Union and there are data to maintain Portugal and Italy are also very interested in the same question. Again, to know better the experience of those not so distant countries is a worthy task today.

I know here I have presented an ambitious goal that, at best, will need more efforts than this book represents. Nevertheless I find very stimulating the opportunity we have had to advance in this direction and to clarify a little the future of some intermediate countries of which Spain is a very clear international example.

ORGANIZATION AND CONTENT OF THE BOOK

To achieve those objectives the book has been organized in two parts. The first one deals with the new perspectives of international competitiveness, with special attention devoted to the role of MNCS in the creation of technological capabilities. The second part has to do with case studies covering most South European economies and recent Latin American experiences.

The contributions of the first half combine the accumulation of international empirical evidences with the analytical work. Thus, Cantwell starts from a new concept of innovation and enters into the analysis of a new vision of technology creation and transfer which takes into account two components: first is the public knowledge element of technology, and second a cluster of tacit elements embodied in the organizational routines of the firms. A crucial part of the chapter consists of the analysis of the role those aspects play in the creation of international capabilities.

The development of global technological advantage is the topic of Patel & Pavitt's contribution. They also start from the fact that it is widely recognised that accumulation of technology is a necessary condition for improved economic performance and international competitiveness. Nonetheless the debate continues to surround the degree of importance of large firms in accumulating technology and the nature and degree of the links between such large firms and their home country. The paper presents evidence in order to clarify this debate using data from more than 500 of the world largest companies from the 11 leading countries.

Chesnais' chapter refers to international competition in the context of global markets. Thus, the "global" economy is the locus of the decisive forms of competition; a single but differentiated arena as the basis for global oligopoly and the new modes of rivalry, allowing for interfirm agreements among oligopolists; standards and norms as key issues in the competition/cooperation relationship; home economies as bases for successful rivalry; and governments and firms and the competitiveness of national economies.

Confronted with the existence of market failures Katz discusses the technology policy. After an analysis of the import substitution path to industrialization in most LDCS, the author considers the new requirements of policy actions derived from situations where stabilization efforts are accompanied by the de-regulation of markets, and the opening up of the economy to foreign competition. In this context the problems of market failures in the creation, diffusion and utilization of technical knowledge give way to the need for an explicit technological policy.

The internationalization of the firm is viewed as a learning process by Alonso who deals with the theory of internationalization of the firm combining macro and microeconomic approaches. On the one hand, it debates the available conventional theories and their weaknesses; the alternative consists of the utilization of sectoral classifications close to Pavitt's taxonomy. On the other, the author uses different microeconomic theories to solve most of the deficiencies arising from the macro perspective.

The content of the second part refers to the particular experiences of Europe and Latin America. The analysis of European countries has as a centre the Spanish experience which is compared to the two nearest cases of Portugal and Italy.

Orsenigo concentrates the study on the technological innovation and international competitiveness of the Italian economy. Two clusters of problems arise in this study; in the first, the author analyses the main features of the Italian "National System of Innovation" and the evolution of innovative activities in order to show the structural features of the sectoral patterns of Italian innovative activities. In the second, he deals with the patterns of internationalization of Italian industry in relation to its trade performance.

The innovation and internationalization of the Portuguese industry is dealt with by Simoes on the basis of a new perspective for the study of "middle of the road" countries which refers to innovation patterns in Portuguese industry. Taking this framework into consideration, the author studies the innovation and foreign investment in Portugal. A crucial complement for the understanding of this case is the role played by licensing and technology upgrading in Portuguese firms.

The analysis of the Spanish case is carried out through two contributions coming from the same research programme. In the first one Molero, Buesa & Casado discuss the reasons underlying the fast growth of FDI in the Spanish industry. As the international literature shows, one of the most significant factors is the role of the domestic market, vis-a-vis the international one. Thus, the study continues by debating the strategic behaviour of MNCS operating in Spain with regard to the balance between local and external markets.

The second chapter on Spain is devoted to the analysis of the role of MNCS in the technological development of the Spanish industry. To achieve this goal, the study is organized in two complementary parts. The first has to do with the study of the technological strategies of MNCS' subsidiaries, based on samples covering German and Dutch firms operating in Spain. The second refers to a comparison of technological regimes of foreign firms with Spanish innovative companies, on the basis of other research done with a large group of innovative firms (national and foreign) established in the Madrid region.

The last chapter of the book undertakes the analysis of the changing role of MNCS in recent Latin American industrialization. Chudnovsky studies the recent recovery in foreign direct investment in Latin America industry under the light of the changing conditions that have prevailed in the region in the 1980s. The implementation of stabilization-cum-structural adjustment programmes aims to transform the traditional import substitution industrialization process into an outward oriented one. Hence, one principal objective of the study is to know the strategies played by MNCS throughout this change in which regional integration tendencies have a revitalizing role.

REFERENCES

Buckley, P. (1993): "The role of management in internationalisation theory". *Management International Review*, 3/93.

Buesa, M. & Molero, J. (1988): *Estructura Industrial de España.* Fondo de Cultura Económica. Madrid.
Cantwell, J. (1991): "The International Agglomeration of R & D". In: Casson (1991).
Cantwell, J.(1993): *Multinational Corporations and Innovatory Activities*: Towards a New, Evolutionary Approach. Included in this book.
Cantwell, J. (1993a): *The Internationalisation of Technological Activity in Historical Perspective.* Proceedings of the 19th Annual Conference of EIBA. Lisbon, December.
Casson, M. (Ed.) (1991): *Global Research Strategy and International Competitiveness.* Basil Blackwell. Oxford.
Cohen, W.M. & Levinthal, D.A. (1989) "Innovation and Learning: the two faces of R & D". *The Economic Journal*, 99. September.
Chesnais, F. (1991a): "Preface". In L.K.Mytelka (ed), (1991).
Chesnais, F. (1991b): "La competitividad tecnologica como competitividad estructural". In F. Chesnais: *Competitividad Internacional y Gastos Militares.* Ediciones Ejercito. Madrid.
Chudnovsky, D.(1994): *The TNCS's changing strategies in the Latin American manufacturing sector.* Included in this book.
Donoso,V.; Molero,J; Munoz,J. & Serrano,A (ed). (1980). *Transnacionalización y Dependencia.* Cultura Hispánica. Madrid.
Dosi, G. (1984): Technical Change and Industrial Transformation. Macmillan. London.
Dosi, G. et al.(1988): *Technical Change and Economic Theory.* Pinter. London.
Dosi, G.; PAvitt, k & sOETE, L. (1990). *The economics of technical change and international trade.* Harverster-Wheatsheaf. London.
Dunning, J. (1993): *The Globalization of Business.* Routledge. London.
Dunning, J. (1994): "Multinational enterprises and the globalization of innovatory capacity". *Research Policy*, 23.
Fagerberg, J. (1988) "Why growth rates differ", In Dosi et al (ed), (1988).
Fajnzylber, F: (1990): "Sobre la impostergable transformación productiva de América Latina". *Pensamiento Iberoamericano*, 16.
Freeman, Ch. (1982): *The Economics of Industrial Innovation.* (2°_ edition) Pinter. London.
Freeman, Ch & Oldham, C. H. G. (1991). "Introduction: beyond the single market". In, Freeman, Ch.; Sharp, M. & walker, W. (eds)(1991): *Technology and the future of Europe.* Pinter. London.
Freeman, Ch. & Perez, C. (1988): "Structural crisis of adjustment, business cycles and investment behaviour". In: G. Dosi et al. (1988).
Freeman, Ch. (ed) (1990): *The economics of innovation.* Aldershot, Edward Elgar. London.
Hirschman, A. (1980): "Auge y ocaso de la teoría del desarrollo". *El Trimestre Económico, n_ 188, Octubre-Diciembre.*
Hufbauer, G. (1986): *Synthetic Materials and the Theory of International Trade.* Harvard University Press. Cambridge, Mass.
Kamien, M.I. & Schwartz, N.L. (1982): *Market Structure and Innovation.* Cambridge University Press. Cambridge.
Katz, J. (1976): *Importación de Tecnología, aprendizaje e Industrialización Dependiente.* Fondo de Cultura Económica. México.

Katz, J. (1993): *Organización Industrial, Competitividad Internacional y Política Pública en la Década de los Anos Noventa.* Mimeo. ECLA. Santiago.
Krugman, P. (1993): "Toward a counter- counterrevolution in Development Theory". In *Proceedings of the World Bank annual Conference on Development Economics.* Washington, 1993.
Lall, S. (1987): *Developing countries as exporters of technology: a first look at the Indian experience.* McMillan. London.
Lucas, R. E. (1988): "On the mechanics of economic development". *Journal of Monetary Economics,* 22.
Michalet, Ch-A. (1991) "Strategic partnerships and the changing internationalization process". In L. K. Mytelka (ed), (1991).
Molero, J. (1986): "La exportación de tecnología y la experiencia de América Latina". In: Minian, I. (ed): *Industrias Nuevas y Estrategias de Desarrollo en América Latina.* CIDE. México.
Molero, J. (1993): La internacionalización de la empresa española en América Latina: inversiones directas y transferencia de tecnología. Workshop on "Foreign Direct Investment in The Third World: The case of Latin America". IRELA&EEC. Segovia, 10/12 June.
Molero, J. & Buesa, M. (1987): "Las relaciones económicas entre España y Portugal. Informe sobre las estructuras productivas y comparadas de ambos paises, las inversiones españolas en Portugal y la exportación de tecnología española a empresas portuguesas". In G. Clausse & M.C. Esteves: *As relaÇoes Luso-espanholas no contexto de adhesao a CEE.* Instituto de Estudos para o Desenvolvimento, Lisbon.
Molero, J. & Bastos, L. (1991): "As relaÇoes Económicas entre Espanha e Portugal após a Entrada na CEE". *Vertice,* n° 44. Noviembre.
Mytelka, L. K.(ed) (1991): *Strategic Partnerships and the World Economy.* Pinter. London.
Nelson, R. R. & Winter, S. G. (1982): *An evolutionary theory of economic change.* Harvard University Press. Cambridge, Mass.
OECD (1992): *Technology and the Economy. The key relationship.* Paris.
Orsenigo, L. (1989): *The Emergence of Biotechnology.* Printer. London.
Patel, P. & Pavitt, K. (1991): "Large firms in the production of the world's technology: an important case of non-globalization". *Journal of International Business Studies,* vol. 1.
Patel, P & Pavitt, K. (1991a): "Europe's technological performance". In.: CH. Freeman; M. Sharp & W. Walker (eds) *op. cit.*
Pavitt, K. (1984): "Sectoral patterns of technical change: towards a taxonomy and theory". *Research Policy,* 6.
Porter, M. (1990): *The Competitive Advantage of Nations.* Free Press, New York.
Posner, M. V. (1961): "International trade and technical change". *Oxford Economic Papers,* vol. 13.
Rosenberg, N. (1975): *Perspectives on Technology.* Cambridge University Press. Cambridge.
Romer, P. (1990): "Endogenous technological change". *Journal of Political Economy,* 98.
Scherer, F. M. (1980): *Industrial Market Structure and Economic Performance.* Houghton Mifflin Company. Boston.

Vaitsos, C. (1977): *Intercountry Income Distribution and Transnational Enterprises*. Clarendon Press. London.

Vernon, R. (1966): "International investment and International Trade in the Product Cycle". *Quarterly Journal of Economics*. vol. 80.

Wells, L.T. (1969). "Test of a product cycle model of international trade: US export of consumer durables". *Quarterly Journal of Economics*. vol. 13.

Williamson, O.E. (1985): *The Economic Institution of Capitalism*. The Free Press. New York.

PART I
NEW PERSPECTIVES ON INTERNATIONAL COMPETITIVENESS

Multinational Corporations and Innovatory Activities: Towards a New, Evolutionary Approach

John Cantwell[1]

I. THE DEVELOPMENT OF THE CONCEPTS OF INNOVATION AND TECHNOLOGY

Innovation entails a change in production, either in the processes employed or in the products created. Innovations normally involve a combined or related change of both processes (including organisational methods) and products. The most notable feature in the development of some of the recent literature on multinational corporations (MNCs) and innovatory activities has been a growing convergence in the use made of the concepts of innovation and technological change. The earliest literature on MNCs and innovation certainly focused on technological progress, but it did not usually treat technological improvements as synonymous with innovation. Instead, technological change was viewed as a special case of a change in production (see, for example, Mansfield, 1974). The typical definition of technology was a narrow one, an engineering concept which described the mechanics of production processes and the physical characteristics of the products made. In

[1] I am grateful to Mark Casson, John Dunning and Karl Sauvant for helpful comments on an earlier draft. This paper is adapted from my introduction to the book I have edited on *Transnational Corporations and Innovatory Activities*, which will be published as Volume 20 in the United Nations Library on Transnational Corporations (London, Routledge, forthcoming).

this narrow sense technology can be understood as the output of the research and development (R&D) and production engineering functions of a firm. This narrow definition of technology remains the accepted orthodoxy in the passing references made to technology in many other areas of economics, but it has been gradually abandoned by most economists working on technology (and innovation) as such. In the current literature on MNCs and technology a division now exists between scholars who continue to use the narrow definition, and those that have adopted the new approach.

The new definition of technology is the broader one that describes the features of an entire production system, a concept which encompasses all aspects of the organisation of production. Using this definition there is no longer any need to separate technological innovation from organisational innovation, as technological progress encompasses organisational change. Organisational changes had appeared either as an afterthought or as a quite separate matter in some of the earlier literature. Under the wider definition of technology, innovation and technological change are brought into a closer correspondence with one another, at least with respect to production systems (excluding financial innovations or marketing innovations). Changes in engineering design are closely allied to changes in the collective capabilities of production teams and their methods of work, and all such changes can be viewed as part of the common process of technological innovation. Technology in the broader sense can also be appreciated as crucial to service sector MNCs, where the analysis of technology in the narrower perspective is generally restricted to firms in manufacturing and resource-based activities.

One reason why the narrow definition of technology as an engineering concept was so readily accepted in the literature on MNCs and innovation was that MNCs were regarded as being distinctive from other firms only for their role in international technology transfer or diffusion. Therefore, even writers whose interests extended beyond technology transfer to issues of innovation, generally began by considering innovation as it applied to all firms, before considering the particular contribution of MNCs as agents of technology diffusion (see, for example, Parker, 1974). What is internationally diffused both between firms and within MNCs is principally scientific and engineering knowledge, and so it was natural to focus upon this. It is only quite recently that attention has shifted away from the MNC for its contribution to technology transfer, and towards the MNC as an institution for international technology creation and innovation (Chesnais, 1988a). With an increasing intra-firm integration of affiliates since the late 1960s (Dunning, 1992), MNCs have established international networks for combined cross-border technological development (Cantwell, 1989). This involves a coordinated change in production structures, or in other words technological change in its broadest sense conducted at an international level.

There can be little doubt about the significance of MNCs as sources of technological innovation, and not just of international diffusion. The world's largest 700 or so industrial firms, which are comprised mainly of the leading MNCs, account for around half of the world's commercial inventions as measured by patent counts (Cantwell and Hodson, 1991; Patel and Pavitt, 1991a). Most of these MNCs originate from the major centres for production – the US, Japan, Germany, and a few other European countries – and this is also where their innovative activities are concentrated. The leading MNCs play an especially important role in the creation of science-based technologies in the fields of chemicals and electrical equipment, but they also feature prominently in other sectors in which mechanical or non-industrial technologies are to the fore (Patel and Pavitt, 1991b).

By comparison with the traditional literature on MNCs and technology transfer, some new discussions of MNCs and innovatory activities have started to find it convenient to take a wider view of technology, even though the measurement of technology continues to rely on more restrictively defined proxies such as R&D expenditure or patent counts. The new approach to MNCs and innovation has drawn heavily on an evolutionary view of the firm and the industry (Nelson and Winter, 1982), examining the accumulation of technology within the international networks of MNCs as a path-dependent corporate learning process (Cantwell, 1989; 1992a). Other representatives of this new evolutionary approach have focused on organisational change within the MNC as a learning process (Kogut, 1990; Teece, 1991). Successful learning establishes technological competence (Cantwell, 1992a) or organisational capabilities (Teece, 1991). What is specific about MNCs in this respect is their use of international networks for innovation, which is one aspect of the recent growth of network organisation in the MNC (Hedlund, 1986; Bartlett and Ghoshal,

1989). The new approach to MNCs and innovation also implies a different perspective on technology transfer, being concerned with its interaction with learning processes and not just with the immediate exchange of knowledge, as will be explained further below.

Under the new broader definition of technology as a system for production, two components of technology can be distinguished. First is the public knowledge element of technology, which encompasses codifiable items as represented in the engineering blueprints and designs and the scientific knowledge that constitute the narrower definition of technology, and to which can be added management manuals, handbooks describing organisational methods and the like in the new broader definition. However, even this first element of technology ranges somewhat beyond the underlying scientific and engineering (or management) principles that can be easily written down and (when they are novel) patented. The public element of technology includes individual practitioners' knowledge of the way such scientific and engineering principles are applied, or in other words the way things work in practice (Nelson, 1990). While this type of knowledge may be difficult or cumbersome to write down in full and needs to be individually learned through practice to be completely understood, it is possible to communicate such practical information between those that are already skilled in the art in question. Taken as a whole, this public aspect of technology is therefore analogous to information, in that in principle it can be exchanged between knowledgeable scientists, engineers and practitioners or managers. The term public knowledge is used here in the sense of being at least potentially public, even though devices such as patents or secrecy may delay its actual entry into the public domain.

Unlike the first, the second element of technology is not akin to information but is tacit, and is specific to particular firms or MNCs. This tacit element of technology is embodied in the organisational routines and collective expertise or skills of specific production teams (Nelson and Winter, 1982). This is the part of technology which differentiates firms or MNCs, and which cannot be exchanged between them as it is derived from and tied to the localised and collective learning experience of the teams of a given company through their own development of production. Hence, the new more comprehensive definition of technology incorporates that element which describes firm-specific competence in production. While the first element of technology may be traded between firms, the second element is the essence of firm-specific competitive advantage, which is non-tradable and relies instead on internal group learning processes.

The two elements of technology are strictly complementary, and cannot be used to create a functioning production system without one another. Thus, even though public knowledge can be exchanged, to make it operational it is necessary to develop some supporting expertise of a tacit kind. In doing so it is possible for one firm to imitate the tacit capability of another, but it can never copy it exactly since the learning experience of each firm and the route actually followed by a production team is unique. The precise course taken by any firm depends partly on chance but also upon its own past technological experience as encapsulated in its existing routines and team skills. Where inter-firm agreements for technological cooperation extend to technical assistance the costs of imitation may be reduced, but it is still necessary for each firm to go through its own particular learning process, with or without assistance.

The firm-specific character of the tacit element of technology is also likely to lead to a differentiation of the codifiable knowledge and designs that are actually used, and to lead to some public knowledge remaining firm-specific for a time. This is obvious where there are major differences in the technological competence of firms. The nature and the range of scientific principles and engineering designs employed by General Electric and by a Latin American based MNC producing electrical goods are quite different, even where they are serving the same market. Yet there is also a differentiation of the blueprints and knowledge used by say, General Electric, Westinghouse and Philips when serving the same market. The specific organisational routines of each company run in parallel to specialised knowledge in certain branches of science and engineering and to a particular set of codes devised to represent the designs in use in a style that is familiar to the members of its own production team. Thus, even the codifiable element of technology requires adaptation if it is exchanged between firms. Specific blueprints and the practical skills that accompany them sometimes appear to be technological advantages, partly because the blueprints can be patented, but more importantly because these designs and skills provide a reflection of a firm's tacit capacity, which is the true source of such competitive advantage.

Nelson (1982; 1990) has described the two complementary components of technology as its public and private elements. The public element of technology is an expression of generic knowledge, or of knowledge which is potentially generic in the sense that it is capable of being understood by suitably trained scientists, engineers and practitioners or managers in other firms or other countries. All that is needed is some translation of the specific codes typically used to articulate the knowledge for the purposes of the company that originally developed and applied it. Summarising information in a form in which it can be disseminated externally is sometimes undertaken by the firm itself, where it is involved in the exchange of knowledge or in a patent application. The first element of technology is a combination of actual and potential generic knowledge. It is a latent public good, in that once it has been created (and after allowing for the costs of adaptation to a general form) it can be made freely available to others. It is this aspect of technology that is rightly the focus of attention in studies of innovation diffusion, such as Griliches' (1957) classic investigation of the diffusion of hybrid corn, and similar studies of international diffusion processes (Hufbauer, 1965). Subject to the constraints of patenting and secrecy, all firms can gain access to a common pool of generic knowledge. Where a newly developed technological system is superior all surviving firms must manage a transition to a new production method (such as the take up of the Bessemer process in the steel industry) or a new product (such as hybrid corn or synthetic materials), by drawing on some common areas of generic knowledge. It is the generic properties of a technology that make it possible to give it a label that is widely understood (such as computerised and numerically controlled machine tools), and this public characteristic represents the part of technology that can be in principle systematically copied by all firms in the same industry or in different countries. It can therefore serve as a target towards which a collection of competitors all aim as occurs in the event of innovation diffusion.

However, diffusion usually follows a logistical process (described by a S-shaped curve), involving an initially gradual switch between one kind of technology and another. One reason for the slow take up of a superior new type of technology is uncertainty over its success, until it is clearly shown to reduce costs or raise product quality and hence demand. However, another reason is that in order to make the switch firms must undertake a costly learning process, in which they develop the tacit capability required to operationalise the generic knowledge associated with the new technology. It is the difficulty of doing this that constitutes the major barrier that delays international diffusion, especially to developing countries. Indeed, the initial uncertainty over the success of a new type of technology is itself an uncertainty over the outcome of the processes of learning by doing and using in the pioneer firms. The achievements they make in the course of critical revision of the new system may be matched in the first instance by continued or renewed learning as part of a response by competitors that retain the older type of technology.

The remainder of the paper begins with a reassessment of the association of MNCs with relatively high levels of R&D, and with R&D-intensive industries. Section II considers the role of the R&D function in the MNC in the light of the broader definition of technology outlined above. In sections III and IV the way in which various authors have interpreted the high R&D-intensity of MNCs is critically examined; some have viewed R&D as a principal source of the competitive advantages of MNCs, while others have explained the international operations of MNCs as a consequence of their internalisation of cross-border technology flows. Sections III and IV redirect attention to the overall innovatory capability of MNCs, and in this respect MNCs are distinguished from other firms (non-MNCs) not so much by their R&D-intensity as by their deployment of international networks for innovation and learning, which is the subject of section V. Some empirical evidence on the significance of these networks is also briefly reviewed. Section VI turns to the technological competitiveness of both new and established MNCs, and the impact of their activities on the competitiveness of countries. In the context of the broader recent evolutionary approach to MNCs and innovatory activities, some concluding remarks on the prospects for future research are set out in section VII.

II. THE ROLE OF THE R&D FUNCTION

Understanding technological innovation as a collective learning process has helped to clarify many of the issues raised in the literature on MNCs and innovation. This learning process brings together the creation, assimilation and adaptation of codifiable and other public knowledge on the one hand with the accumulation of tacit capability embodied in organisational routines on the other. One issue that has become better understood is the importance of research and development (R&D) to many MNCs. While some writers have focused exclusively on the R&D function, corporate research is just one of the contributors to the learning process. For MNCs, R&D is usually the most important source of new public knowledge. The significance of R&D varies between sectors, just as the relationship between public or potentially generic knowledge and tacit capability differs between industries. R&D and the creation of new public knowledge plays a more prominent role in the science-based industries that rely on chemical and electrical technologies, and is less prominent (although still significant) in the scale-intensive or specialised supplier lines of business which depend more heavily on mechanical technologies.

The contribution of R&D to technological innovation is of two kinds. R&D may be directly tied to production, for instance where it is required to devise and adapt products or processes in accordance with local conditions. Alternatively, the contribution of R&D to innovation may be indirect where it is less immediately tied to any particular production facility, while of course remaining cognisant of the overall needs and strategy of the firm. In this event R&D personnel may be called upon to assess or to attempt to recognise new technological opportunities through monitoring advances in generic knowledge made elsewhere, and increasing the ability of the firm to imitate the achievements of others more rapidly. This latter type of activity is more important in the science-based industries in which there are a broader range of potential technological opportunities and a greater variety of new generic knowledge to take into account.

R&D contributes to technological innovation by providing a supply of public knowledge which is used in harness with the systematic development of tacit capability through the evolution of collaborative skills and organisational routines. Therefore it is misleading to think of R&D as in general driving innovation (even though it plays a crucial role in the science-based sectors), since it also reflects what is achieved in the broader learning process, and thus what types of knowledge have become useful to the firm or at least worth exploring. Indeed, appreciating that innovation is a collective learning process helps to resolve the old debate over whether the essential source of technological change is science or research-push (sometimes called technology-push by those using the old narrower definition of technology) or demand-pull (Mowery and Rosenberg, 1979). Innovative learning instead gathers a certain cumulative and incremental logic of its own (Rosenberg, 1982; Pavitt, 1987), which interacts with but is not driven by the development of either science or market demand. Technology affects science and demand as much as the other way round. For example, the improvement of instrument technology has had a major impact on what is feasible in various branches of science. Likewise, it is the steady progress of computer technology that has created the growth in demand for computerised equipment rather than some exogenous change in consumer tastes or preferences.

It remains true that the R&D function gains in importance as technological development becomes more complex and sophisticated. A higher level of team skills and organisational expertise is associated with the creation and use of larger amounts of state of the art knowledge. Hence, R&D-intensity is greater in industries in which production tends to be more heavily differentiated across firms and dependent on specific skills, and the presence of MNCs tends to be more pronounced in these high research-intensive sectors. Similarly, within an industry, companies that have built up a more sophisticated technological competence tend to rely more on R&D than their competitors, and so MNCs (which on average have relatively high levels of accumulated expertise or competence) tend to be more research-intensive than other firms in the same sector. MNCs originating from more highly developed and hence technologically advanced countries also tend to run more extensive R&D operations than do MNCs based in less developed countries.

III. THE FIRST APPROACH TO THE HIGH R&D-INTENSITY OF MNCS: THEIR COMPETITIVE ADVANTAGES

Such observations have given rise to two separate accounts of why R&D-intensive firms are more likely to become MNCs. These two accounts, and criticisms of them, have come to dominate much of the literature on MNCs and innovation. The two strands of argument relate respectively to what Dunning (1988a) has termed the ownership advantages and internalisation advantages of MNCs. That is to say, R&D can be treated as a source of competitive advantage relative to other firms which enables MNCs to expand internationally (it provides them with ownership advantages); or alternatively R&D can be thought of as a source of highly specific intermediate products and knowledge, in which international transactions are most efficiently organised internally within MNCs (conferring internalisation advantages).

Both these lines of reasoning have been adapted somewhat as the discussion has developed more recently. In the first case some early debates had revolved around whether R&D was a more important source of competitive strength by comparison with the contribution made by the other functions or divisions of a MNC such as in advertising and marketing (Caves, 1982). Sceptics termed this the search for the elusive secret ingredient underpinning competitive success, and labelled more eclectic reviews of the same range of potential assets a shopping list of variables. However, cross-sectional empirical evidence did suggest that MNCs have a stronger presence in industries with higher R&D-intensity and higher advertising-intensity, and both these factors tend to be associated with higher industrial concentration at least up to some upper bound concentration ratio.

The reappraisal of the nature of technological innovation that began with Nelson and Winter (1982) has led to a more coherent view of corporate competence. Competence resides in the tacit capability of the firm that results from a process of continued and collective learning, and is embodied in the firm's localised skills and organisational routines. It is this aspect of technology which is strictly specific to the firm and cannot be exactly copied by others (Nelson, 1991; Cantwell, 1992a). While patents, brand names and industrial secrets provide temporary advantages, the process or product knowledge they are associated with can be bought and sold and otherwise copied by others, and used at a cost if perhaps with a delay (after inventing around a patent, establishing or acquiring their own brand names and so forth). In imitating or emulating one another in this way companies still rely on building upon their own differentiated form of expertise, and because tacit capability is always distinctive and non-tradable (since it is created only through an internal collective learning process) it marks out the specific competence of the firm.

Although a reasonable degree of technological competence is a necessary condition for competitive success in international markets, it may not be sufficient. David Teece (1986) explores how firms also gain advantage from linking innovative capability with complementary or co-specialised assets. These typically lie downstream from production expertise, most notably in the form of distribution networks. The scope of the distribution system that a firm has access to may act as a constraint compelling the firm to follow some avenues rather than others in its technological learning, or it may become a constraint on its ability to capitalise on its existing technological capability by developing a new related product range. Thus, for example, IBM's transition along a technological path that led from expertise in mechanical typewriters to computers was facilitated by the company's establishment of a distribution network for the sale of office equipment. The influence of such downstream co-specialised assets could be thought of as a constraint on technological development mainly from the product demand or user side, just as the extent of the firm's R&D facilities provides a constraint on the side of the availability of the requisite scientific and engineering knowledge.

Another way of viewing these relationships is to start from the continual construction of tacit capability in each firm under the pressures of competition, which can be described as a process of technological accumulation (Cantwell, 1989). In the course of accumulation the complexity of production expertise and organisational routines is steadily increased, and with it the requirements of the firm are gradually changed and extended in terms of its R&D and co-specialised assets such as distribution networks. This is the normal course of economic growth or development. An increase in R&D and the international expansion of the firm's activity as a MNC are therefore both partly reflections of the progress of technological accumulation. Thus from this perspective it is misleading to treat high R&D-intensity as the cause of greater internationalisation, a point taken up in a different context by Hirschey (1981). High R&D-intensity and internationalisation are both handmaidens to the accumulation of a more sophisticated level of technological capability or competence; they feed the progress of such accumulation and themselves in turn feed from it.

IV. THE SECOND APPROACH TO THE HIGH R&D-INTENSITY OF MNCS: THEIR INTERNALISATION OF INTERNATIONAL TECHNOLOGY FLOWS

Similar comments apply with respect to the second major issue, the internal exploitation of technological capability within the MNC. High R&D-intensity is as much an outcome of a sophisticated internal production system based on a learning process as it is the cause of such an internal system. To further develop its specific abilities in production the firm needs to draw upon the knowledge and ideas generated by its R&D department, and the goals of the R&D division are set with the existing problem-solving activity and corporate strategy of the firm in mind. Of course, some of the knowledge created by a research facility may be of equal or greater use to other companies, and in this event it can be bought and sold subject to the costs of adapting it to the specific codes or systems of other firms. However, given that corporate R&D is under the control of a particular firm, most of the contribution to public knowledge which it makes will be of greatest relevance when combined with the tacit capability and specialised learning of the company in question.

The earliest literature in this area instead sought to explain the association between R&D-intensity and MNC activity by focusing on the problems involved in the exchange of knowledge through external markets (Buckley and Casson, 1976; Komus, 1983). These may be summarised as the problems of ensuring appropriability of the economic rents from knowledge creation, and providing for proper coordination between the producers and users of complex products. Since R&D is an uncertain process the results of projects are difficult to forecast, and even after an invention has been made its commercial value may be unclear. This implies that it is troublesome for inventors to ensure that they are fully rewarded for their efforts through contracts with other parties who prior to the completion of a deal lack information on the true value of what they are purchasing. Without the control of downstream production it is thus difficult to appropriate a full return on R&D (Magee, 1977).

In addition, using or applying the knowledge gained from R&D in production is likely to require a regular flow of information and other contacts between the laboratory and the plant. Managing such a high intensity of transactions by negotiated contracts is likely to prove costly, and it is also subject to the limitations on the complexity of contractual agreements imposed by bounded rationality (Williamson, 1975). Both the problems of appropriability and coordination are related to the possibility of opportunistic behaviour by either agent; most notably, the buyer of knowledge may refuse to share unanticipated returns on it with the seller, and may in turn sell the knowledge to others (so the seller fails to appropriate rents on earlier investments in R&D); or the seller may not fully cooperate in terms of being sufficiently willing and available to handle further enquiries and to provide other supporting information so as to enable the buyer to realise the full worth of the knowledge (so coordination between the two does not function properly).

Such arguments are summarised by the view that the transaction costs involved in the exchange between independent agents of public knowledge or information tend to exceed the transaction costs associated with the internal organisation of technology transfer and usage within the MNC. Hence, where the R&D-intensity of production is high MNCs will be more likely to manage international operations and thereby to internalise the creation and transfer of technology. Conditions of lower R&D-intensity offer a greater scope for the inter-firm diffusion of knowledge, and so independent local companies retain a higher share of activity relative to MNCs.

Much of the force of arguments of this kind depended upon the older narrow definition of technology as being analogous to information and thus in principle fully tradeable. Once tacit capability is also taken into consideration it becomes clear that technology as a whole cannot be traded or exchanged. Only the public knowledge component is tradeable and therefore liable to be assessed in terms of the transaction costs of alternative modes of exchange.

Indeed, it now seems probable that in some of the earlier literature the problems associated with the exchange of public knowledge were overstated. In recent years there has been a steadily rising number of technology-based strategic alliances, one of the incentives for which has been the sharing of information between companies. This helps to illustrate that inter-firm exchanges of knowledge actually tend to be greater in more R&D-intensive sectors, rather than less. Even before considering alliances which entail collaborative R&D ventures, informal exchanges between company scientists, engineers and other skilled personnel tend to be more prevalent in R&D-intensive branches of activity. In the chemicals industry, for example, MNCs have long been involved in extensive cross-licensing arrangements.

In other words, when using a narrow notion of technology as akin to information and so concentrating on the organisation of the exchange of such information, there was a tendency to overemphasise the problems of appropriability (Mowery and Rosenberg, 1989). The return on innovation to a firm is in fact principally a return on its creation of tacit capability, a process supported by but not reducible to the generation of new public knowledge. This new knowledge can come from outside the firm, either from public institutions such as universities or from other companies. That the supply of knowledge from outside the MNC does not simply replace its own R&D department is due to two considerations. First, by controlling its own R&D department the firm is able to address more directly the problems and potential opportunities it has encountered in its own development of production, and it is able to ensure the regular feedbacks between research and production that are required when critically revising a new technology (the problems of coordination mentioned by the transaction cost economists).

Second, the firm's R&D division has an important monitoring function, since in order to understand the potential relevance of knowledge generated outside the firm it is necessary to be already actively engaged in a related research programme. From this perspective the objective of corporate research is not especially to attempt to be the first to create new knowledge, a form of competition sometimes depicted as a patent race. The motive behind R&D is rather that, as emphasised by Penrose (1959), what a firm sees in its environment, and thereby the opportunities it is able to exploit, is conditional on its existing capability, the problems it is currently trying to resolve and the opportunities it is already aware of. Thus, the difficulty of appropriating a full return on a particular item of knowledge is not normally of overriding concern to a firm (Cohen and Levinthal, 1989). Firms are not especially worried about the leakage of information provided that exchanges form part of a mutual consensus and do not run in only one direction. Therefore in taking measures to guard industrial secrets firms may often simply be trying to ensure a fair exchange, rather than excluding the possibility of exchange altogether.

To recap, a firm that has accumulated a greater level and more sophisticated range of technological competence tends to rely more extensively on R&D. This implies not only that such a firm is more dependent on new scientific and engineering knowledge than others, but also that it is making a greater contribution to the public or generic knowledge base than are other companies. However, the more competent firm is also better able to gather relevant knowledge from its environment and to use it in productive applications that are not well understood or not perceived so quickly by lesser able competitors.

For the purposes of illustration, consider a comparison between a high research-intensive and competent MNC and a low research-intensive firm with a more narrowly specialised and weaker competence in the same industry. The MNC provides a much greater supply of knowledge than does the other firm, but the MNC may also be able to make better use of the limited new knowledge created by the other company, and to implement this knowledge more effectively. In contrast the other firm may be unable to perceive much usefulness to itself at all in the extensive research output of the MNC. Indeed, even if it were able to appreciate the potential of some of the new knowledge generated by the MNC it may lack the tacit capability needed to exploit it. Thus, in a process of technological competition in which all firms develop new competence, they have an incentive to match this with investments in R&D, without being over-concerned about the appropriability of returns on the new public knowledge that they themselves will thereby create. The recently strong innovative performance of Japanese MNCs has been linked to a greater ability to monitor and utilise the public knowledge created externally by other firms, by comparison with US and European MNCs (Mansfield, 1992).

However, the knowledge created by a firm's R&D facility is in general of greatest relevance to the learning process underway in the same company, rather than the somewhat different paths to learning being followed in other companies. Where the technological traditions of two companies are quite different, the costs of imitation in a less amenable environment may exceed the original costs of innovation (Mansfield, Schwartz and Wagner, 1981; Levin, Klevorick, Nelson and Winter, 1987). As a result the most efficient and effective way to exploit this knowledge is for it to be fed in as a contribution to innovation within the same firm. Where necessary the firm can extend its own production system incrementally to take advantage of new knowledge, probably giving rise to further related problems that require the R&D facility to continue or adapt its investigation. In this respect, the issue of appropriability remains relevant as well as the need to coordinate the interchange between R&D and production to increase the rate of generation of new technology, and not just to raise the efficiency with which a particular piece of knowledge is used.

However, the major reason why the appropriability of returns to R&D tends to be greater when knowledge is used within the same firm is essentially the complementarity between the tacit capability of the firm and the activity of its own R&D facilities. This complementarity, and as a secondary factor the costs of translation into different codes that must be incurred when providing knowledge to another firm, ensures that as a rule the knowledge generated by an R&D department is more valuable to its own firm than to any other corporation. Thus, differences in appropriability have more to do with the different degrees of relevance that any new item of knowledge has for alternative processes of learning and innovation, rather than problems associated with the act of exchanging knowledge. In an early challenge to the then conventional view that MNCs retain strict control over the knowledge they create as it would otherwise flow easily to other firms and remove their incentive to conduct R&D, David Teece (1977) showed that the transfer of knowledge and its use in other firms was a difficult and costly process.

So MNCs tend to be research-intensive due to the needs of the continuing innovation process within the firm. The problems of the appropriability of returns on new knowledge and of coordinating R&D and production are both relevant to explaining the intra-firm linkage between scientific and engineering advances and technological accumulation, but appropriability and coordination are not at root problems that stem from the dangers of opportunistic behaviour in contractual relationships. Some recent accounts of the internalisation of international technology flows within the MNC have thus drawn on but also moved beyond the transaction cost approach, which has become the mainstream framework in many other branches of the literature on MNCs.

V. MNC NETWORKS FOR INNOVATION AND LEARNING

The increasing appreciation of the role of technological accumulation and learning within the MNC has been facilitated by the recent trend for MNCs to establish international networks to support this process. These networks are of two kinds. First are the networks of international production and international R&D facilities organised within MNCs. Such networks are the logical outcome of the shift by MNCs away from local market-oriented investments towards internationally integrated strategies that began in the late 1960s (Hedlund, 1986; Bartlett and Ghoshal, 1989; Dunning, 1992). An interactive international network of MNC affiliates replaces a system of satellites or miniature replicas. Second are the inter-firm networks in which MNCs increasingly participate. These include the growing number of strategic alliances between MNC competitors, and a greater variety of local networks that link MNC affiliates with their suppliers and customers. Although each of these networks has various purposes, perhaps the most prominent motive prompting MNCs to enter into them has been that joint learning processes are believed to be a means of raising the rate of innovation of the MNC, and hence its technological competitiveness.

The establishment of integrated internal networks of R&D and production within MNCs has helped to foster a growing interest in the internationalisation of R&D, and a gradual change in the way in which the literature has viewed this phenomenon. The early literature on the internationalisation of R&D (reviewed by Pearce, 1989) tended to depict R&D as a centrally provided service within the firm, the location of which may be partially dispersed according to the strength of centripetal forces relative to the significance of centrifugal forces. In other words, the R&D requirements of individual affiliates by and large could be treated separately. The central R&D facilities of the firm would provide knowledge to all the affiliates, and whether particular affiliates had locally supporting R&D of their own depended (for example) on the size of their local market and on the extent of its differentiation from the home market. The extent of the need for local testing, the adaptation of products to local requirements, the use of locally available materials and meeting local government regulations could then be assessed against the gains from economies of scale in the locational concentration of R&D.

Many of the early writings on international R&D were also aware that it may have a monitoring function, tapping into local skills and acquiring foreign knowledge, as is clear in the paper by Mansfield, Teece and Romeo (1979), and was originally outlined by Dunning (1958). However, some early articles spoke of this as 'reverse technology transfer', the implication being that knowledge was essentially disseminated outwards from the centre of the MNC, with allowance for feedbacks from the recipient affiliates. The notion of an active interchange between parts of an MNC network has only been picked up more recently, as MNCs have adopted internationally integrated strategies in a number of industries (Granstrand, 1979; Granstrand, Håkanson and Sjölander, 1992). One reason why this possibility was not noted previously is that much of the earlier work understated the significance of the internationalisation of R&D, asserting that as a rule the bulk of R&D is centralised in the parent company. It now seems clear that the empirical basis for this contention was the relatively low share of R&D located abroad by US MNCs. While US and Japanese MNCs incur less than 10% of their total world R&D expenditure in foreign facilities, for the MNCs that emanate from all the more industrialised European countries the equivalent proportion is at least 10%. As shown in Table 1, based on patent data, the foreign research ratio is considerably higher (approaching 50% or more) for the major MNCs based in the UK, Belgium, the Netherlands and Switzerland (Cantwell, 1992b).

For many European MNCs, R&D has been quite strongly internationally dispersed since at least the 1960s. For these firms it is an easier process to switch towards the establishment of international networks for knowledge generation. They have often, although not always, geared affiliate R&D towards the fields of local technological specialisation as a means of accessing the most relevant new knowledge being created in other major centres (Cantwell and Hodson, 1991). As shown in Table 2, the internationalisation of R&D has been greatest in the food products, chemicals and pharmaceuticals, non-metallic mineral products and coal and petroleum products industries.

With the shift towards international networks for technology creation, US and Japanese MNCs have begun to follow suit. For this purpose, American MNCs have been steadily increasing the

Table 1 The share of US patents of the world's largest firms attributable to research in foreign locations (outside the home country of the parent company), organised by the nationality of parent firms, 1969–86 (%)

	1969–72	1983–86
USA	4.28	7.40
Japan	2.85	1.24
Germany	13.57	14.43
UK	43.27	44.91
Italy	20.11	11.72
France	10.23	10.92
Netherlands	63.93	70.04
Belgium	49.62	71.32
Switzerland	44.94	42.59
Sweden	20.94	31.30
Canada	42.06	35.52
Others[1]	32.76	23.10
TOTAL	9.80	10.63

Source: Cantwell (1992b).

[1] Excluding companies registered in Panama.

internationalisation of their R&D facilities, as indicated in Table 1. This has not been true of Japanese MNCs, in which the very rapid growth of R&D in Japan has outstripped the extension of their operations abroad. However, the R&D of Japanese MNCs located in the US and Europe has also been growing quite fast, and it seems that such Japanese-owned R&D has been especially aimed at tapping into the strongest areas of local expertise and skills (Kogut and Chang, 1991; Mowery and Teece, 1992; Graham, 1992; Ozawa, 1991). In other words, in the international R&D that Japanese MNCs have undertaken, technology acquisition has been a prominent and perhaps the most important motive.

In the formation of a network for technological learning and research the location of R&D may again be subject to forces that point to either centralisation or decentralisation. On the one hand, R&D is increasingly drawn to the major centres of excellence in which the best researchers and most skilled production teams are clustered. This tends to increase the locational concentration of R&D and its centralisation in the home country centre vis-á-vis countries in which local technological capability is weak. On the

Table 2 The percentage share of US patents of the world's largest firms attributable to research in foreign locations (outside the home country of the parent company), organised by the industrial group of parent firms, 1969–86

	1969–72	1983–86
1. Food products	16.63	23.96
2. Chemicals nes	12.18	12.73
3. Pharmaceuticals	17.69	17.79
4. Metals	10.64	9.18
5. Mechanical engineering	10.60	14.73
6. Electrical equipment nes	7.71	7.92
7. Office equipment	5.03	11.96
8. Motor vehicles	4.59	6.83
9. Aircraft	2.09	2.66
10. Other transport equipment	9.70	5.24
11. Textiles	5.88	3.90
12. Rubber and plastic products	6.53	5.13
13. Non-metallic mineral products	11.38	15.43
14. Coal and petroleum products	14.87	13.22
15. Professional and scientific instruments	6.68	3.31
16. Other manufacturing	5.03	12.69
TOTAL	9.80	10.63

n.e.s. = not elsewhere specified
Source: Cantwell and Hodson (1991).

other hand, as part of the same process some R&D projects may be moved out of the home country to important foreign centres better able to undertake them, which contributes to decentralisation. To examine conflicting trends of this kind further it is necessary to move beyond the rather simple single dimensional measure that has dominated the literature in this area to date, namely the share of R&D located abroad. A more complex indicator of geographical dispersal is required, and the data that are now available (Casson, 1991) make this feasible, although progress in this direction is only just beginning.

Among the issues to be addressed concerning the international location of R&D by MNCs, two strands of analysis can be discerned. First, there are scholars that are interested in the R&D function as such, and with the changing requirements for the management of international R&D in the MNC (Håkanson, 1990; De Meyer, 1992; Pearce, 1989; Casson, Pearce and Singh, 1991;

Pearce and Singh, 1992). This has become an important area of investigation as MNCs increasingly integrate their international R&D networks, and as there is a continuing rise in the reliance of innovation on new scientific and engineering know-how, the public knowledge component of technology. However, this line of enquiry examines only one aspect of the international creation of technology by MNCs, since as argued above technology is not reducible to the output of R&D facilities. Instead, the R&D function is one (particularly important) contributor to the learning process that characterises innovation, and leads to the creation of new technology in the sense of new production systems.

The second type of analysis directs attention to the international networks of MNCs that support technological innovation as a whole, through the development of new production systems (Cantwell, 1989, 1992b; Teece, 1986; Patel and Pavitt, 1991a). In this kind of study, evidence on the internationalisation of R&D and knowledge creation or invention is typically used as a proxy measure rather than as a means of focusing on the R&D function as such. The R&D-intensity of production is a measure of the technological sophistication of activity in each location, while the specific types of knowledge being created reflect the fields in which tacit capability or competence has been especially accumulated (that is, they provide a measure of technological specialisation).

Of course, basic R&D may be located away from tacit capability, feeding knowledge to more development-based R&D facilities in other production centres. This is one important reason for preferring patent statistics (as illustrated in the accompanying tables) in place of data on R&D facilities when measuring the international location of inventions by MNCs from the perspective of the broader process of technological innovation. Patent statistics generally provide a better indication of the location of the development component of R&D which tends to be linked to local production, rather than the location of pure research. Hence, patent grants better measure the location of underlying technological capability or competence. Equally, they may be misleading with respect to the location of basic R&D facilities. For example, the international location of basic R&D by Japanese MNCs is probably understated in Table 1, which may be a drawback for those who wish to focus on the internationalisation of the R&D function as such.

There is some evidence that the creation by MNCs of international networks to support their own technological innovation may help to reinforce existing patterns of national specialisation. For instance, it has been shown that German MNCs are especially prone to locate international production in the US in industries in which the US is comparatively technologically strong, while US MNCs are particularly drawn to Germany in industries in which Germany is comparatively technologically advantaged (Cantwell, 1989). This has contributed towards a trend to intra-industry direct investment between the major centres of excellence in a sector, accompanied by intra-industry technological activity supported by cross-investments in research within the international industry in question.

The issue then becomes whether these cross-investments help to strengthen intra-industry specialisation as well as inter-industry technological specialisation. That is, within an industry certain areas of tacit capability and knowledge creation are concentrated in some centres rather than others. In the pharmaceutical industry, for example, in which international R&D runs principally between the major centres (Dunning 1988b), research into heart disease and the related drug production may be concentrated in one location, while work on skin ailments agglomerates in a different country. The extent to which the affiliates of MNCs specialise within their industry across national boundaries in accordance with the comparative advantages of local expertise seems to depend upon the degree of locational hierarchy that exists between alternative centres. In the European chemical and pharmaceutical industry Germany is the dominant centre, the UK is a second-order centre, and Italy is of the third-order. The evidence suggests that in this sector the affiliates of German MNCs are technologically specialised in the other European centres in accordance with the local strengths of the centre in question, and the same is true of British chemical and pharmaceutical MNCs in Italy (Cantwell and Sanna-Randaccio, 1992).

However, British MNCs in chemicals and pharmaceuticals when operating in Germany follow a pattern of technological specialisation that accords with their own comparative advantages in the industry and those of their home centre, the UK. They do not appear to be especially prone to try and tap into the areas in which German expertise is relatively greatest, but rather treat Germany as a general reservoir of skills that can be used principally to extend those lines of operation on which they are already focused. In other words, firms based in higher-order centres are more likely to establish a locationally specialised network of technological activity in support of corporate innovation than are firms that originate from lower-order centres. Thus, at least until now, patterns of technological specialisation within an industry seem to have been strengthened only by the networks of MNCs from the leading centres.

In any case, even where MNCs establish networks in which technological activity is locationally specialised across the major centres this does not usually destroy the distinctiveness of their national origins. As stressed above, firms follow differentiated paths to learning even when their fields of research are similar. Hence the nature of their tacit capability is path dependent, and reflects their starting point in nationally differentiated types of expertise (see, for example, Kogut, 1987; 1990). Moreover, the home centre of the MNC normally continues to be the most important individual source of knowledge and capability, a theme that is emphasised by Patel and Pavitt (1991a). As shown in Table 3, the largest MNCs generally account for a substantial proportion of R&D in their home centre, although foreign-owned MNCs play a greater role in Belgium and Canada. While the international R&D of MNCs is certainly significant it is quite possible that by reinforcing locational specialisation among the major centres it may sustain rather than erode national systems of innovation (Archibugi and Michie, 1993).

Nonetheless, as MNCs have moved towards the construction of international networks, so the number of overlaps in their areas of knowledge creation in a given industry has increased. Nationally specific but overlapping patterns of technological development have helped to promote international joint ventrues (Mowery and Rosenberg, 1989). In addition, technological relatedness has been rising such that formerly separate branches of technology have been increasingly brought together in recent innovations. An important element in this process has been described as a trend towards technology fusion (Kodama, 1991; 1992). While it is true that, as argued previously, the knowledge created by a firm is usually of greatest value to itself given its own particular experience in production, it may still be of some value to other companies after allowing for the costs of converting it for use in a somewhat different setting. R&D projects also tend to create potential spinoffs that the firm itself decides not to pursue, but

Table 3 Large Firms in National Technological Activities, 1981–86

Country	National Sources of Patenting in US (3 columns add up to 100%			Patenting in US by Nationally Controlled Firms from Outside Home Country (% of National Total)
	Large Firms			
	Nationally Controlled	Foreign Controlled	Other	
Belgium	8.8	39.7	51.5	14.7
France	36.8	10.0	53.2	3.4
Germany	44.8	10.5	44.2	6.9
Italy	24.1	11.6	64.3	2.2
Netherlands	51.9	8.7	39.4	82.0
Sweden	27.5	3.9	68.6	11.3
Switzerland	40.1	6.0	53.9	28.0
UK	32.0	19.1	49.0	16.7
W. Europe	44.1	6.2	49.7	8.1
Canada	11.0	16.9	72.1	8.0
Japan	62.5	1.2	36.3	0.6
USA	42.8	3.1	54.1	3.2

Note: All columns as percentage of total national patenting in US, 1981–86.
Source: Patel and Pavitt (1991a).

which are increasingly likely to be of interest to some other firms as the extent of technological overlaps rises.

The increasing scope for technological interchanges between MNCs has provided a greater incentive for companies not to restrict themselves to creating their own intra-firm international networks but also to join with other MNCs in inter-firm networks in selected areas of parallel lines of activity. There are now a growing number of such technology-based strategic alliances (Chesnais, 1988a; 1988b; Hagedoorn and Schakenraad, 1990; Gugler and Dunning, 1992). Their purpose is not only to extend the existing arrangements for information sharing between firms, by regulating for and promoting the mutual exchange of knowledge. The objective is also to organise collaborative efforts in joint ventures where the paths of learning being followed by the firms are complementary to one another. Joint ventures may be superior to cross-licensing agreements as a means of mutual assistance towards technology imporvements where tacit capability is more complex and most important relative to the sharing of knowledge

(Mowery and Rosenberg, 1989). The production and research set up in these joint ventures thereby establish a common learning experience on which all partners to a venture can draw, in return for their own specific contribution. The need for such ventures is further evidence of the difficulty of technology transfer between firms, requiring close cooperation if the tacit capabilities of different MNCs are to be combined in some way. Of course, from the viewpoint of the R&D function as such, a further reason for entering into alliances is to share the very high costs of some R&D projects.

The increasing significance of technological interrelatedness and fusion is one aspect of what has been described as a new technology paradigm (Freeman and Perez, 1988). In this context a technological paradigm is a system of scientific and productive activity based on a widespread cluster of innovations that represent a response to a related set of technological problems, relying on a common set of scientific principles and on similar organisational methods. The old paradigm was based on energy and oil related technologies, and on mass production with its economies of scale and specialised corporate R&D. In recent years this has gradually been displaced by a new paradigm grounded on the economies of scope derived from the interaction between flexible but linked production facilities, and a greater diversity of search in R&D. Individual plant flexibility and network linkages both depend upon the new information and communication technologies.

Another aspect of the new paradigm is that firms have moved away from a reliance on large scale plants in favour of a more complex range of agreements with subcontractors. For example, legal and repair services and some assembly activities that were previously undertaken in-house within a major industrial company may now be provided to it by a local network of smaller suppliers. Japanese firms have been in the forefront of the new technology paradigm and it is they that have demonstrated most clearly how innovation can be raised in flexible manufacturing systems supported by a network of cooperative agreements with other companies. Specialised suppliers can contribute a good deal to innovation through their relationship with a larger producer. Japanese MNCs have also been leading the way in trying to establish such local contractual networks, an issue raised by Ozawa (1991).

VI. INNOVATION AND THE INTERNATIONAL COMPETITIVENESS OF FIRMS AND COUNTRIES

The establishment of international networks by MNCs and their involvement in networks of cooperation with other firms if successful helps to increase their ability to innovate and thus their international competitiveness. Innovation is the process by which corporate technological competence is constructed, as discussed in section III above. The tacit capability embodied in the collective skills and organisational routines of the firm is the product of continual problem solving and learning, which is in turn enhanced in a MNC through combining complementary avenues of technological development in an international network. While technological advantage or competence forms the essential basis of the competitiveness of MNCs in world markets (Berlin and Wyatt, 1988), the international networks of MNCs help to reinforce such capability through mutually assisted learning between affiliates, and an enhanced ability to engage in purposeful R&D (Hirschey, 1981).

Greater advantages are provided by internationally integrated strategies at a time when the potential for technology fusion is rising, and the costs of maintaining international networks are falling due to advances in information and communication technology. These advantages have increased the competitive pressure on firms to become MNCs, such that companies now tend to internationalise their production and research at a much earlier stage of their development. Historically, most of the major MNCs in manufacturing originated from among a narrow range of backgrounds. Many were based in countries that were or had been technological leaders (the US or Britain), and allied to this they began from a position of innovative strength in international competition in their industries. Most other industrial MNCs with substantial foreign manufacturing production emanated from smaller economies that were highly technologically developed (Switzerland or the Netherlands) despite the limited size of their own local markets.

While today the strongest internationalisation of all is being mounted by the industrial firms of the new technology leader (Japan), the geographical origins of MNC outward investment is becoming much more widely dispersed. The best illustration of this is provided by the rise of Third World MNCs, based mainly in the newly industrialised countries (NICs). As with the internationalisation of the firms of the earlier industrialised countries the growth of Third World manufacturing MNCs is linked to an internal process of technological accumulation (Lall, 1983; Tolentino, 1992). Third World MNCs like others have a technological competence that derives from their own localised learning experience in developing country conditions. Although they sometimes use the kinds of technology that were last used by industrialised country MNCs many years ago, the paths taken by innovative change are to a large extent irreversible, and the new MNCs thus have advantages in operating more effectively technologies that are well suited to a Third World environment.

For the same reason Third World MNCs are much less reliant on R&D and new knowledge creation than are other MNCs. Much of the knowledge they require in their technological development is already freely available and is familiar to the production engineers they employ. However, even this lower degree of research-intensity of Third World MNCs has begun to change recently (Lall, 1991; Tolentino 1992). As technological improvement has taken off in the Asian NICs so they have increasingly come to depend upon R&D inputs to support their continued accumulation of tacit capability (Lall, 1992). For example, the share of R&D expenditure in sales of Korean electrical equipment companies rose from 1.3% in 1978 to 3.0%in 1983; and Korea's total national R&D as a share of GDP was planned to rise from 0.6%in 1978 to 2.5%in 1991, which would put her on a par with the major industrialised countries (Enos and Park, 1988). Indeed, both Korean and Taiwanese MNCs now have significant research-related investments in the US and Europe as a means of tapping into local expertise and creating the kind of international networks for technological accumulation discussed in the previous section.

Trends such as these are at odds with earlier interpretations of Third World MNCs in terms of the product cycle model, in which it is argued that standardised technologies gradually trickle down and production is relocated in countries at lower levels of development (Wells, 1983). The product cycle model is of greatest relevance in an unchanged technological paradigm, in which the ladder of technological leadership has become well established and is sustained over time. The technology leader enjoys a higher level of R&D relative to GDP, higher productivity, higher incomes and thus higher domestic demand for more sophisticated products.

Home country firms have high export shares in international markets for research-intensive products, and home country MNCs establish international production in less research-intensive lines in countries with steadily lesser levels of local capability as products mature and standardise (Vernon, 1966; Hirsch, 1967). Indigenous firms in these countries can in their turn develop exports and international production in the equivalent lines of activity.

In this form the product cycle model cannot cope satisfactorily with three of the recent phenomena just outlined. First, technological leadership has shifted with a change in paradigm. The institutional structure of the firms of Japan and the Asian NICs is more attuned to the flexible manufacturing systems required under the new paradigm. Thus they have initiated innovative investments at home and abroad, rather than just relying on a trickle down effect from American and European technologies. Largely as a consequence of their successful development, R&D has been increased faster than elsewhere. As argued in section III, R&D-intensity is as much a reflection of accumulated competence as it is a precondition for it. However, it should also be noted that in most less developed countries, especially in Africa, indigenous firms still have only rather weak technological capabilities (Cantwell, 1991). Second, MNCs have increasingly turned to integrated networks in support of an international system of innovation. This has weakened the usefulness of the notion that international production replaces exports to countries with lower R&D-intensity as products mature (Vernon, 1979). Third, irrespective of changes of technological leadership but due to the potential offered by international networks, there has been a growth in internationalisation by the firms of all countries. This has included some cross-investments in similarly R&D-intensive lines of activity in the same industry.

This less hierarchical pattern of international trade and production can be explained by thinking of the technological capability of countries in similar terms to the competence of firms. Tacit capability and hence innovation is differentiated across countries just as it is between firms, owing to the different nature of their traditions as encapsulated in the particularity of their institutions (Nelson, 1992). Just as a number of different firms can all be competent within an industry in their own specific ways, so a variety of major locational centres can co-exist in international competition, each with their own fields of expertise and thus competitive strength (Dosi, Pavitt and Soete, 1990). Major centres of this kind will all prove attractive to MNCs in determining the location of those of their investments that are undertaken with a view to the construction of international networks capable of supporting their technological development.

The growth of MNC networks for innovation is thus likely to lead to a positive interaction between the competitiveness of the leading MNCs and the competitiveness of the major centres. By integrating across national borders teams that draw on the agglomerations of expertise in each of the centres MNCs enhance their learning capability and hence their technological competence. For their part the local technological activities of foreign MNCs contribute to the strength of innovation in a location, both directly and indirectly through the competitive stimulus they provide to other firms and through the active assistance provided to partner companies. However, the inward investment of MNCs does not always enhance the technological competitiveness of a host country. The evidence of US direct investment in Europe in the post-war period suggests that local technological activity was boosted as a result in some industries but not others. The most important consideration seems to be the initial level of capability in indigenous firms. Where local firms are technologically strong or have notable technological traditions that can be revived, the local presence of competent foreign MNCs is more likely to induce beneficial spillover effects (Cantwell, 1989). Not only is there more likely to be a positive competitive interaction between firms (which may be part of a broader process of international competition through cross-investments between centres as local companies themselves become MNCs), but there is also a greater scope for collaborative agreements and local exchanges of new knowledge.

The exchange of knowledge between foreign-owned and local firms benefits innovation in indigenous companies with their own distinctive technological traditions in the host country, and it also contributes to the learning process underway elsewhere through the MNC networks that link affiliates to related activities in other countries. In some cases the acquisition of knowledge and the development of mutual assistance in problem-solving activity across countries may be a principal motive for MNC investments. This applies to intra-industry direct investments between major centres of innovatory activity, such as that between the US and Germany in the chemicals industry, as noted above. It has also applied to a good deal of the recent investment by Japanese MNCs in the US and Europe (Ozawa, 1992a). In instances such as these there are likely to be spillover benefits in home countries due to the linkages between MNC parent companies and their local suppliers, customers and competitors, (see Ozawa, 1991; 1992b for some similar arguments on outward investment and home country economic development).

Where MNC networks span the major centres of innovation in an industry the greatest likelihood exists of a favourable consolidation of technological capability in both home and host countries. However, centres of only intermediate significance can be subject to the erosion of local technological capacity as international economic integration increases, in part through the changing locational decisions of MNCs (Cantwell and Dunning, 1992). A host country in this position may lose as foreign MNCs make greater use of the local knowledge they gain in production abroad, while establishing only technologically less sophisticated or assembly types of production locally. A home country may suffer where local MNCs relocate a significant part of their higher grade operations in some foreign centre. Various interactions between both inward and outward MNC investments and national technological capability are thus possible (Cantwell, 1992c). What matters is not so much the general levels of inward and outward investment, but the structure of production and its degree of technological sophistication in each location. Intermediate centres are more likely to be sustained where countries have some particularly distinctive fields of technological sophistication that are not easily emulated or substituted through an extension of the activities being conducted in the leading centres.

VII. THE AGENDA FOR FUTURE RESEARCH

Work on MNCs and innovatory activities has now moved beyond the focus of early writers on MNCs as agents of international technology transfer, whether from the standpoint of the product cycle or internalisation traditions. In the new evolutionary approach that has been outlined the focus is instead on MNCs as agents of the generation of new technology. MNCs are distinguished from other firms through their deployment of international networks for innovation. Associated with this new approach is a broader view of technological innovation as a problem-solving and learning process through which the systems of production are gradually changed. Technology is accumulated not only in the form of the new knowledge incorporated in the scientific and engineering characteristics of products and processes, but also in the form of the tacit capability that is embodied in the production systems of firms. From this perspective technology transfer is merely one element in internationally coordinated learning processes. The central objective of the international networks of MNCs is to increase the innovativeness of their overall system of production, subject to the constraint of having suitably complementary distribution networks.

The agenda for future research now lies in at least three areas: the theory of the firm (sections I to IV), MNC networks for innovation (section V) and the impact of MNCs on the international location of innovatory capabilities (section VI). With respect to the theory of the firm, the new evolutionary approach to technology suggests a theory of the firm or the MNC which is different from the normal transaction cost theory of the firm (on which much other MNC literature is based). In the theory of technological competence the firm is viewed as a cohesive social unit or a system of production, rather than as a nexus of contracts. The firm as a social unit has an inherent capability to learn or innovate, and to gradually change its system of production over time, and it can be argued — following Schumpeter — that this is the basis for profits. The firm becomes a repository of accumulated productive capability which is much more than the sum of the knowledge or ability of the individuals that work for it (Winter, 1991; Cantwell, 1992a). By contrast, the Coasian or transaction cost theory views the firm as an ownership or legal unit, within which transactions are organised by hierarchy, and outside of which transactions are organised through arms-length contracts or market relationships. The notion of technological competence or productive capability is not addressed by the transaction cost theory.

The evolutionary theory of the firm or MNC carries various implications that can be usefully explored in further research. One in particular is that the theory suggests that for successful long term growth the firm must be a cohesive unit, and not simply a collection of disparate activities. This implies that international acquisitions may be more difficult to manage and to integrate than greenfield ventures, unless they have well defined purposes (such as the acquisition of R&D facilities that are known to be potentially useful as a source of knowledge for other parts of the MNC network). It also implies that international acquisitions which are motivated by short term financial motives must be treated quite differently, and in principle they would be better excluded from direct investment statistics.

More work remains to be done on this and other issues raised by the establishment of MNC networks for cross-border learning or innovation. A better understanding is needed of the way in which the internationalisation of R&D and the transmission of public knowledge across countries contributes to problem-solving and learning in geographically distant production plants. It would also be useful to know more of the effects of collaborative agreements between MNCs on the exchange of knowledge between them, and on how this relates to the development of tacit capability in each partner firm. In addition, as mentioned earlier, it is possible now to examine in greater depth the precise geographical dispersion of technological activity in MNCs. Until now, due to data constraints, the literature on MNCs in this area like others has tended to restrict its attention to a binary measure of multinationality, distinguishing only between home and foreign activity. With the development of networks it becomes more important to understand how different types of activity are locationally dispersed. The data now available make it feasible to extend work in this direction.

In their turn, discussions of the changing international division of labour within MNCs feed into those concerned with the impact of MNCs on the location of innovatory capabilities. Different types of effect of MNCs on home and host country capabilities have been identified, but more research needs to be done on the circumstances that surround either beneficial or detrimental interactions between MNC activities and national systems of innovation. Of course, this is quite closely related to policy debates. For example, the governments of Japan and Korea have followed different strategies from those of Singapore or Mexico towards obtaining foreign technological knowledge. The first type of strategy relies on indigenous firms to independently develop their tacit capability, while encouraging them to acquire the most relevant public knowledge created abroad by various means. The second type of strategy is more concerned to promote joint learning processes between foreign MNCs and local companies. The conditions under which each type of strategy is most appropriate need to be articulated more clearly, with reference to the different size of countries and to different national systems of innovation.

REFERENCES

Archibugi, Daniele and Jonathan Michie, "Myths and realities of the globalisation of technology: a reexamination of the evidence" (Cambridge University, *mimeo, 1993*), 34 pp.

Bartlett, Christopher A. and Sumantra Ghoshal, *Managing Across Borders: The Transnational Solution* (Boston, Mass., Harvard Business School Press, 1989), 274 pp.

Bertin, Gilles Y. and Sally M.E. Wyatt, *Multinationals and Industrial Property* (Hemel Hempstead, Harvester Wheatsheaf, 1988), 177pp.

Buckley, Peter J. and Mark C. Casson, *The Future of the Multinational Enterprise* (London, Macmillan, 1976), 116 pp.

Cantwell, John A., *Technological Innovation and Multinational Corporations* (Oxford, Basil Blackwell, 1989), 239 pp.

Cantwell, John A., "Foreign multinationals and industrial development in Africa", in Peter J. Buckley and L. Jeremy Clegg, eds., *Multinational Enterprises in Less Developed Countries* (London, Macmillan, 1991), pp. 183–224.

Cantwell, John A., "The theory of technological competence and its application to international production", in Donald G. McFetridge, ed., Foreign Investment, Technology and Economic Growth (Calgary, University of Calgary Press, 1992a), pp. 33–67.

Cantwell, John A., "The internationalisation of technological activity and its implications for competitiveness", in Ove Granstrand, Lars Håkanson and Sören Sjölander, eds., *Technology Management and International Business: Internationalisation of R&D and Technology* (Chichester, John Wiley, 1992b), pp. 75–95.

Cantwell, John A., "Innovation and technological competitiveness", in Peter J. Buckley and Mark C. Casson, eds., *Multinational Enterprises in the World Economy: Essays in Honour of John Dunning* (Aldershot, Edward Elgar, 1992c) pp. 20–40.

Cantwell, John A. and John H. Dunning, "Multinationals, technology and the competitiveness of European industries", *Aussenwirtschaft*, **46** (1991), pp. 45–65.

Cantwell, John A. and Christian Hodson, "Global R&D and UK competitiveness", in Mark C. Casson, ed., *Global Research Strategy and International Competitiveness* (Oxford, Basil Blackwell, 1991), pp. 133–182.

Cantwell, John A. and Francesca Sanna-Randaccio, "Intra-industry direct investment in the European Community: oligopolistic rivalry and technological competition", in John A. Cantwell, ed., *Multinational Investment in Modern Europe: Strategic Interaction in the Integrated Community* (Aldershot, Edward Elgar, 1992), pp. 71–106.

Casson, Mark C., ed., *Global Research Strategy and International Competitiveness* (Oxford, Basil Blackwell, 1991), 312 pp.

Casson, Mark C., Robert D. Pearce and Satwinder Singh, "A review of recent trends", in Mark C. Casson, ed., *Global Research Strategy and International Competitiveness* (Oxford, Basil Blackwell, 1991), pp. 250–271.

Caves, Richard E., *Multinational Enterprise and Economic Analysis* (Cambridge, Cambridge University Press, 1982), 346 pp.

Chesnais, François, "Multinational enterprises and the international diffusion of technology", in Giovanni Dosi, Chris Freeman, Richard R. Nelson, Gerald Silverberg and Luc L.G. Soete, eds., *Technical Change and Economic Theory* (London, Frances Pinter, 1988a), pp. 496–527.

Chesnais, François, "Technical cooperation agreements between firms", *STI Review*, 4 (1988b), pp. 51–119.

De Meyer, Arnoud, "Management of international R&D operations", in Ove Granstrand, Lars Håkanson and Sören Sjöander, eds., *Technology Management and International Business: Internationalisation of R&D and Technology* (Chichester, John Wiley, 1992), pp. 163–179.

Dosi, Giovanni, Keith L.R. Pavitt and Luc L.G. Soete, *The Economics of Technical Change and International Trade* (Hemel Hempstead, Harvester Wheatsheaf, 1990), 303 pp.

Dunning, John H., *American Investment in British Manufacturing Industry* (London, Allen and Unwin, 1958), 365 pp.

Dunning, John H., "The eclectic paradigm of international production: a restatement and some possible extensions", *Journal of International Business Studies*, 19 (Spring 1988a), pp. 1–31.

Dunning, John H., *Multinationals, Technology and Competitiveness* (London, Unwin Hyman, 1988b), 280 pp.

Dunning, John H., *Multinational Enterprises and the Global Economy* (Wokingham, Addison-Wesley, 1992), 687 pp.

Enos, John L. and Woo-Hee Park, *The Adoption and Diffusion of Imported Technology: the Case of Korea* (London, Croom Helm, 1988), 272 pp.

Freeman, Christopher and Carlota Perez, "Structural crises of adjustment, business cycles and investment behaviour", in Giovanni Dosi, Christopher Freeman, Richard R. Nelson, Gerald Silverberg and Luc L.G. Soete, eds., *Technical Change and Economic Theory* (London, Frances Pinter, 1988), pp. 38–66.

Graham, Edward M., "Japanese control of R&D activities in the United States: is this a cause for concern?", in Thomas S. Arrison, C. Fred Bergsten, Edward M. Graham and Martha Caldwell Harris, eds., *Japan's Growing Technological Capability: Implications for the US Economy* (Washington DC, National Academy Press, 1992), pp. 189–206.

Granstrand, Ove, Technology Management and Markets: An Investigation of R&D and Innovation in Industrial Organisation (Göteborg, Svenska Kulturkompaniet, 1979), pp. 107–129.

Granstrand, Ove, Lars Hákanson and Sören Sjölander, eds., *Technology Man-*

agement and International Business: Internationalisation of R&D and Technology (Chichester, John Wiley, 1992), 254 pp.

Griliches, Zvi, "Hybrid corn: an exploration in the economics of technical change", *Econometrica*, **25** (1957), pp. 501–522.

Gugler, Philippe and John H. Dunning, "Technology based cross-border alliances" (Rutgers University, *mimeo*, 1992), 52 pp.

Hagedoorn, John and Jos Schakenraad, "Inter-firm partnerships and cooperative strategies in core technologies", in Christopher Freeman and Luc L.G. Soete, eds., *New Explorations in the Economics of Technical Change* (London, Frances Pinter, 1990), pp. 3–37.

Håkanson, Lars, "International decentralisation of R&D — the organisational challenges", in Christopher A. Bartlett, Yves Doz and Gunnar Hedlund, eds., *Managing the Global Firm* (London, Routledge, 1990), pp. 256–278.

Hedlund, Gunnar, "The hypermodern MNC: a heterarchy?", *Human Resource Management*, 25 (Spring 1986), pp. 9–25.

Hirsch, Seev, *Location of Industry and International Competitiveness* (Oxford, Oxford University Press, 1967), 133 pp.

Hirschey, Mark, "R&D intensity and multinational involvement", *Economics Letters*, 7 (1981), pp. 87–93.

Hufbauer, Gary C., *Synthetic Materials and the Theory of International Trade* (London, Duckworth, 1965), 165 pp.

Kodama, Fumio, *Analysing Japanese High Technologies: The Techno-Paradigm Shift* (London, Frances Pinter, 1991).

Kodama, Fumio, "Japan's unique capability to innovate: technology fusion and its international implications", in Thomas S. Arrison, C. Fred Bergsten, Edward M. Graham and Matha Caldwell Harris, eds., *Japan's Growing Technological Capability: Implications for the US Economy* (Washington DC, National Academy Press, 1992), pp. 147–164.

Kogut, Bruce, "Country patterns in international competition: appropriability and oligopolistic agreement", in Neil Hood and Jan-Erik Vahlne, eds., *Strategies in Global Competition* (London, Croom Helm, 1987), pp. 315–340.

Kogut, Bruce, "The permeability of borders and the speed of learning among countries", in John H. Dunning, Bruce Kogut and Magnus Blomström, *Globalization of Firms and the Competitiveness of Nations* (Lund, Lund University Press, 1990), pp. 59–90.

Kogut, Bruce and Sea J. Chang, "Technological capabilities and Japanese foreign direct investment in the United States", *Review of Economics and Statistics*, **73** (1991), pp. 401–413.

Komus, David W., "The level of research and development activity of multinationals", in Alan M. Rugman, ed., *Multinationals and Technology Transfer: the Canadian Experience* (New York, Praeger, 1983), pp. 11–25.

Lall, Sanjaya, ed., *The New Multinationals: The Spread of Third World Enterprises* (Chichester, John Wiley, 1983), 268 pp.

Lall, Sanjaya, "Direct investment in S.E. Asia by the NIEs: trends and prospects", *Banca Nazionale del Lavoro Quarterly Review*, **179** (December 1991), pp. 463–480.

Lall, Sanjaya, "Technological capabilities and industrialisation", *World Development*, **20** (1992), pp. 165–186.

Levin, Richard C., Alvin K. Klevorick, Richard R. Nelson and Sidney G. Winter,

"Appropriating the returns from industrial research and development", Brookings Papers on Economic Activity, 3 (1987), pp. 783-820.

Magee, Stephen P., "Information and multinational corporations: an appropriability theory of direct foreign investment", in Jagdish Bhagwati, ed., *The New International Economic Order* (Cambridge, Mass., MIT Press, 1977), pp. 317–340.

Mansfield, Edwin, "Technology and technological change", in John H. Dunning, ed., *Economic Analysis and the Multinational Enterprise* (London, Allen and Unwin, 1974), pp. 147–183.

Mansfield, Edwin, "Appropriating the returns from investments in R&D capital", in Karel Cool, Damien J. Neven and Ingo Walter, eds., *European Industrial Restructuring in the 1990s* (New York, New York University Press, 1992), pp. 331–356.

Mansfield, Edwin, Mark Schwartz and Sam Wagner, "Imitation costs and patents: an empirical study", *Economic Journal*, **91** (December 1981), pp. 907–918.

Mansfield, Edwin, David J. Teece and Anthony Romeo, "Overseas research and development by US based firms", *Economica*, **46**, (1979), pp. 187–196.

Mowery, David C. and Nathan Rosenberg, "The influence of market demand upon innovation: a critical review of some recent empirical studies", *Research Policy*, 8 (April 1979), pp. 103–153.

Mowery, David C. and Nathan Rosenberg, *Technology and the Pursuit of Economic Growth* (Cambridge, Cambridge University Press, 1989), 330 pp.

Mowery, David C. and David J. Teece, "The changing place of Japan in the global scientific and technological enterprise", in Thomas S. Arrison, C. Fred Bergsten, Edward M. Graham and Martha Caldwell Harris, eds., *Japan's Growing Technological Capability: Implications for the US Economy* (Washington DC, National Academy Press, 1992), pp. 106–135.

Nelson, Richard R., "The role of knowledge in R&D efficiency", *Quarterly Journal of Economics*, **96** (1982), pp. 453–470.

Nelson, Richard R., "On the public and private elements of technology" (Columbia University, New York, mimeo, 1990), 47 pp.

Nelson, Richard R., "Why do firms differ, and how does it matter?", Strategic Management Journal, 12, (1991), pp. 61–74.

Nelson, Richard R., "National innovation systems: a retrospective on a study", *Industrial and Corporate Change*, **1** (1992), pp. 347–374.

Nelson, Richard R. and Sidney G. Winter, *An Evolutionary Theory of Economic Change* (Cambridge, Mass., Harvard University Press, 1982), 437 pp.

Ozawa, Terutomo, "Japan in a new phase of multinationalism and industrial upgrading: functional integration of trade, growth and FDI", *Journal of World Trade*, **25** (1991), pp. 43–60.

Ozawa, Terutomo, "Cross-investments between Japan and the EC: income similarity, technological congruity and economies of scope", in John A. Cantwell, ed., *Multinational Investment in Modern Europe: Strategic Interaction in the Integrated Community* (Aldershot, Edward Elgar, 1992a), pp. 13–45.

Ozawa, Terutomo, "Foreign direct investment and economic development", *Transnational Corporations* **1** (February 1992), pp. 27–54.

Parker, John E.S., *The Economics of Innovation: the National and International*

Enterprise in Technological Change (London, Longman, 1974), 396 pp.
Patel, Pari and Keith L.R. Pavitt, "Large firms in the production of the world's technology: an important case of 'non-globalisation' ", *Journal of International Business Studies*, **22** (1991a), pp. 1–21.
Patel, Pari and Keith L.R. Pavitt, "Europe's technological performance", in Christopher Freeman, Margaret L. Sharp and William Walker, eds., *Technology and the Future of Europe: Global Competition and the Environment in the 1990s* (London, Frances Pinter, 1991b), pp. 37–58.
Pavitt, Keith L.R., "International patterns of technological accumulation", in Neil Hood and Jan-Erik Vahlne, eds., *Strategies in Global Competition* (London, Croom Helm, 1987), pp. 126–157.
Pearce, Robert D., *The Internationalisation of Research and Development by Multinational Enterprises* (London, Macmillan, 1989), 209 pp.
Pearce, Robert D. and Satwinder Singh, *Globalising Research and Development* (London, Macmillan, 1992), 213 pp.
Penrose, Edith T., *The Theory of the Growth of the Firm* (Oxford, Basil Blackwell, 1959), 272 pp.
Rosenberg, Nathan, *Inside the Black Box: Technology and Economics* (Cambridge, Cambridge University Press, 1982), 304 pp.
Teece, David J., "Technology transfer by multinational firms: the resource costs of transferring technological know-how", *Economic Journal*, **87** (1977), pp. 242–261.
Teece, David J., "Profiting from technological innovation: implications for integration, collaboration, licensing and public policy", *Research Policy*, **15** (1986), pp. 285–305.
Teece, David J., "Reconceptualising the corporation and competition", in Gerald R. Faulhaber and Gaultiero Tamburini, eds., *European Economic Integration: the Role of Technology* (Boston, Mass., Kluwer, 1991), pp. 177–200.
Tolentino, Paz E.E., *Technological Innovation and Third World Multinational Corporations* (London, Routledge, 1992).
Vernon, Raymond, "International investment and international trade in the product cycle", *Quarterly Journal of Economics*, **80** (May 1966), pp. 190–207.
Vernon, Raymond, "The product cycle hypothesis in a new international environment", *Oxford Bulletin of Economics and Statistics*, **41** (November 1979), pp. 255–267.
Wells, Louis T., *Third World Multinationals: The Rise of Foreign Investments from Developing Countries* (Cambridge, Mass., MIT Press, 1983), 206 pp.
Williamson, Oliver E., *Markets and Hierarchies: Analysis and Antitrust Implications* (New York, Free Press, 1975), 286 pp.
Winter, Sidney G., "On Coase, competence and the corporation", in Oliver E. Williamson and Sidney G. Winter, eds., *The Nature of the Firm: Origins, Evolution and Development* (Oxford, Oxford University Press, 1991), pp. 179–195.

The Localised Creation of Global Technological Advantage

Pari Patel and Keith Pavitt

1. INTRODUCTION AND PURPOSE

In this paper, we shall use recently developed data, based on US patenting, to evaluate the importance of the technological activities of the world's largest firms in different sectors and countries. There are at least two interrelated reasons for doing this.

The first is that technological change is a central feature in economic development, structural change and improvements in efficiency in all countries. Recent studies have shown that technological activities – as measured through R & D and international patenting – are statistically significant determinants of differences in export and productivity performance amongst the major OECD countries (Soete, 1981; Fagerberg, 1987, 1988). At the same time, major international differences have emerged over the past 25 years in trends – and subsequent levels – of these activities, both in these countries and in the large firms based on them (Franko, 1988; Patel and Pavitt, 1988). Briefly stated, the Japanese have had the strongest upward trend, the Anglo-Saxons (UK and USA) and the Dutch the weakest, and the other continental Western Europeans have grown at rates between the two. By the end of the 1980s, the countries spending the highest proportion of national resources on business-funded technological activities were Sweden, Switzerland, FR Germany and Japan, followed at some distance by the USA, and then by Belgium, Canada, France, the Netherlands and the UK.

The second is that the debate continues about the degree to which these technological activities are localised in large firms. The heavy concentration of R & D activities in large firms (Freeman, 1982) has led some analysts to conclude that they have a dominant position in countries' development of new technology. On the other hand, a number of studies using other measures show that R & D activities considerably underestimate the volume of technological activities in firms that are too small to have functionally specialised R & D departments (Acs and Audretsch, 1989; Kleinknecht, 1987; Pavitt et al., 1987). A parallel debate is taking place about the extent and the implications of the international concentration of large firms' technological activities, most often when technology has been made a central explanatory variable in the internationalisation of business[1]. In Vernon's early formulation (1966) and in subsequent analyses by Dunning (1980) and Cantwell (1989), home markets are important determinants of large firms' technological advantage, through the nature and extent of inducement mechanisms that stimulate technical change, and of positive externalities that influence the effectiveness of firms' response to these stimuli. However, in later formulations Vernon (1979) and Dunning (1994) suggest that large firms are increasingly footloose in their R & D activities, thereby weakening the links between the development of their technology and their home country.

In this paper, we present evidence clarifying this debate. Our main data source is systematic information of US patenting by more than 500 of the world's largest technologically active firms, broken down by each firm's nationality (headquarters country), principal product group, by technical field and by the country of origin of the inventor of each patent[2]. Using these data we address two interconnected questions.

- How important are large firms' technological activities in the technologically most advanced countries?

[1] See in particular Vernon (1966, 1979), Buckley and Casson (1976), Cantwell (1989).

[2] These firms have been chosen from the list of world's largest firms published in the Fortune magazine in 1988. For a detailed description of the characteristics and method of compilation of the database see Patel and Pavitt (1991).

- How far do large firms concentrate their technological activities in their home countries?

2. HOW IMPORTANT ARE LARGE FIRMS TO COUNTRIES?

Table 1 shows the share of our large firms in total US patenting, in aggregate and broken down into 34 technical fields. Large firms dominate technology production in R & D intensive sectors, plus automobiles and hydrocarbons. They are relatively less important in non-electrical machinery, but still play an important role as sophisticated users. Overall, they develop about 45% of the world's new technology.

Table 2 shows that large national firms produce more than 30% of national technology in 6 out of the 13 technologically most active OECD countries. Foreign large firms account for more than 10% only in 4 of the 13. Smaller (mainly national) firms and other institutions account for more than 50% in 10 out of 13 countries. R & D statistics underestimate the important role of these smaller firms.

3. HOW IMPORTANT ARE HOME COUNTRIES TO LARGE FIRMS?

Table 3 shows that large firms performed only about 11% of their technological activities outside their home countries in the late 1980s — a 1% increase on the early 1980s. As might be expected, firms based in smaller countries tended to have a higher proportion of technological activities outside their home country. More generally, the proportion of a large firms' technological activities outside its home country is explained statistically by its proportion of production outside its home country (Cantwell, 1992). But foreign production is significantly less technology intensive than home production, since the technical function is generally one of local support and adaptation. Table 3 also shows that most of the foreign technological activities of large firms are not globalised, but concentrated in the USA and Germany.

This pattern suggests at least one compelling reason why companies concentrate a high proportion of their technological

Table 1. Importance of Large Firms in 34 Technical Fields: 1985–90.

Percentage Shares of Total US Patenting Accounted for by Large Firms	
Photography & photocopy	79.7
Semiconductors	76.7
Hydrocarbons, mineral oils, fuels etc.	72.7
Organic Chemicals	72.5
Agricultural Chemicals	71.5
Calculators, computers, & other office equip	65.9
Road vehicles & engines	65.1
Image & sound equipment	64.0
Induced Nuclear Reactions	60.3
Power Plants	59.2
Inorganic Chemicals	59.1
Bleaching Dyeing & Disinfecting	57.9
Materials (inc glass & ceramics)	56.7
Telecommunications	56.7
Metallurgical & Metal Treatment proc.	55.7
Mining & wells: mach. & proc.	52.2
Plastic & rubber products	50.8
Chemical Processes	50.7
Electrical devices & systems	49.2
Drugs & Bioengineering	48.9
Aircraft	47.5
Instruments & controls	47.4
General Electrical Ind. Apparatus	46.1
Food & Tobacco (proc. & prod.)	40.1
General Non-electrical Ind. Equip.	38.9
Apparatus for chemicals, food, glass etc.	33.7
Metallurgical & metal working equip.	31.7
Assembling & material handling app.	27.8
Other transport equip. (exc. aircraft)	24.1
Non-electrical specialized ind. equip.	21.8
Miscellaneous metal products	20.2
Dentistry & Surgery	18.6
Other - (Ammunitions & weapons, etc.)	11.1
Textile, clothing, leather, wood products	10.0
All Patenting	44.8

Table 2. Large Firms in National Technological Activities, 1985–90

	Large Firms		Other Firms and Institutions	Total
	National	Foreign		
Japan	64.9	0.7	34.4	100.0
Netherlands	53.5	8.1	38.4	100.0
Germany	43.0	9.9	47.1	100.0
UK	28.8	17.7	53.5	100.0
Switzerland	37.6	5.8	56.6	100.0
Belgium	7.1	35.8	57.1	100.0
France	31.5	9.3	59.2	100.0
United States	37.0	2.6	60.5	100.0
Sweden	20.5	11.5	68.0	100.0
Italy	19.0	9.0	71.9	100.0
Norway	13.9	9.2	76.9	100.0
Canada	7.6	13.5	78.9	100.0
Finland	20.7	0.2	79.1	100.0

activities in one location. The development and commercialisation of major innovations requires the mobilisation of a variety of tacit (person-embodied) skills, and involves high uncertainties. Both are best handled through intense and frequent personal communications and rapid decision-making — in other words, through geographical concentration[3].

This is confirmed by Table 4, showing that firms making products with the highest technology intensities are amongst those with the lowest degrees of internationalisation of their technological activities: those producing aircraft, instruments, motor vehicles, computers and other electrical products are all below the average for the population of firms as a whole. In all these products, links between R & D and design, on the one hand, and production, on the other, are particularly important in the launching of major new products, and benefit from geographical

[3] It is worth noting that the rapid product development times in Japanese firms (Clark et al., 1987) have been achieved from an almost exclusively Japanese base, whilst the strongly globalised R & D activities of the Dutch Philips company are said to have slowed down product development.

Table 3. Geographic Location of Large Firms' US Patenting Activities, According to Nationality: 1985–90.

Percentage Shares Firms' Nationality	Home	Abroad	Of Which USA	Europe	Japan	Other
Japan (143)	98.9	1.1	0.8	0.3	–	0.0
USA (249)	92.2	7.8	–	6.0	0.5	1.3
Italy (7)	88.1	11.9	5.4	6.2	0.0	0.3
France (26)	86.6	13.4	5.1	7.5	0.3	0.5
Germany (43)	84.7	15.3	10.3	3.8	0.4	0.7
Finland (7)	81.7	18.3	1.9	11.4	0.0	4.9
Norway (3)	68.1	31.9	12.6	19.3	0.0	0.0
Canada (17)	66.8	33.2	25.2	7.3	0.3	0.5
Sweden (13)	60.7	39.3	12.5	25.8	0.2	0.8
UK (56)	54.9	45.1	35.4	6.7	0.2	2.7
Switzerland (10)	53.0	47.0	19.7	26.1	0.6	0.5
Netherlands (9)	42.1	57.9	26.2	30.5	0.5	0.6
Belgium (4)	36.4	63.6	23.8	39.3	0.0	0.6
All Firms (587)	89.0	11.0	4.1	5.6	0.3	0.9

Note: The parenthesis contains the number of firms based in each country.
Source: Based on data supplied to SPRU by the US Patent and Trademark Office.

proximity.[4] By contrast, we also see a high proportion of foreign R & D in industries, where some localised technological activities are required, either to adapt products to differentiated local tastes, or to exploit local natural resources: food, drink and tobacco, building materials, mining and petroleum. These differences between product groups suggest that localised, "low-tech" products require global R & D, whilst global "high tech" products do not.

Finally, our evidence shows that:

- the level, rate of change, and sectoral patterns of specialisation of large firms' technological activities are strongly determined by the conditions in their in their home country;
- what large firms do technologically abroad is significantly related

[4] The one technology intensive exception is pharmaceutical products, where the share of foreign R & D is high, but where the links between R & D and production are unimportant compared to the links with high quality basic research.

Table 4. Geographic Location of Large Firms' US Patenting Activities, According to Product Group: 1985–90.

Percentage Shares. Product Group	Abroad	Of Which USA	Europe	Japan	Other
Drink & Tobacco (18)	30.8	17.5	11.1	0.4	1.8
Food (48)	25.0	14.8	8.5	0.1	1.7
Building Materials (28)	20.6	9.1	9.8	0.1	1.6
Other Transport (5)	19.7	2.0	6.8	0.0	10.9
Pharmaceuticals (25)	16.7	5.5	8.3	1.1	1.7
Mining & Petroleum (47)	15.0	9.7	3.5	0.1	1.6
Chemicals (72)	14.4	8.0	5.1	0.3	1.0
Machinery (68)	13.7	3.5	9.1	0.1	1.1
Metals (57)	12.8	5.4	5.7	0.1	1.6
Electrical (58)	10.2	2.6	6.8	0.3	0.4
Computers (17)	8.9	0.1	6.6	1.1	1.1
Paper & Wood (34)	8.1	2.4	4.9	0.1	0.7
Rubber & Plastics (10)	6.1	0.9	2.4	0.4	2.4
Textiles etc. (18)	4.7	1.4	1.8	0.8	0.6
Motor Vehicles (43)	4.4	0.9	3.2	0.1	0.2
Instruments (20)	4.4	0.4	2.8	0.5	0.8
Aircraft (19)	2.9	0.3	1.8	0.1	0.7
All Firms (587)	11.0	4.1	5.6	0.3	0.9

Note: The parenthesis contain the number of firms in each product group.
Source: Based on data supplied to SPRU by the US Patent and Trademark Office.

to local patterns of specialisation in only 3 out of the 11 major countries (Patel and Pavitt, 1991).

This is reflected in Table 5, where the national (or regional) origins of the top 20 firms in the worlds in 11 major technological fields reflect the relative technological strengths of the three regions. Thus, as summarised in Table 6, Japanese firms make up 11 of the top 20 firms in motor vehicles and 14 in consumer electronics and photography, US firms make up 16 of the top 20 in raw materials and 15 in defence, whilst European firms have their largest numbers in chemicals.[5]

In addition to uneven development of large firms in each technological field according to their nationality, there has also

[5] For a more systematic statistical proof, see Patel and Pavitt, 1991.

Table 5. Shares of US Patenting for Top 20 Firms in 11 Technical Fields: Sorted According to Shares in 1985–90.

Fine Chemicals	Nationality	1969–74	1985–90
1 Bayer	FRG	2.84	3.70
2 Hoechst	FRG	1.61	2.53
3 Merck	USA	2.57	2.44
4 Ciba-Geigy	Switzerland	4.33	2.27
5 Imperial Chemical Industries	UK	1.98	1.98
6 E. I. Du Pont De Nemours	USA	1.48	1.79
7 Warner-Lambert	USA	0.71	1.58
8 Eli Lilly Industries	USA	1.67	1.46
9 Dow Chemical	USA	1.21	1.24
10 BASF	FRG	0.58	1.19
11 Pfizer	USA	1.17	1.09
12 American Cyanamid	USA	2.43	1.04
13 Johnson + Johnson	USA	0.36	1.03
14 Boehringer Mannheim	FRG	1.00	1.01
15 Hoffmann-La Roche	Switzerland	1.59	0.96
16 Smithkline Beckman	USA	1.40	0.96
17 Monsanto	USA	2.87	0.88
18 Squibb	USA	1.03	0.88
19 Takeda	Japan	1.21	0.83
20 Beecham	UK	0.23	0.82

Other Chemicals	Nationality	1969–74	1985–90
1 Bayer	FRG	2.57	2.77
2 Dow Chemical	USA	2.40	2.67
3 Hoechst	FRG	2.37	2.45
4 BASF	FRG	1.40	2.31
5 Ciba-Geigy	Switzerland	2.54	1.92
6 General Electric	USA	1.39	1.86
7 E. I. Du Pont De Nemours	USA	3.29	1.68
8 Imperial Chemical Industries	UK	2.14	1.16
9 Shell Oil	Netherlands	0.85	1.09
10 Eastman Kodak	USA	1.33	1.03
11 Union Carbide	USA	1.11	0.86
12 Exxon	USA	0.79	0.84
13 Allied-Signal	USA	1.62	0.81
14 Henkel	FRG	0.35	0.80
15 Rhone-Poulenc	France	0.63	0.69
16 Phillips Petroleum	USA	1.46	0.66
17 Sumitomo Chemical	Japan	0.55	0.65
18 Texaco	USA	0.41	0.64
19 3M	USA	0.52	0.62
20 Monsanto	USA	2.22	0.61

Materials	Nationality	1969–74	1985–90
1 3M	USA	1.36	2.26
2 Fuji Photo Film	Japan	0.31	2.24
3 Ppg Industries	USA	2.72	1.81
4 General Electric	USA	2.32	1.76
5 E. I. Du Pont De Nemours	USA	3.48	1.57
6 Hitachi	Japan	0.20	1.43
7 Corning Glass Works	USA	2.77	1.13
8 Dow Chemical	USA	1.26	1.11
9 Hoechst	FRG	1.01	1.08
10 Saint-Gobain Industries	France	0.96	0.95
11 Emhart	USA	0.46	0.93
12 TDK	USA	0.10	0.91
13 Owens-Corning Fiberglas	USA	1.83	0.89
14 Allied-Signal	USA	0.65	0.86
15 Toshiba	Japan	0.38	0.80
16 Sumitomo Electric Industries	Japan	0.06	0.75
17 Kimberly-Clark	USA	0.61	0.75
18 W. R. Grace	USA	0.69	0.71
19 Bayer	FRG	0.59	0.69
20 GTE	USA	0.28	0.65

Non-electrical Machinery	Nationality	1969–74	1985–90
1 General Motors	USA	1.23	0.91
2 Hitachi	Japan	0.18	0.88
3 General Electric	USA	1.22	0.80
4 Canon	Japan	0.05	0.71
5 Toshiba	Japan	0.08	0.69
6 Siemens	FRG	0.29	0.65
7 Philips	Netherlands	0.39	0.54
8 United Technologies	USA	0.47	0.54
9 Nissan Motor	Japan	0.12	0.52
10 Westinghouse Electric	USA	0.56	0.51
11 Honda	Japan	0.03	0.51
12 Allied-Signal	USA	0.78	0.50
13 Toyota Jidosha Kogyo	Japan	0.10	0.50
14 Fuji Photo Film	Japan	0.09	0.41
15 Mitsubishi Denki	Japan	0.03	0.38
16 IBM	USA	0.46	0.38
17 ITT Industries	USA	0.35	0.35
18 Robert Bosch	FRG	0.24	0.34
19 ATT	USA	0.56	0.34
20 Aisin Seiki	Japan	0.10	0.31

Vehicles	Nationality	1969–74	1985–90
1 Honda	Japan	0.91	9.12
2 Nissan Motor	Japan	1.74	5.73
3 Toyota Jidosha Kogyo	Japan	0.76	4.84
4 Robert Bosch	FRG	3.79	4.27
5 Mazda Motor	Japan	0.78	2.93
6 General Motors	USA	5.21	2.79
7 Mitsubishi Denki	Japan	0.21	2.78
8 Nippondenso	Japan	1.27	2.57
9 Fuji Heavy Industries	Japan	0.06	2.20
10 Hitachi	Japan	0.38	1.91
11 Yamaha Motor	Japan	0.32	1.85
12 Daimler-Benz	FRG	2.71	1.50
13 Ford Motor	USA	2.41	1.50
14 Brunswick	USA	0.42	1.10
15 Aisin Seiki	Japan	0.34	1.10
16 Lucas	UK	0.95	0.87
17 Porsche	FRG	0.42	0.86
18 Outboard Marine	USA	0.70	0.84
19 Caterpillar	USA	1.99	0.76
20 Kawasaki Jukogyo	Japan	0.08	0.76

Electrical Machinery	Nationality	1969–74	1985–90
1 General Electric	USA	5.77	2.99
2 Westinghouse Electric	USA	3.22	2.68
3 Philips	Netherlands	1.44	2.15
4 Amp	USA	1.10	2.02
5 Mitsubishi Denki	Japan	0.20	1.97
6 Hitachi.	Japan	0.53	1.91
7 Siemens	FRG	1.47	1.85
8 Toshiba	Japan	0.41	1.53
9 General Motors	USA	1.81	1.30
10 GTE	USA	1.20	1.29
11 Motorola	USA	0.51	0.97
12 Matsushita Electric Industrial	Japan	0.85	0.88
13 Asea Brown Boveri Ab	Switzerland	0.83	0.80
14 United Technologies	USA	0.93	0.67
15 NEC	Japan	0.22	0.63
16 ATT	USA	1.25	0.53
17 Robert Bosch	FRG	0.49	0.53
18 Allied-Signal	USA	0.72	0.52
19 Honeywell	USA	0.76	0.51
20 Canon	Japan	0.07	0.51

Electronic Capital Goods & Components	Nationality	1969–74	1985–90
1 Toshiba	Japan	0.53	5.29
2 IBM	USA	8.83	5.25
3 Hitachi	Japan	1.71	4.79
4 Motorola	USA	2.15	2.88
5 Texas Instruments	USA	1.97	2.88
6 NEC	Japan	0.97	2.75
7 Mitsubishi Denki	Japan	0.13	2.73
8 Fujitsu	Japan	0.38	2.59
9 General Electric	USA	6.77	2.50
10 Philips	Netherlands	2.81	2.43
11 ATT	USA	6.05	2.09
12 Siemens	FRG	1.75	1.79
13 Honeywell	USA	2.23	1.08
14 Unisys	USA	3.47	1.03
15 Sharp	Japan	0.05	1.03
16 Canon	Japan	0.04	0.97
17 General Motors	USA	1.36	0.92
18 Tektronix	USA	0.26	0.89
19 Thomson-Csf	France	0.32	0.81
20 Sony	Japan	0.43	0.79

Telecommunications	Nationality	1969–74	1985–90
1 ATT	USA	5.97	4.24
2 Siemens	FRG	2.22	3.25
3 General Electric	USA	4.29	2.89
4 Philips	Netherlands	1.54	2.55
5 Motorola	USA	1.02	2.55
6 NEC	Japan	0.61	2.43
7 Westinghouse Electric	USA	3.30	1.79
8 Toshiba	Japan	0.26	1.64
9 Mitsubishi Denki	Japan	0.21	1.49
10 ITT Industries	USA	3.55	1.41
11 Hitachi	Japan	0.43	1.41
12 General Motors	USA	1.57	1.30
13 Thomson-Csf	France	0.82	1.26
14 GTE	USA	1.49	1.21
15 IBM	USA	1.19	1.12
16 Northern Telecom	Canada	0.54	1.02
17 Fujitsu	Japan	0.20	0.86
18 Rockwell International	USA	0.63	0.77
19 CGE	France	0.58	0.75
20 Alps Electric	Japan	0.13	0.74

Electronic Consumer Goods	Nationality	1969–74	1985–90
1 Canon	Japan	0.95	6.51
2 Fuji Photo Film	Japan	2.12	6.21
3 Eastman Kodak	USA	6.24	3.32
4 Toshiba	Japan	0.42	3.27
5 General Electric	USA	3.97	3.06
6 Philips	Netherlands	2.38	3.04
7 Sony	Japan	1.02	2.94
8 Hitachi	Japan	0.62	2.89
9 Minolta Camera	Japan	0.88	2.47
10 Xerox	USA	3.79	2.29
11 Konica	Japan	0.52	1.95
12 Ricoh	Japan	1.00	1.87
13 Matsushita Electric Industrial	Japan	1.20	1.61
14 Sharp	Japan	0.00	1.60
15 IBM	USA	2.92	1.44
16 Pioneer Electronic	Japan	0.18	1.44
17 Olympus Optical	Japan	0.14	1.22
18 Mitsubishi Denki	Japan	0.07	1.11
19 NEC	Japan	0.36	1.05
20 Siemens	FRG	0.59	1.01

Technologies for Extracting and Processing Raw Materials	Nationality	1969–74	1985–90
1 Mobil Oil	USA	2.17	4.91
2 Exxon	USA	3.00	2.25
3 Halliburton	USA	0.60	1.62
4 Chevron	USA	2.66	1.47
5 Philip Morris	USA	1.32	1.42
6 Baker Hughes	USA	0.41	1.38
7 Texaco	USA	2.49	1.36
8 Phillips Petroleum	USA	2.35	1.36
9 Nabisco Brands	USA	0.32	1.29
10 Amoco	USA	0.18	1.28
11 Shell Oil	Netherlands	2.13	1.26
12 Allied-Signal	USA	3.00	1.17
13 Atlantic Richfield	USA	0.89	1.10
14 Deere	USA	1.04	0.89
15 Union Oil Of California	USA	0.57	0.83
16 E. I. Du Pont De Nemours	USA	0.87	0.67
17 Nissan Motor	Japan	0.03	0.61
18 Schlumberger	USA	0.85	0.55
19 British-American Tobacco	UK	0.19	0.55
20 Nestle	Switzerland	0.15	0.55

Defence-related Technologies	Nationality	1969–74	1985–90
1 Boeing	USA	1.06	4.29
2 MBB	FRG	1.18	2.50
3 General Electric	USA	1.58	1.44
4 Oerlikon-Buhrle Ag	Switzerland	0.89	1.35
5 British Aerospace	UK	0.66	1.28
6 Morton Thiokol	USA	0.93	1.11
7 Feldmuhle	FRG	1.56	1.08
8 General Dynamics	USA	0.29	1.08
9 Imperial Chemical Industries	UK	1.33	0.95
10 Honeywell	USA	0.31	0.93
11 United Technologies	USA	1.04	0.82
12 Aerospatiale	France	0.35	0.82
13 General Motors	USA	0.54	0.80
14 Westinghouse Electric	USA	0.15	0.80
15 Olin	USA	1.16	0.71
16 Lockheed	USA	0.79	0.69
17 Grumman	USA	0.02	0.66
18 Ford Motor	USA	0.08	0.51
19 Sundstrand	USA	0.02	0.51
20 Rockwell International	USA	0.83	0.46

Source: Based on data supplied to SPRU by the US Patent and Trademark Office.

been an uneven degree of stability (or instability) in the firms' shares and rankings within each technological field. A casual reading of Table 5 shows that in some fields, the leaders of the early 1970s continued to be so into the late 1980s, whilst in others new leaders emerged during the period. This is shown statistically in the final column of Table 6, which presents the correlation of the shares of the top 20 firms in 1985–90 with their shares in 1969–74.

Thus, the low (and statistically insignificant) correlations in motor vehicles and in electronic consumer goods mainly reflect the emergence of Japanese firms as technological leaders in these fields, whilst the high (and statistically significant) correlations in electrical machinery and telecommunications reflect mainly a re-enforcement of the dominance of established US and some European firms. The more stable shares in industrial chemicals reflect the continuing strength of mainly European firms.

Table 6. Nationalities of the Top 20 Firms in US Patenting: 1985–90.

	Japan	United States	West Europe	Correlation of Shares of the Top 20: 1969–74 to 1985–90
Defence Related Technologies	0	14	6	0.37
Fine Chemicals	1	12	7	0.54
Industrial Chemicals	1	11	8	0.66*
Raw Materials Based Technologies	1	16	3	0.45
Materials	4	13	3	0.41
Electrical Machinery	6	10	4	0.68*
Telecommunications	6	10	4	0.70*
Electronic Capital Goods	8	9	3	0.51
Non-Electrical Machinery	9	8	3	0.41
Motor Vehicles	11	5	4	0.15
Electronic Consumer Goods	14	4	2	0.27

Note: *Denotes a correlation coefficient significantly different from zero at 5% level.
Source: Based on data supplied to SPRU by the US Patent and Trademark Office.

4. CONCLUSIONS

A numbers of clear conclusions emerge from the above analysis.

First, the relative importance of large firms in the generation of new technology varies widely across technical fields.

Second, most technologically advanced countries depend very little, in general, on the technological activities of foreign large firms, and on any large firms for the development of capital goods technologies.

Third, the technological links between large firms and their home country are in general very close. The latter has a major influence on the rate and direction of technological activities in the former.

Fourth, there are no inherent tendencies for technological activities to spread out around the globe. Foreign production by large firms requires foreign technical support activities; firms' shares of foreign technological activity are therefore largely explained by their shares of foreign production. As a counterbalancing force, effective management of innovation requires close physical proximity between the technological activities and the main centres of production and sales. For this reason, most technological activities in large firms are concentrated at home, and otherwise in the USA and Germany.

These conclusion have two major implications for countries at intermediate stages of technological development:

- in the short term, they can with the appropriate policies expect foreign large firms to develop local capacities to adapt foreign technologies to local conditions, and to stimulate the development of capacities in local suppliers of capital goods;
- in the long term, they cannot expect foreign large firms to create major innovation-launching capabilities in their country.

REFERENCES

Acs, Zoltan and Audretsch, David 1989. *Small Firms and Technology*, Directorate of Technology Policy, Ministry of Economic Affairs, the Hague.

Cantwell, John 1989. *Technological Innovation and Multinational Corporations*, Oxford: Blackwell.

Cantwell, John 1992. "The Internationalisation of Technological Activity and its Implications for Competitiveness", in Granstand, Ove; Hakanson, Lars: and Sjolander, Soren (eds.), *Technology Management and International Business: Internationalisation of R & D and Technology*, Wiley, Chichester.

Dunning, John 1980. "Towards an Eclectic Theory of International Production: Some Empirical Tests", Journal of International Business Studies, Spring/Summer 1: 9–31.

Dunning, John 1994. "Multinational Enterprises and the Globalisation of Technological Capacity", *Research Policy*, **23**: 67–88.

Fagerberg, Jan 1987. "A Technology Gap Approach to Why Growth Rates Differ", *Research Policy*, **16**: 87–99.

Fagerberg, Jan 1988. "International Competitiveness", *Economic Journal*, **98**: 355–374.

Franko, Lawrence 1989. "Global Corporate Competition: Who's Winning, Who's Losing, and the R & D Factor as One Reason Why", *Strategic Management Journal*, **10**: 449–474.

Freeman, Christopher 1982. *The Economics of Industrial Innovation*, London: Pinter.

Kleinknecht, Alfred 1987. "Measuring R & D in Small Firms: How Much are we Missing?", *Journal of Industrial Economics*, **36**: 253–256.

Patel, Parimal and Pavitt, Keith 1988. "The International Distribution and Determinants of Technological Activities", *Oxford Review of Economic Policy*, Winter, 4: 35–55.

Pavitt, Keith. Robson, Michael and Townsend, Joe 1987. "The Size Distribution of Innovating Firms in the UK: 1945–83", *The Journal of Industrial Economics*, **35**: 297–316.

Soete, Luc 1981. "A General Test of Technological Gap Trade Theory", *Review of World Economics*, **117**: 638–666.
Vernon, Raymond 1966. "International Investment and International Trade in the Product Cycle", *Quarterly Journal Of Economics*, **80**: 190–207.
Vernon, Raymond 1979. "The Product-Cycle Hypothesis in a New International Environment", *Oxford Bulletin of Economics and Statistics*, **41**: 255–267.

World Oligopoly, Rivalry between "Global" Firms and Global Corporate Competitiveness

François Chesnais[*]

The aim of this paper is to contribute to a clarification of the terms "globalisation" and "global" in relation to the waging of competition and the location of production in manufacturing industry (the service industries are not dealt with here). The most widely used definition is still the one given by Porter (1986). Porter opposes "multidomestic" and "global" industries and goes on to make three propositions regarding the latter:

1) "a global industry (. . .) is an industry in which a firm's competitive position in one country is significantly affected by its position in other countries or vice versa" (p. 18)
2) "therefore, the international industry is not merely a collection of domestic industries but a series of linked domestic industries in which the rivals compete against each other on a truly world-wide basis" (p. 18) and;
3) "in a global industry, a firm must in some way integrate its activities on a worldwide basis to capture the linkages among countries" (p. 19).

As Imai and Baba (1992) have suggested, while Porter acknowledges the existence of fairly severe Japanese and European competition to US multinationals, his approach remains extremely

* Département de sciences économiques et de gestion, Universtité de Paris XIII, 93430 Villetaneuse, France.

"US- centric". Porter's "global strategy" is directed at US corporations and is basically asking them to *"think of the world as one market, instead of a collection of domestic markets, and to coordinate world-wide R&D, marketing production and distribution in order to gain efficiency in the overall " global factory" system"* (Imai and Baba, 1992, p. 396). The setting of Porter's analysis is still implicitly the worldwide outward extension of US domestic oligopoly first studied by Hymer, Caves and Knickerbocker. The "rivals (who) compete against each other on a truly world-wide basis" are still US rivals. Porter is not yet really contemplating today's real "global oligopoly" marked by the presence of large oligopolistic rivals coming from the three poles of the "Triad" and a situation where for the first time in their history, US firms are now confronted with a novel situation of "global mutual market dependence" involving large foreign rivals with whom they may never be able to establish the type of oligopolistic understanding they had previously worked out among themselves (see in section II our presentation of Kogut' insights on this point).

Porter's definition is thus no longer satisfactory. The first argument this paper makes is that "a global industry" is an industry in which it is *competition* that has become "global", as distinct from corporate industrial integration as such. It is an industry in which international cross-investment and transnational concentration (Chesnais, 1993) have brought about a situation of " mutual global market dependence" which shapes quite strongly the competitive position and strategic decisions of the large multinational firms. In such an industry a firm's competitive position in one country will be significantly affected (to paraphrase Porter) by its position in other countries, as determined both by its own capacity to manage the coordination and integration of activities at an international level and by the moves of its oligopolistic rivals (see Vernon, 1992, pp. 29–30 for a clear discussion of this aspect).

In transnationally concentrated industries or product groups, competition is "global" in that it takes place essentially in the same "world market" (which consists mainly of markets within the "Triad", where most of the world's purchasing power is to be found), and is fought out among and between firms capable of waging oligopolistic competition on a "world" scale. On the "supply-side" it involves fairly small numbers of true rivals who entertain a complicated mix of relationships combining cooperation and cut-throat competition. On the "demand-side" it calls on a fairly similar common set of "values", shaped by ideology of the media and activated by commercial publicity, which both boost final consumption and ensure its homogeneity internationally.

The global character of competition does not however ipso facto make "the international industry (. . .) a series of linked domestic industries" (Porter's second proposition). Competition is global, but it is still waged from fairly separate industrial bases at the three poles of the "Triad". In the case of Japan the industrial base is in fact still a highly distinctive one, only very weakly linked to those of the other poles. While the number of industries truly marked by ever stronger interconnections between countries is growing fast, it is at each (or at least at two poles of the "Triad", the EC and NAFTA), hence at a "regional" (e.g. continental) level rather than a "global" one, that they are to be found.

There a real "linking" of industries can certainly be observed; the linkages "captured" by large firms (Porter's third proposition) being often those that they have consciously *built* through their own strategies. This will invariably go hand in hand with corporate policies for the sourcing of key inputs (strategic raw materials on a truly world-wide basis incorporating countries outside the "Triad" as suppliers whenever this is still justified, and technology and R&D-intensive sophisticated intermediate inputs inside the OECD countries), but otherwise manufacturing is less "global" — more centered on the three poles of the "Triad" — than it was twenty years ago. There are important technological and organisational reasons for this. The pervasive technological changes associated with the emergence and constant improvement of manufacturing-related micro-electronics have gone hand in hand with the adoption of new methods of organising and controlling manufacturing production, with the extensive use of subcontracting close to final assembly and "just-in-time" delivery. It is also on this "regional" basis that a large part of the increasingly strongly customized marketing and selling takes place, which means of course that it is at a "regional" level the greater part of what is still deemed "international trade" occurs, both in intermediate and in final goods. In many industries this will establish "globalization", as defined by van Tulder and Ruigrok (1993) as the most efficient way of organizing production and marketing and so of waging global competition. Seen in this context "globalisation" and "regionalisation" should be viewed as representing today two largely complementary processes (Oman, 1994).

The new international telecommunication technologies have made differentiated strategies for the sourcing and deployment of resources much easier to manage. It is ever easier for large firms to distribute manufacturing and marketing facilities in a number of different national locations on a regional basis and their R&D facilities possibly on a worldwide one, to source key technological and intermediate product inputs internationally and to manage their value and profit creating activities in real time. The advent of a new type or"style" of transnational firm, the "network firm" (Antonelli, 1988, Dunning, 1988, Imai and Baba, 1991) is the organisational expression of corporate strategies aimed at seizing these new opportunities.

In section I, the paper begins with a general discussion of "globalisation". Section II examines the basis of world oligopoly and the nature of the competition waged by "global" firms. Section III takes a closer look at the foundations of corporate competitive advantages and looks at the way firms engaged in intra-triadic "global competition" will attempt to combine the "firm-specific" competitive advantages they generally still derive from their home "national systems of innovation", with "regional" strategies for the location of manufacturing and marketing.

I. GLOBALISATION AS A NEW PHASE OF INTERNATIONALISATION.

Globalisation is a term coined by journalists and politicians. It was thrust on the academic community, which has often rejected it, characterising it simply as a catchword (this is of course largely true). The term is often wrongly understood to refer to the effects of a multilateral lowering of tariff and non-tariff barriers to trade and so associated principally with the outcome of trade liberalisation (see Oman, 1994 for a useful discussion of this error). Globalisation has essentially to do with the dynamics of capital accumulation and technological change and is "personified" so to speak by the international investment activities of large corporations. On account of this MNEs seem to "personify" globalization so to speak, explaining why business economists were quick to use the term "global" to characterise the newer forms of corporate strategy.

This means that globalisation falls totally within the bounds of internationalisation or international production. This is perhaps why many scholars working on internationalisation have tended to equate globalisation with earlier international production. They have viewed the extensive and very fashionable use of the new term as a belated and partly skewed recognition of a process they have long studied, be it from a variety of methodological standpoints, and have not approached globalisation as representing something new. In France Michalet (1991 and 1993) and myself have taken a somewhat different position. We have decided that, despite its non-academic origin, the term reflected some major changes in the world economy and, notwithstanding fairly significant differences in focus between us, we have both sought to define globalisation as a specific phase within the much longer process of internationalisation, a phase possessing a number of new characteristics. Some rudimentary lineaments of my own approach are discernible in the final report of the Technology/-Economy Program (OECD, 1992a) as well as in two pieces written about the same time (Chesnais, 1992 and 1993). Today my position can perhaps be set out a little more clearly than before.

Trade-created internationalisation and "multinationalisation".

The term internationalisation is generic (Chesnais, 1988a); it encompasses the numerous different processes whereby previously fairly separate national economies have become increasingly inter-related and interdependent. A convenient analytical approach is offered by establishing a basic distinction between the nature and implications of trade-created internationalisation and those of international production or "multinationalisation" as it is called in French. Although the two processes have become increasingly closely inter-twined and are harder and harder to disentangle in their effects, it is worth attempting to point to some differences between them.

International trade theory postulates the existence of separate, clearly identifiable national economies (even if, as in the case of neo-classical theory, countries are only defined by their overall factor endowment). Trade can be viewed as pertaining to a logic of the *extension of the productive* forces and the *full exploitation* of the *potentialities of an international division of labour*. The logic is that of the "Wealth of Nations" and Adam Smith's central proposition that the division of labour (including the division of labour in the process of production within firms, hence productivity and technical progress) is dependent on "the extent of the market". Considered in isolation from the process of concentration and centralisation of capital and the formation of very large firms, this logic points to processes such as the growth in international trade, the increasing complexity of patterns of international trade specialization, arm's length trade in technology, and the constitution of a common pool of scientific knowledge at the international level open to all those with the level of competence required to understand it.

In contrast with trade-created internationalisation, *multinationalisation* pertains to the accumulation, centralisation and deployment of *capital* across national borders within large corporations and so the formation of *transnationalised internal corporate markets* organised within the structure of large multinational firms and banks operating in a number of countries. One moves from the logic of the Wealth of Nations to that of the chapters on the concentration and centralisation of capital of Marx's theory of long term capital accumulation. Once capital becomes centralised within large profit-making centers, a number of consequences will follow. In particular, the subsequent deployment of this capital will be commanded by strictly defined criteria of profitable value creation and/or rent-based value appropriation and so to the conditions (both geographically and activity-wise) which appear to fit this requirement best at any given moment. The MNE examines the allocation of productive and R&D resources between the different countries where it operates and the type of operations assigned to each plant or laboratory from its own centralised view point and strategy (Michalet, 1976/86).

The growth of strongly concentrated capital has its own internal logic which *combines* the search for industrial *profit* through industrial production, the reaping of *rent* from corporate assets in various forms including technology and numerous varieties of speculative financial earnings. Highly concentrated capital, as recognised by the best literature on MNEs, possesses a capacity not open to smaller firms for reaping "appropriable rents" or "quasi rents"; for exerting numerous forms of monopolistic and monopsonic market power; and for exploiting situations where as Dunning (1981) puts it,

> "the deliberate organisation of 'market failure' and the subsequent extension of internalisation" should be seen as "a

> powerful motive for takeovers or mergers and a valuable tool in the strategy of oligopolists" (op. cit. p.28).

Once it consolidates its international operations, the MNE acquires what Dunning defines as the specific ownership advantage stemming from

> "the ability to organise related productive activities more efficiently than the market"

which

> "confer an important economic on the firms possessing them" (Dunning, 1988a, p. 11).

The specific features of globalisation

It is against this background that globalisation can be discussed. In my view it is characterised in particular by two decisive features. The first is the advent of totally internationalised financial and monetary markets. While this development does not herald "the end of geography" (O'Brien, 1992) in the field of finance if only because it also strengthens a number of hierarchical relationships between States , it does represent a qualitative step forward in the process of internationalisation. Over the past three decades concentrated money capital possessing extremely strong rentier traits has gained tremendous power (or perhaps better regained it after the loss suffered during the Great Depression , the Second World War and the subsequent Keynesian cum Socialist policies). Since the start of the 1980s it has played an ever more important role. Besides the sway now exerted by financial markets and their operators over the exchange rates of supposedly sovereign countries, this role includes the increasingly strong attraction concentrated money capital exerts on all profit-making centers, including productive capital lodged within firms, as well as the capacity it now has to impose its demands (in particular the defense of rentier earnings in the face of inflation as well as of political insecurity) on OECD governments as well, of course, as on those of weaker debtor nations.

The *second* feature, on which this paper concentrates, is the extremely rapid growth in the 1980s of FDI taking principally the form of international cross-investment in and between the three poles of the "Triad". This has led to the generalisation of global oligopoly as the most significant type of supply structure, as distinct from the earlier situation where an essentially US domestic oligopoly extended out into the world.

The pattern of world trade reflects these two key developments. The trade of many newly industrialised and developing countries as well as their current investment and growth, are shaped to a large extent by the burden of their debt to the private financial system. Among OECD countries, recent developments in the pattern of trade such as the notable growth in the foreign sourcing of intermediate inputs, can only be understood against the background of the pattern of FDI at the three poles of the "Triad". Trade liberalisation, both within GATT and at a "regional" level in the EC and NAFTA, has facilitated intra-industry /intra-firm trade flows, thus strengthening the interconnection between MNE activity and the pattern of trade.

The process leading to globalisation was driven by capital accumulation and technological advance, but it was strongly aided by political developments. The central role should be attributed to capital accumulation, fueled by the sustained and particularly high rates of growth of the "Golden decades", but also with respect to the accumulation of money capital by the inflationary policies adopted by most governments and more important still the huge amount of debt and hence credit money created through the floating of loans required to finance the US federal deficit. The formation, outside the sphere of domestic capital markets and the regulatory control of Central Banks, of the Eurodollar market laid the foundation for financial globalisation and the formation of totally internationalised financial and monetary markets which are now strong enough to exert their sway over government monetary and foreign exchange policies in all but the strongest countries. But large scale capital accumulation also set the scene for the spectacular growth of foreign direct investment during the 1980s despite the context of economic turbulence, slow growth and/or outright recession which has marked the world economy since the second sharp 1979-81 downturn. While other factors discussed below are also at work the main form taken by FDI, namely *transnational acquisitions and mergers*, cannot be dissociated from the part now played by financial globalisation.

The technological basis for financial globalisation as well as the growth of contemporary "network firms", has been provided by telematics and the facilities it offers multinational banks and

MNEs for establishing world-based intra-corporate IT networks. The progress made in international telecommunication technologies and networks, the convergence of previously separate functions and the rapid decline in telecommunications and computing costs, have provided a strong and extremely efficient technological foundation for the interconnection of domestic capital markets and stock exchanges, the consolidation of the international banking system and that of the transnational Eurobond and foreign exchange markets. Large firms have also used the new technological opportunities to organise the regional or worldwide location of their manufacturing and marketing or their R&D facilities in a number of different national locations, to source key technological and intermediate product inputs internationally and to manage their value and profit creating activities in real time on a global basis.

The third set of factors behind globalisation are political. They concern of course the enacting in GATT and OEEC/OECD of numerous codes, agreements and treaties for the liberalisation of international trade, FDI and services, further consolidated in Europe by the Common Market and its subsequent developments now leading up to 1993 and the new treaties now under ratification within the EC. But they also concern all the policies associated with the triumph of Reaganism and Thatcherism since the start of the 1980s and their subsequent amplification with the collapse after 1989 of Stalinist-inspired command communism in Eastern Europe and the ex-USSR. The part played by these policies cannot be underestimated. Taken in conjunction with the first two sets of driving forces, privatisation, deregulation and trade and capital-market liberalisation have seriously impaired the capacity of governments to enhance structural competitiveness and social cohesion through industrial policy. It is worth repeating that in the case of OECD countries, this loss is not *simply* a consequence of the objective tendencies at work in relation to nation-States and the process of internationalisation. It is *also* quite as strongly the outcome of the economic policies, in particular financial deregulation, advocated by neo-liberal economists. These policies obviously reflect the pressures coming from the constant increase in the degree of internationalisation, but the extent and the way in which these pressures have been accommodated has opened the door to today's almost unbridled domination of capital at world level.

The overall result of these developments has been the renewal of a strong trend towards rampant unequal development or to use a more familiar expression, towards economic and social *divergence* and *polarisation* as distinct from convergence and increased income equality, both *between* and *inside* countries. The marginalisation of an increasing number of developing countries within the structure of world investment and trade flows cannot be abstracted from an overall discussion of globalisation and an appraisal of its consequences.

II. WORLD OLIGOPOLY AND THE CONFIGURATION OF GLOBAL COMPETITION

The advent of world oligopoly represents one of the features which characterise globalisation as a specific phase. In an international or "world" context the notion of oligopoly requires appropriate handling. For reasons which have to do both with "supply" and with "demand", it cannot be used exactly the way it is in the context of a closed domestic economy. In a domestic context because of the strong overlap between the two, the term "supply structure" tends to be used to refer indifferently to the firms producing and selling in a given market and to the industrial base qua base. This strong overlap or near identity disappears when one moves to the level of "global" oligopoly. The formation, through the combined effect of domestic and transborder acquisitions and mergers of a single concentrated "supply structure" with reference to the number of firms still remaining in the market as producers, does not imply that this has yet led to the formation of a single industrial base. Similarly in a global context the "market" is much more elusive than in a domestic setting where it can be delimited with precision. The "world market" qua selling place or market where goods are sold is something very flexible, delimited by effective purchasing power and effective access, which can evolve in relation to cyclical processes and political events.

Both these dimensions mean that global oligopoly cannot be equated automatically, as in a domestic context, with the capacity by firms collectively to control quantities and prices. Global oligopoly has welfare implications, but these concern other aspects than consumer prices, for instance the capacity to bar the access to technology to firms who are not members of the oligopoly.

Consequently the notion of "world oligopoly" is used in this paper to designate *the set of dynamic* (rather than static as in standard oligopoly theory) *relationships of competition and cooperation* linking the small group of large corporations which are in a position to wage effective oligopolistic rivalry in a given industry or product group, alone or with the support of their "home country" administration and government. The configuration of the oligopoly taken in this meaning, demarcates at any given point in time the *economic* and in particular the corporate strategic *boundaries* of what business management economists call "global competition". The actual *geo-political* limits of the arena where such competition is waged will depend on the exact location at a given time of the markets where effective purchasing power is to be found and goods can be sold and also where strategic productive inputs (in particular technology) can be sourced. It should be perfectly clear that *neither are "global" in the sense of incorporating the world.* "Global competition" involves the firms that are capable of waging competition effectively in many markets. "Global markets" are exclusively markets where purchasing power and intermediate inputs are effectively located (primarily at the three poles of the "Triad" and in the NIEs).

Industrial concentration as an international process.

Global oligopoly is intimately linked with international cross-investment. Below "mutual invasion" will be looked at from the standpoint of oligopolistic rivalry. Here we examine international cross-investment in relation to the process of transborder and transoceanic industrial concentration which represents one of the foundations of world oligopoly. Internationally highly concentrated supply structures are the outcome of two related but nonetheless distinct processes, that of *internationalisation* and that of *industrial concentration.* They emerge when in a given industry i) industrial and technological development has created extremely both opportunities and constraints on firms (notably in the form of large R&D costs which must be recouped) to produce for world markets as distinct from even the largest domestic markets and to source key inputs to production, notably in the form of scientific and technological advances made in foreign countries on a worldwide basis; and ii) when concentration after developing principally on a domestic basis, has evolved as an international process involving transnational cross-investment occurring in the form of acquisitions and mergers.

Work on concentration at an international level is very behind hand (Newfarmer, 1985) . Measures of concentration (e.g. market shares by the first 4, 8 and 20 firms) are still being carried out *mostly on a purely domestic basis* at a time when the most significant indicator of concentration now pertains to *global, e.g. world market shares.* Data showing similar concentration in aggregate *world* assets or sales have begun to be collected in the context of industrial sector studies carried out over recent years at OECD, the EC (FAST) and the United Nations. They have been put together in the OECD study (see OECD, 1992a, pp. 222–223, tables 46, 47 and 48) and show that in a wide range of industries and product groups the world market is shared by 10–12 firms, and often fewer. This provides an initial way of determining, for a given industry or product group, the identity of the small group of large corporations which are in a position to display effective oligopolistic rivalry, to build and consolidate entry barriers in particular through the individual and collective protection of their technological advance, and also, when conditions permit, to limit price-competition around the world (as has been the case for instance for certain pharmaceutical products).

Oligopoly and mutual recognition in a global setting.

The single most important proposition established regarding oligopoly is that it is marked not simply by fewness, but more decisively by *interdependence* and *mutual recognition.* Oligopolists

> "respond not to impersonal market forces, but personally and directly to their rivals"
>
> (Pickering, 1974).

Or again,

> "the key distinguishing feature (. . .) is that oligopolists are strategically linked to one another. The best policy for one firm is dependent on the policies being followed by each rival firm in the market"
>
> (Friedman, 1983).

This proposition was first applied in an international setting in relation to the study of outward FDI by large US firms in the

1950s and 1960s. S. Hymer and his associates and friends at Harvard (in particular R. Caves and Knickerbocker), established that the foreign investment of US firms,

> "involved market conduct that extended the recognition of mutual market dependence – the essence of oligopoly – beyond national boundaries"
>
> (Caves, 1971).

In short it represented the extension of US domestic oligopoly to a world arena.

Within the current configuration of tri-polar world oligopoly, strategic interdependence and mutual recognition concern large firms with national trajectories and codes of oligopolistic conduct which differ significantly. As Kogut (1986) has rightly pointed out:

> "an oligopoly is itself an organisation regulated by routines which are not quickly or easily changed; and of great importance, these routines and oligopolistic agreements reflect national traits regarding anti-trust regulations, government intervention, and tolerance of competitive or co-operative behaviour. Thus, there will be a country component which cuts across national oligopolies and which will generate country patterns in trade and international competitive behaviour."

The asymmetrical patterns of conduct which mark "global competition" as waged by Japanese oligopolists on the one hand and their US and European rivals on the other, and so the "misunderstandings" which are continually arising among them, can easily be interpreted in this light. US firms for instance now realise that Japanese oligopolists are, at least at present, unwilling to respect the tacit "rules" of competition and the mutual commitments to deter entry that these firms had previously worked out among themselves in a domestic context and found the large European firms ready to respect.

Technological cooperation and "peaceful" oligopolistic recognition

The tacit codification of oligopolistic competition is likely to take time in an international context, meaning that the present situation of severe rivalry (mainly between the US and Japan because few European firms or governments show much inclination for engaging in a real head-on industrial contest) cannot be expected to disappear rapidly. This does not imply that the process is not at work, notably at the level of technological cooperation. International technological agreements between firms probably represent today the area where large firms otherwise engaged in fierce rivalry can most easily assert a form of non-belligerent mutual recognition and collaboration. This suggests that such alliances must be identified and submitted to special analysis, for instance by taking a closer look at the type of data collected by J. Hagedoorn and his colleagues at MERIT (Hagedoorn and Schakenraad, 1990).

International cross-licensing between large firms which remains a fairly basic form of technical cooperation agreement in some industries, was already a significant feature of the strongly concentrated chemical and heavy electrical equipment industries in the 1920's and 1930's (Newfarmer, 1978). The 1930s also witnessed the establishment of at least one large and very effective research consortium between a number of major oil companies belonging to different countries. Today agreements involving the world's largest firms in strategic industries and R&D intensive product groups and their implications for national systems must necessarily be set in the context of the present trend towards high levels of world concentration. Interfirm technological agreements represent a response to many pressures: the rapid and often cheap (since the risks have been borne by another firm) acquisition of technology or technological knowledge from outside the firm, the pooling of R&D and complementary assets; but also the collusive or quasi-collusive protection by oligopolists of their technological advance vis-à-vis smaller firms and potential entrants (Contractor and Lorange,1985; Porter and Fuller,1986). This is particularly characteristic of international agreements.

Contemporary innovation theory (Dosi et al., 1988) stresses the importance of analysing different "appropriability regimes", e.g. the degree to which an innovation can be protected (ranging from "tight" regimes where technology is extremely difficult to imitate to very "weak" regimes where it is almost impossible to protect). Appropriability must now be considered alongside classical components of entry barriers (e.g. economics of scale, level of marketing expenditures and other absolute cost advantages, etc.). Rapid paradigmatic technological change probably affects appropriability in *two opposite directions*. On the one hand, it will weaken the previous appropriability regime considerably and destroy previous dominant designs. In turn this will lower the technological component of entry barriers, although other components, such as a strong hold over distribution networks as in pharmaceuticals still offer oligopolists a considerable degree of protection against would-be entrants in particular when they are smaller domestic firms. On the other hand, radical technological change creates a constraint on firms to achieve much stronger appropriability. Today, however, it does so within changed international conditions, marked in particular by the fact that potential competitors fall into different groups, the most important division being the one which occurs between those competing firms who are capable of "reading" technological trajectories and understanding what the "other man" is doing, and those which do not have the in-house technological capacity to this. By pooling some of their R&D, or by organising the two way exchange of key complementary technologies (as studied for instance by Hacklisch, 1986, between US and Japanese oligopolists), the firms in the first grouping while still competing between themselves, can nonetheless constantly increase their lead over other firms and raise the technological entry barriers facing potential entrants.

International cross-investment and asymmetry in "mutual invasion".

In contrast with technological cooperation, international cross-investment or "mutual invasion" as it has aptly been called (Erdileck,1985), is a highly rivalistic way of recognising mutual market dependence. Studying European FDI into the US economy in the 1970s, Graham noted that it occurred mainly in industries which had previously attracted US investment in Europe and suggested that it had begun to be driven by the requirements of oligopolistic rivalry, in particular the capacity

> "to replicate the cost and benefit trade off experienced by US rivals in the development of new product technologies"

and the

> "capacity of European firms to pose a threat to US rivals on their 'home turf' " (Graham, 1978).

Cars, tyres and parts of the chemical industry were sectors where the capacity to counter severe rivalry in one market area with retaliation in another began to shape the conduct of international oligopolists from the early 1970s onwards. European MNEs tended however to remain cautious and not provoke the US leaders too strongly. The entry of the Japanese Keiretsu as major global oligopolistic rivals in the late 1970s and their large scale penetration through investment into the US economy modified this situation radically. It made global oligopoly irreversible and international cross investment a strategic imperative for large firms in their fight for survival.

Other theoretically-minded business management economists stress that

> "cross-subsidisation between markets and products is the essence of global competition"

and that

> "the process of globalisation involves a new sequence of competitive action and reaction (..)
> 1) An aggressive competitor decides to use the cash flows generated in its home market(s) to cross-subsidise an attack on the home market(s) of foreign-based competitors.
> 2) A defensive-minded competitor then retaliates not in its home market(s) where the attack was staged, but in national markets where the aggressor firm is most vulnerable in a cash-flow sense"
>
> (Hamel and Pralahad, 1988 p.138).

During the 1980s US oligopolists were subjected to such competition in an acute manner as shown by the scale of FDI channeled to acquisitions and mergers rather than *ex novo* investment. Even if the process is not documented as clearly as in the case of the US, the same thing occurred in many European countries, with the notable exception of Germany. The asymmetry between Japan's *outward* and *inward* FDA as compared with its main OECD competitors is now documented (see, in particular OECD, 1992b p. 125).

Asymmetry in the degree of penetration into rivals' home industrial and technological bases is an important handicap for the waging of successful rivalry in oligopolistic industries. This is why it has become an important source of international friction today. One of the many reasons behind Japan's large and very stable long-term trade surplus in manufactured products, the relatively low level of its intra-industry trade and its superiority in global oligopolistic competition, is the capacity of the keiretsu system of financial and industrial organisation to limit quite severely the degree of foreign penetration into Japan's NSI and production system at a time of rapid expansion abroad. This is so to the extent that the collective ability to pose a counter-threat depends on the possibility for all rivals in the global oligopoly to operate in more or less equal conditions in one another's markets via cross-investment. The success of Japanese firms, through their system of dense capital cross-ownership, in severely limiting inward investment by their US and European rivals has given them an important extra source of competitive advantage in addition to all the others.

III. THE TECHNOLOGICAL AND MANUFACTURING BASIS OF CORPORATE COMPETITIVE ADVANTAGE.

We must now rapidly discuss the foundations of corporate competitive advantages. Here the argument is that today the competitiveness of large firms engaged in intra-triadic global oligopolistic rivalry is built on the combined effects of the technology-based "firm-specific" competitive advantages corporations generally still derive from activities located in their home "national systems of innovation", and of their capacity to enact successful strategies for manufacturing, marketing and distribution at the "regional" (e.g. continental) level.

Nurturing the domestic technological base and sourcing in foreign ones

In the case of most "global" firms the foundation of corporate competitive advantage remains the firm's home technological and industrial base. This is why oligopolistic rivalry involves simultaneously a capacity to nurture and protect one's "home" technological base and to "invade" that of one's rivals.

In numerous articles P. Patel and K. Pavitt have rightly argued that MNEs continue to keep in their home countries, near to their corporate headquarters, a much higher fraction of their R&D than of their manufacturing activities (*see inter alia* Patel and Pavitt, 1990). This is uncontestable and is one expression of the recognition by oligopolists of the importance of the "home" technological base. British multinationals represent the exception which "confirms the rule". Along with Canada, the United Kingdom has long been the G7 country having opened its technology base the most broadly to foreign (mainly US firms), whose UK affiliates accounted by 1986 for more than 20 per cent of total UK patenting in the United States. As part of their move

> "to escape from the deteriorating UK economy by investing in more dynamic markets overseas"
>
> (Jones, 1993, p. 30),

UK firms seem to have begun to shift not only their production abroad but also a large part of their R&D. Of all the G7 countries (which are also in absolute terms the large OECD R&D spenders) the United Kingdom has the largest figure for patenting outside the home base, superior to 25 per cent. Given the size of the United Kingdom's technology base and the long tradition of UK science, this is a rather remarkable figure, raising the question of the solidity of these firms' relation to their domestic technological base. In the case of the United States, Germany and France, let alone Japan, key R&D activities as partially expressed by patenting data, remains located at home.

The point I have been trying to make in my long-standing argument with P. Patel and K. Pavitt really concerns the second complementary dimension of corporate technological strategies. One will generally find that while most oligopolists locate their R&D at home and interact with their domestic technological base, they will also seek to get a foot *inside the technological bases of their rivals.* This will generally imply the setting up of laboratories abroad, whose main mission however may not be that of undertaking sophisticated R&D work of the type which is likely to be patented, but to

> "act as a window on foreign science"
>
> (Fusfeld, 1986).

As far as I am concerned this falls completely within the notion of the "globalisation of technology" even if it does not show up in the patent data. It will also include other forms of scientific and technological scanning on a global scale and lead to the (paid or unpaid) acquisition and centralisation of knowledge to the laboratories and centers where the firm's vital R&D is being carried out. Today this will often entail the setting up of technological cooperation and sharing agreements with foreign universities as well as with smaller R&D intensive small firms (as in the case of biotechnology where European and Japanese MNEs have set up many agreements with small US firms). Cantwell (1990) argues that in any given industry,

> "technological activity is locationally differentiated, as part of different national systems of innovation. The distinct characteristics of innovations in each country provide MNEs with an incentive to *disperse research facilities* to gain *access to complementary paths of technological development* which they can then *integrate at a corporate level."*
>
> (our stress).

This is quite certainly true, but does *not* occur solely or perhaps in some cases even principally by the delocation of formal R&D; external sourcing of foreign technology through scientific scanning and then the setting up of non-equity agreements can be just as important.

Home country networks and national systems of innovation.

The domestic technology base is not simply the R&D base. It encompasses the numerous facets of the national system of innovation. Among "evolutionary economists" there is now a broad common understanding that the existence and working of national economies cannot be reduced simply to a question either of more or less efficient markets or of appropriate or inappropriate government policies, but that their performance points to deeper factors of cohesion involving both the role of institutions and the existence of non-market or para-market relationships between economic agents. Among industrial economists interest for the role played by such factors was stimulated both by the performance of the Japanese economy per se and by the original thinking of Japanese industrial economists (K.J. Imai, H. Itami, M. Aoki, Y. Baba, A. Goto, etc.). They have shown why successful innovation calls for cooperation among numerous firms and institutions, and may even depend (as argued by Imai and Itami, 1984), on the degree to which the "Schumpeterian entrepreneur" is consciously understood to be a *"system"* made up of a set of inter-related firms and institutions involved in a complex mix of competition and cooperation.

The new focus has also built on the work of economists specialised in technological change, in particular those who have worked on the inter-sectoral diffusion of technology (Pavitt et al., 1987); the role of tacit knowledge (Dosi et al, 1988); the interactive character of technological innovation (Kline and Rosenberg, 1986), the quality of interfirm user/producer relationships (Lundvall, 1988) and the role played by technological cooperation. Since the mid-1970s, the pressure towards inter-institution and inter-firm cooperation in technology, and the premium on success in organising joint research, alliances and partnerships have increased dramatically as a result of the generic features of contemporary core technologies and the importance of synergies and interfaces between previously separate know-how (see Chesnais, 1988 for an overview).

The notion of national systems of innovation coined by Freeman (1987) and Andersen and Lundvall (1988) has been developed with the aim of encompassing these numerous facets and of showing that the performance of national economic may depend on the manner in which *organisational and institutional arrangements and linkages conducive to innovation and growth* have been permitted to thrive in different countries (see Lundvall, 1992, for an overview). These institutions and linkages are not the making of governments alone; many of them have as much to do with socio-historical factors shaping the behaviour and strategies of *firms* than with action by the State. As some American scholars now argue, while firms may often be tempted to view their national environment as something they can "take for granted", this environment is in fact strongly affected by the collective views, decisions and intangible investments of firms (Hollingsworth, 1991). National environments will furnish a climate conducive to competitiveness to the extent that cooperation, in various forms, is recognised and valued by firms and that economy-wide externalities are developed through public but also private intangible investments (OECD, 1992a).

In a situation where generic technologies permit strong inter-industry interactive relationships between complementary technologies, firms and countries which have succeeded in appropriating the results of these interactions individually and collectively (through the process Dosi (1984) names *"the internalisation of untraded technological interdependencies"*) are likely to demonstrate high levels of international competitiveness in a fairly wide range of partially interconnected industries. Work by Guerrieri (1992) on the structure of Japanese as compared to US exports has given some statistical support to this hypothesis. His starting point is

> "technological change is that it affects a wide range of structural relationships linking different industries. Some sectors will be more productive in terms of innovations while others will be users of innovations developed by others. So, the linkages among various parts of the production system can assume great importance, in terms of technological complementarities and interdependencies affecting competitiveness of each sector and hence of the industrial system as a whole" (p. 30).

On this basis, Guerrieri refers to the systemic dimensions contained in Pavitt's well-known taxonomy of industrial innovation and applies it to the study of Japanese, US and German exports.

Japan's exports show the highest concentration among the three countries compared in its exports of products in the three key inter-connected groups of scale intensive, specialised supplier and science-base industries. It is also the only country where the weight of both the last groups has risen and been accompanied by gains in competitiveness across all three types of industries as well as a much lower level of intra-industry trade than all other OECD countries. These features all bear a close relationship to the technological complementarities and inter-industry linkages arising from the specific features of the Japanese industrial system, including those of the *keiretsu* corporate group structures with the synergies, the capacity for "collective internalisation" and the protection from takeovers these structures provide (see Freeman, 1987 for some aspects).

More is known about the US R&D base than about the US national system of innovation as such and its relation to the competitiveness of US MNEs. The deterioration of US industrial competitiveness has still to be studied from this perspective. The notable erosion of US technological advantages during the last decade obviously has many causes. One has certainly to do with the fact that many key relationships within the US national system of innovation depend on military R&D outlays possessing very weak links to the civilian sector. The MIT report on US competitiveness (Dertousous et al. 1989) has highlighted many facets of US corporate culture and business conduct having negative effects on industrial performance. The difficulty of US firms in recognising that interfirm and inter-institutional cooperation, in various forms might "represent a specific source of increasing returns" (Ferguson, 1991) has been identified as a strong potential source of weakness. Porter's (1990) study on the"competitive advantage of nations" can be read as a call on US firms to giver a much higher priority to the strengthening of their domestic "diamonds of industry-level competitive advantage".

An interesting study by Scherer has attempted to test the relation between the performance of US firms and the nature of their reactions to foreign rivalry, domestic market structures and the extent of corporate multinationalisation. Scherer finds that *"import penetration rose more rapidly in concentrated industries"* and that government support tended to increase rather than to limit *"submissive reactions"* to successful foreign rivalry. His conclusions are less clear-cut regarding multinationalisation and suggests that *"MNEs reacted more heterogeneously". According to his data, "companies with R&D operations outside the US had on average zero reactions to changes in net exports, whereas US market specialists had strongly submissive reactions. Case study evidence suggested that R&D multinationals reacted differently because they were able to offset falling exports with imports from overseas subsidiaries, because they could change overseas as well as domestic R&D programs in response to altering strategic threats, and because their overseas operations provided a 'distant early warning line' (about competition and new products)"* (Scherer, 1992, p. 175). This would imply that it was the foreign rather than the home segment of their corporate R&D which permitted the more successful US firms to face foreign rivalry. It is obvious from such findings that the debate about the internationalisation of R&D and its advantages and disadvantages is still at its beginning.

MNEs as active forces in the process of "regionalisation"

We must now turn to the other major source of corporate competitiveness, namely the linkages which large firms may succeed in "capturing" (to use Porter's expression) between separate or at least previously separate national industries, but which they may in fact often have consciously *built* through their own strategies of cross-border industrial coordination and integration. This is the process which has been occurring since the 1980s thus making the "linking" (e.g. corporate integration of national industries) a "regional" (e.g. continental) level rather than a "global" one, and thus "regionalisation" and "globalisation" something like the two sides of a same coin.

One of the most significant features of the 1980s and early 1990s has been the trend towards a "regional" clustering of trade and investment at each of the three poles of the Triad and the formation of regional trading blocks. At the European and North American poles this has taken the form of negotiated "Regional Trading Arrangements" provided for by article 24 of the GATT, e.g. customs unions as in the case of the Rome Treaty and the EC in its subsequent more closely organised institutions, and free trade areas involving several countries as in the case of EFTA, the US-Canada trade agreement and now the North America Free Trade Area (NAFTA). In the case of the South-East Asian Japanese-dominated zone, it has taken the form of quite tightly knit regional multinational trade relationships which have developed independently of any formal trade agreement.

The UNCTNC has suggested that although the dividing line can be blurred, one may usefully distinguish between "policy-led" regional integration initiated by governments and "FDI-led integration". The essential characteristic of the former is that the political and institutional framework for integration precedes integration at the production level. In contrast, FDI-led or MNE-led integration occurs when firms are the driving force (UNCTNC, 1992). While MNE-driven integration is now playing an increasingly important role, it is true that in the EC the process has been strongly policy-led and also marked by particularly intensive intra-industry trade in which *medium* and even in many cases *small* firms, played an active role. In South East Asia, but also in North America integration has, on the contrary, been very strongly led by FDI and marked principally by the activity of MNEs.

In South East Asia a strong process of FDI-led integration is underway since the late 1970s. As a result of the building of regional production networks by Japanese MNEs intra-regional, intra-industry trade has grown rapidly among a group of countries which other members of, or neighbours to, the Asian Pact. Most of the intra regional trade is in capital and intermediary goods, one part of which originates in Japan, the rest consisting of trade among Japanese foreign affiliates and non-affiliated local subcontractors situated in a number of countries in the region. The structure of sales for final products is significantly different: only a small part of output is exported back to Japan, the bulk of output being shared between sales in domestic markets, within the region, exports to the rest of Asia and quite high exports to the US and also to a much lesser degree to Europe.

Thanks to the staff of the UNCTNC, quite detailed data is available for the electrical and electronic and the automobile industry. In the case of purchases of capital goods and intermediate products, Asia – including Japan – dominates purchases, accounting for 92 per cent and 99 per cent of the total for automobile and electronics affiliates, respectively. In the case of automobiles, the North American affiliates of some of the Japanese MNEs provide about 7 per cent of their Asian affiliates' purchases of intermediate products, all the trade being intra-firm. Overall, however, supply networks existing among affiliates are largely contained within the region. Integration occurs through intra-firm trade as well as through trade between unaffiliated firms, who have in common the fact that they are component suppliers and sub-contractors to the same group of hub corporations. This trade involves an international division of labour and country specialisations which permit the fulfillment of scale economies through the network of regional trade. Figure 1 illustrates this for the affiliates of Toyota, but the process is in fact more advanced in the electronics industry than in automobiles.

In the case of NAFTA, the MNE-led integration of a developing country into a more advanced economic zone is, for the time being at least, but probably for a long time to come essentially limited to one country, Mexico. Well before the signature of the NAFTA Treaty, Mexico's trade was characterised by intra-industry trade flows overwhelmingly dominated by the intra-firm trade of a few US corporations. For these firms Mexico's geographical proximity, its low wage rates and the free-export zones (maquiladoras) on the US–Mexican border, represented a way of safely "retreating" to a "regional" strategy after their earlier attempt at truly "global" industrial integration through a delocation of selected low-skill,

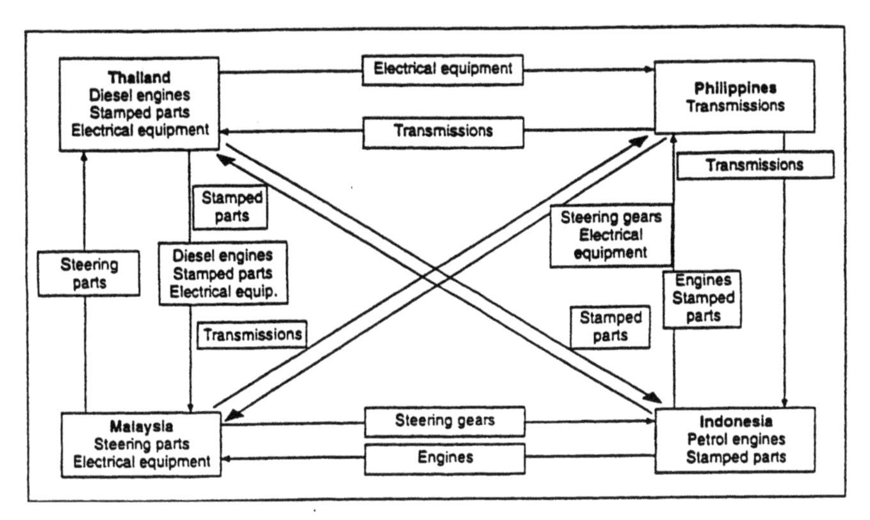

Figure 3.1 Specialisation and intra-firm trade among Toyota's Asian subsidiaries.
Source: Far Eastern Economic Review (1989, p. 73)

low wage segments of manufacturing to South East Asia. No other national group of corporations has delocated manufacturing and intermediate product-sourcing operations to low-wage production sites to the extent that the US MNEs have, nor been so attracted to the concept of the "hollow corporation". Today the location of plant in Mexico permits these firms to reconcile, at least partially, within the framework of "adapted Fordism", traditional strategies based on cheap labour, with the opportunities offered by automation and the imperatives of customisation.

The semiconductor industry is a case in point (Henderson, 1989). In the late 1970s when hourly wages seemed to be the key issue and when wafers could still be assembled manually in competitive conditions, this stage in the manufacturing process was delocated to the Philippines, Thailand, Indonesia and Malaysia. During the 1980s the constant updating of equipment and the need to use frontier technology became the overriding factor. As semiconductor technology became ever more sophisticated, there were also considerable benefits in terms of quality and output to be gained from assembling the devices automatically. This has been the case especially for the more advanced semiconductors based on VLSI (very large scale integration) technology which require the "bonding" of many more connections than simpler devices. The other development of the 1980s was the increasing demand for customised semiconductors as distinct from standardised ones. This was partly the result of the increasing significance of military and space markets following the "Star War" program and the military buildup under Reagan, but has also arisen from increasing demand for customised products in industrial microprocessor and even in consumer electronics markets. Customer monitoring calls for "regional" rather than "global" industrial integration. When production processes are spread across the globe, user-producer relationships are harder and more expensive to manage than if processes are spatially concentrated.

US firms will not be the only firms to benefit from NAFTA as a market and as a cheap labour resource base. The few European and the numerous Japanese MNEs which have set up integrated manufacturing plant in automobiles or electronics in the North American zone are in a position to do so as well. Nissan has a large plant supplying motors in Mexico. In general, however, the strategy of Japanese firms has consisted in transplanting "Toyotism" and the just-in-time system within the US industrial base, both through the delocation of their domestic component suppliers and through the progressive build up of sub-contracting networks with indigenous US small and medium firms (see Mair, 1993 on the Honda system).

Organising and capturing "regional" linkages between industries

Europe is of course the region of the world where the opportunities for internationally integrated production offered by large markets characterised by high income, homogeous demand and falling tariffs are the oldest and where the experience of large firms in "linking" previously separate national industries is the greatest. This was already the case in the period of "rationalised", "internationally integrated" Fordism practised by Ford and General Motors (Dicken, 1992), but is more so in the context of "Toyotism" and a full exploitation of the potentialities offered simultaneously by the Single Market the new technologies and the new industrial management paradigm.

Large scale industrial restructuring characterised by a switching and reorganisation of MNE operations between countries grew in Europe in the later half of the 1980s both as a result of the perspective of the 1992 Single Market and of the rapidly growing differentiation in wage levels inside and between EC member countries as a consequence of Thatcherism. To some extent inside the EC there are regions, in particular in the British Isles, which occupy basically the same function as the Mexican low-wage, free-export zones (the maquiladoras) with the additional important advantage of calling on a labour force which has been disciplined and trained by a century and a half of capitalist production.

Initially industrial restructuring primarily concerned the sites and production facilities which foreign MNEs (essentially US ones) had previously built on a "multidomestic" basis and were now able to reorganise on the basis of the Single Market, but it also involved the growth, through international (e.g. intra-continental) acquisitions and mergers, of European firms that had previously only been mainly large domestic or regional concerns. The reorganisation and restructuring by MNEs of production facilities within Europe (Savary, 1993; Howells and Wood, 1993; van Tulder and Ruigrok, 1993) has involved a simultaneous process of focusing and switching of activities by MNEs among their previous production sites. Replica subsidiaries previously set up to cater for home markets have progressively been closed down. Production is organised on the basis of internationally interdependent production facilities which are increasingly centralised in a small number of important affiliates to which world or more often "regional" (e.g. European) product mandates have been assigned. This has already led to the closure of many plants with more closures in the offing (Hamill,1993) as well as to the *upgrading or downgrading* of the facilities that stay open (Dunning and Cantwell, 1991). National manufacturing industries are subjected to a process of upgrading, downgrading and hierarchical ranking with which governments are asked, in the name of the free play of the "market" not to interfere.

With the advent of "Toyotism", its acclimatization through Japanese investment as in the UK and its adoption by US and European business management experts in the form of "lean production" (Womack et al., 1992), a further round of industrial restructuring is now underway. The feature which has the greatest implications for the location of production and what remains of industrial employment is the kanban or "just-in-time" manufacturing system. This system calls for highly synchronised and continual deliveries of components and materials from the hub corporation's component suppliers and sub-contractors, thus requiring that these suppliers produce in spatial proximity to their principal customers. The industrial upgrading and downgrading effects of restructuring and relocation appear to be compounded by those of the new investment aimed specifically at establishing the "lean production" model. For reasons related to unionisation and the bargaining of wages and working conditions, firms are prone to locate this investment in other areas of host EC countries than the old industrial regions which remained so long fortresses of the labour movement.

CONCLUSIONS

Inside the "Triad" globalisation and "regionalisation" are proceeding hand in hand for reasons which have to do with politics, geography and history as well as with the present foundations for successful oligopolistic rivalry.

The increasingly concentrated market structures resulting from transnational mergers delimit the arena where effective "global" competition takes place; the sourcing of key inputs, in particular scientific and technological inputs, is organised on a truly worldwide basis; production however takes place essentially on a "regional" (e.g. continental) basis, where a large part of marketing, and so of "trade", also occurs. The effect is to make trade and competitiveness among the advanced countries, both within the three "regional" groupings and between them, to a large extent the outcome of corporate strategies, many of which are dictated by the "global", oligopolistic character of corporate rivalry.

Following the technological and managerial developments of the last fifteen years, along with the effects of deregulation and liberalisation, the competitive advantages of the large firms engaged in global competition are based on a *mix* of "ownership" advantages, many of which are still strongly related to *home country* "locational advantages" in the form of national R&D outlays and the strengths of national innovation systems, and of "internalisation" advantages relating to multinationality. Today the latter include the capacity for global sourcing and the effective use of monopsonic power (for instance with regards to the technological assets owned by smaller firms). However competitive advantages of effective or would-be world oligopolists are also increasingly based on their capacity to exploit and/or create linkages between previously separate national industries and organise a mix of horizontal and vertical industrial integration in the most efficient manner.

The precondition for this is the acquisition of what Ohmae (1985) has named *"global insider"* status. In an age of true "Triadic" global oligoplistic rivalry, the fate of erstwhile "national champions" will increasingly be sealed by their capacity to be "inside" both the national innovation system, the manufacturing base and the "regional" (e.g. continental) market at the other two poles of the "global" competitive arena. Seen from a European standpoint the outlook is bleak. Whatever appraisal one has of globalisation one thing is certain. Today the waging of competition requires both technological, industrial, commercial and hence centralised and voluntaristic political approaches which both Japan and the United States possess, but which the defenders of the "Europe of Maastricht" seem determined not to acquire and even to impede its acquisition.

At the level of the world economy, the issue today may well be one of knowing whether the foundations on which world oligopoly is built and the basis on which rivalry among global oligopolists is shown really permit growth outside the "Triad" and the countries and regions immediately associated with the three poles. In many parts of the world it was only on account of trade barriers and other political constraints that FDI was undertaken and foreign production set up by MNEs. These firms cooperated for a time and to a much more limited extent than is generally recognised (for instance with respect to the type of technology transferred) in "import-substituting" industrial capacity building. But for them it was always very much a *"second best"* imposed on them because of the international situation which existed in the late 1950s — early 1960s after the Bandung conference, the arrival of Kruschev at the head of the USSR and the Cuban Revolution.

Today a totally different political and ideological situation exists expressed *inter alia* by the so-called "Washington consensus" (see Oman, 1994 for a clear analysis), the power of the IMF and the triumph of trade liberalisation, privatisation and dereglementation in the largest part of the "Third World". Barring a few (temporary ?) exceptions such as China, both the incentives and the constraints for investing in countries not directly associated with one of the three poles are almost gone. Taken as a bloc the global oligopoly has, furthermore, just scored at the end of the Uruguay Round a major victory by imposing the introduction of industrial property rights (IPRs) into the GATT instruments, thus creating further barriers to technology access by firms and countries which were in fact already barred on account of their non-participation in international networks of interfirm technological agreements. At the *very same time*, as has just been discussed, an ever more powerful productive capacity than before has been built inside the "Triad" for the imperatives of global competition. The status now reserved for all but the very closest associates of the G7 is essentially that of serving as markets, e.g. outlets, albeit extremely poor ones in most cases and when it is appropriate resource bases. Industrialisation is unwanted; countries will have to *fight for it alone* on the basis of their own determination and resources. A discourse on the "alleviation of poverty" is surreptitiously replacing the earlier ones on development, in particular in the case of Sub-Saharan Africa.

In their "Evolutionary Theory of Economic Change" (1982), Nelson and Winter demonstrate through a combination of case study evidence and formal modeling how the combined advent of concentrated supply structures and strong technological change are capable of leading to the "endogenous generation of market structure and technological performance" marked among other things by the emergence of "reverse causation" in which technological change far from reducing concentration can in fact reinforce it. One of the hypotheses raised by the advent of world oligopoly and the waging of global competition from the bases in the "Triad" could be that of the formation of a cumulative process of closer and closer integration at the core of the "Triad" which might go hand in hand with a complementary process of marginalisation or "deconnection" for other parts of the world economy. As was said earlier it seems increasingly difficult to abstract a discussion of the renewal of a strong trend towards economic and social divergence and polarisation between and inside countries from the overall analysis of globalisation.

BIBLIOGRAPHY

Antonelli, C. (1988),"The Emergence of the Network Firm", in Antonelli, C. (ed),

New Information Technology and Industrial Change: The Italian Case, Kluwer Academic Publishers, Dordrecht.

Cantwell, J. (1989), *Technological Innovation and Multinational Corporations*, Oxford, Brasil Blackwell.

Cantwell, J. (1990), *The Technological competence Theory of International Production and its Implications*, Reading University Discussion Papers in International Investment and Business Studies, no 161.

Chesnais, F. (1988a), "Multinational enterprises and the international diffusion of technology", in Dosi *et al.* (1988), *Technical Change (. . .)*.

Chesnais, F. (1988b), "Technical Co-operation Agreements between Independent Firms", STI Review, OECD, no 4.

Chesnais, F. (1992), "National systems of innovation, foreign direct investment and the operations of multinational enterprises", in Lundvall, B.A. (ed.), *National Systems of Innovation (. . .)*.

Chesnais, F. (1993), "Globalisation, world oligopoly and some of their implications", in Humbert, M. (Ed.), *The Impact .. op. cit.*

Contractor, F.R. and Lorange, P. (1985), "Why Should Firms Cooperate? The Strategy and Economic Basis for Co-operative Ventures", in F.R. Contractor and P. Lorange, eds., *Cooperative Strategies in International Business*, Lexington Books, Lexington, Mass.

Dosi, G. (1984), Technical Change and Industrial Performance, *The Theory and an Application to the Semiconductor Industry*, London, Macmillan.

Dosi, G., Freeman, C., Nelson, R., Silverberg, G. and Soete, L. (eds.), (1988), *Technical Change and Economic Theory*, London, Pinter Publishers.

Dunning, J.H. (1981), *International Production and the Multinational Enterprise, George Allen and Unwin, London.*

Dunning, J.H., (1988a), Multinationals, Technology and Competitiveness, Unwin Hyman, London.

Dunning, J.H., ed., (1988b), *Explaining International Production*, Unwin Hyman, London.

Dunning, J.H. and J. Cantwell (1991),"MNEs, Technology and Competitiveness of European Industries", Aussenwirtschaft, Vol. 1, no 46.

Erdilek, A. (ed), (1985), *Multinationals as Mutual Invaders: Intra-Industry Direct Foreign Investment*, Croom Helm, London.

Friedman, J. (1983), *Oligopoly Theory*, Cambridge University Press, Cambridge, United Kingdom.

Fusfeld, H.I. (1986), *The Technical Enterprise: Present and Future Patterns*, Ballinger, Cambridge, Mass.

Hagedoorn, J., and Schakenraad, J. (1990), "Interfirm partnerships and cooperative strategies in core technologies" in Freeman, C. and Soete L., *New Explorations in the Economics of Technological Change*, London, Pinter Publishers.

Hamill, J. (1993), "Employment effects of the changing strategies of multinational entreprises", in Bailey,P. (Ed.) *Multinationals and Employment: The Global Economy of the 1990s*, Geneva, ILO.

Graham, E.M. (1978), "Transatlantic Investment by Multinational Firms: A Rivalistic Phenomenom ?", *Journal of Post-keynesian Economics*, No 1.

Graham, E.M. (1985), "Intra-industry Direct Foreign Investment, Market Structure, Firm Rivalry and Technological Performance" in Erdilek, A., (ed.),

Multinationals as Mutual Invaders: Intra-Industry Direct Foreign Investment, 1985, London, Croom Helm.

Guerrieri, P. (1992), "Technological and Trade Competition: The Changing Positions of the United States, Japan and Germany", in *Linking Trade and Technoogy Policy*, National Academy of Engineering, Washington DC.

Haklisch, C.S. (1986), *Technical Alliances in the Semiconductor Industry*, Center for Science and Technology Policy, New York University, mimeo.

Hamel, G. and Prahalad, C.K. " Creating Global Strategic Capability" in N. Hood and J.E. Vahlne (Eds.), *Strategies in Global Competition*, London, Croom Helm.

Henderson, J. (1989), *The Globalisation of High Technology*, London, Routledge.

Howells, J. and Wood, M. (1993), *The Globalisation of Production and Technology*, London, Pinter Publishers.

Humbert, M. Ed., (1993), *The Impact of Globalisation on Europe's Firms and Industries*, London, Pinter Publishers.

Hymer, S. (1960), *The International Operations of National Firms*, The MIT Press, Cambridge, Mass.

Imai, K.J. and Y. Baba (1991),"Systemic Innovation and Cross-Border Networks, Transcending Markets and Hierarchies to Create a New Techno-Economic System", in OECD (1991).

Jones, G. (1993), *British Multinationals and British 'Management Failure': Some Long-Run Perspectives*, Reading University Discussion Papers in International Investment and Business Studies, no 175.

Kline, S.J. and Rosenberg, N. (1986), "An Overview of Innovation", in National Academy of Engineering, *The Positive Sum Strategy: Harnessing Technology for Economic Growth*, The National Academy Press, Washington D.C.

Knickerbocker, F.T. (1973), *Oligopolistic Reaction and Multinational Enterprises*, Harvard University Press, Boston, Mass.

Kogut, B. (1988), "Country Pattern in International Competition: Appropriability and Oligopolistic Agreement," in N. Hood and J.E. Vahlne (Eds.), *Strategies in Global Competition*, London, Croom Helm.

Lundvall, B.A. (1988), "Innovation as an Interactive Process: From User-Producer Interaction to the National System of Innovation", in Dosi et al.

Lundvall, B.A. (ed.) (1992), *National Systems of Innovation – Towards a Theory of Innovation and Interactive Learning*, London, Pinter Publishers.

Mair, A. (1993), *Honda's Global Local Corporation*, London, Macmillan.

Michalet, C.A. (1976), *Le capitalisme mondial*, Paris, PUF (revised edition, 1986).

Michalet, C.A. (1993), "Globalisation, attractiviti et politique industrielle", in Coriat, B. and Taddii, D. *Made in France*, vol.2, Paris, Le Livre de Poche.

Newfarmer, R.S. (1978), *The International Market Power of Transnational Corporations: A Case Study of the Electrical Industry*, United Nations, CNUCED, Geneva.

Newfarmer, R.S. (1985), "International Industrial Organisation and Development: A Survey", in Newfarmer, R.S., *Profits, Progress and Power: Case Studies of International Industries in Latin America*, Indiana, University of Notre Dame Press.

O'Brien,R. (1992), *Global Financial Integration: The End of Geography*, London, Pinter Publishers.

Oman, C.(1994), *Globalisation and Regionalisation: The Challenge for Developing Countries*, OECD Development Centre Studies, Paris.
OECD (1991), *Technology and Productivity: The Challenge for Economic Policy*, Paris.
OECD (1992a), *Technology and the Economy: The Key Relationships*, Paris.
OECD (1992b), *Industrial Policy in OECD Countries*, Paris.
Ohmae, K. (1985), *Triad Power*, The Free Press, New York.
Patel, P. and Pavitt, K. (1990), "Large Firms in the Production of the World's Technology: an Important Case of 'Non-Globalisation' ", University of Sussex Science Policy Research Unit Discussion Paper, January.
Pavitt, K., Robson, M. and Townsend, J. (1987), "Sectoral Patterns of Production and Use of Innovations in the UK: 1945–1983", *Research Policy*, vol 17.
Pickering, J.F. (1972), *Industrial Structure and Market Conduct*, Martin Robertson, Oxford.
Porter, M.E., "Competition in Global Industries: A Conceptual Framework", in M.E. Porter Ed. (1986), *Competition in Global Industries*, Boston Mass., Harvard Business School Press.
Porter, M.E. (1990), *The Competitive Advantages of Nations*, London, MacMillan.
Porter, M.E., and Fuller, M.B., (1986), "Coalitions and Global Strategy", in Porter, M.E. Ed., *Competition in Global Industries*, op.cit.
Savary, J. (1993), "European integration, globalisation and industrial location", in Cox,H. et al. (Eds), *The Growth of Global Business*, London, Routledge.
Scherer, F.M. (1982), *International High-Technology Competition*, Harvard University Press, Harvard.
van Tulder, R. and Ruigrok, W., "Regionalisation, globalisation and localisation: the case of the world car industry", in Humbert, M. (Ed.), *The Impact .. op. cit.*
UNCTC (1991), *World Investment Report 1991: The Triad in Foreign Direct Investment*, New York, United Nations.
UNCTNC (1992), *World Investment Report 1991: Transnational Corporations as Engines of Growth*, New York, United Nations.
Vernon, R. (1992), "Transnational corporations: where are they coming from, where are they headed", *Transnational Corporations*, Vol. 1, No 2, August 1992.

Market Failure and Technological Policy*

Jorge M. Katz

MARKET FAILURE AND TECHNOLOGICAL POLICY

1. From ISI efforts to stabilization programmes

A new breed of market-oriented theoretical ideas and policy proposals seems to be gaining ground throughout the economics profession. Protectionism, inward-orientedness and direct investment subsidies are increasingly identified as the main source of poor economic performance, all of them resulting from a high degree of Government intervention in the economy.

The degree of Government intervention in the economy increased quite considerably — both in DCs and LDCs — during the 1940's and 1950's. It did so in the aftermath of the market failure debate of the 1930's, and it came associated with Keynesian economics, on the one hand, and socialist planning, on the other (Helm, 1990). In most LDCs it took the form of what later on came to be known as the Import Substitution Industrialization (ISI) strategy. Different sources of market failure — micro and macro-originating either on the demand side, on the supply side or in

* Dr. Jorge Katz is Professor of Industrial Economics at the University of Buenos Aires, Argentina. The present paper has been written as a contribution for the discussion of a recent *IDRC draft document entitled IDRC regional strategy for the Latin American and the Caribbean Region.* Comments by Dr. F. Chaparro to a first draft of this paper are hereby acknowledged.

market structure — called for the 'visible' hand of Government to intervene. Also, greater expectations concerning social justice and individual rights laid down the basic principles of the Welfare State.

The breakup of the Gold Standard called for the creation of Central Banks and for the introduction of active monetary policy in many peripheral countries.Economies of scale, — leading to industrial concentration and monopoly pricing — suggested the convenience of nationalization and public production in sectors such as steel or petroleoum. Failure of capital markets induced the erection of financial institutions and development agencies. Failure of the insurance market and imperfect information and preference failure from the part of consumers called for social insurance and for public provision of such goods as health or education. And so on and so forth. A new set of institutions and ideas developed world-wide as a consequence of the emerging new values and principles and the role of the State became central within the new patterns of social organization that resulted thereafter.

It is important to notice that these were years of rapid economic expansion both for DCs and LDCs as well. Within such a climate the world's economy and international trade grew quite significantly for a rather long period of time.Foreign direct manufacturing investment acted as a major growth-inducing force in many peripheral societies, having a considerable impact upon the rate and direction of the industrialization process. Little consideration was then given to the high — and increasing — degree of government intervention in the economy and, in a more general way, to the fact that the Public Sector was gradually taking over initiatives and responsibilities which naturally belonged in the private sector.

External public funds at rather low cost and direct foreign manufacturing investment supplied the resources upon which this model could rapidly diffuse into many Third World countries. Excess domestic demand in the early stages of the ISI process provided the basis for a period of rapid economic growth which took place within the limits of the internal market.

The above mentioned process of rapid economic growth lost momentum in the late 1970's. The international economic scenario suffered a dramatic transformation after the oil shocks of 1973 and 1979, and the Mexican moratorium of 1982. As a result of this the expansionary process of the industrialized world suffered a major setback and it practically ceased to act as a 'growth inducing' force in the peripheral world. On the other hand, a drastic fall in raw material prices, the drying up of external finance and a rocketing rate of interest defined a less friendly world environment for LDCs which thereafter could hardly maintain their attained levels of development, let alone continue with their long term expansion. In addition to the above, the rapid diffusion of microelectronics and of flexible automation production technologies rapidly rendered obsolete many of the technological capabilities aquired by LDCs through 'learning by doing' and 'adaptive' domestic R&D efforts carried out during the years of the ISI process.

As a result of the above the domestic socio-economic environment of many LDCs became increasingly unstable and fragile. A faltering overall economic performance and a massive escalation in social repression — which obtained after military takeovers in countries such as Argentina, Brazil, Chile, Uruguay, Bolivia, etc. — point to the fact that a major transformation of the long term development model of many peripheral societies was clearly in the making. The rate of saving and investment suffered a dramatic contraction and the inflow of foreign manufacturing investment became much less significant than in the immediate post-war years, or ceased altogether in the case of many of these countries. The process of capital accumulation deteriorated badly and public accounts moved into huge deficits which could only be covered through money printing and a rapidly expanding inflationary tax.

Under such critical circumstances many peripheral societies attempted to return to orthodox free market principles during the 1980's. They drastically curtailed the regulatory role of the State and opened up their economies to foreign competition. A new set of institutions, markets and patterns of social organization gradually began to emerge as a consequence of the above. A deep socio-economic transformation started at that point and is now steadily working its way through the socio-economic structure. Such an — as yet unfinished — transformation, whose impact upon production efficiency and social equity is still far from clear, will surely have far-reaching consequences in the years to come. Questions of production efficiency and international competitiveness as well as major issues concerning social equity and political governance seem to be at stake and clearly demand a new and fresh discussion. Once again the role of governments and markets appears to be at stake and a new debate seems to be urgently needed concerning the massive process of 'creative destruction' many Third World countries are presently going through.

It goes without saying that the above mentioned transformation both in values and principles as well as in the rate and nature of the growth process has strongly affected the way in which economists – and social scientists in general – are presently looking at development problems. Based on ideas emerging from strict conventional neoclassical thinking many professional economists are nowadays negatively judging the ISI strategy and passing a highly critical message concerning 'government failure' during the post-war period. From this extreme perspective the Import Substitution Industrialization process has left LDCs with distorted and inefficient production systems resulting from long-standing protectionism. Inward-orientedness, low international competitiveness and income-seeking behaviour from the part of local businessmen are all regarded as the result of excessive government intervention in the economy. Such an extreme view – although a popular one – is probably false, as the last Annual World Bank Report argues in its introductory page when it says: "this is not a question of intervention vs laissez-faire. ... Competitive markets are the best way yet found for efficiently organizing the production and distribution of goods and services. ... But markets can not operate in a vacuum. They require a legal and regulatory framework that only governments can provide. *(Besides) markets sometimes prove inadequate or fail altogether."* (World Bank, 1991).

Thus, and in spite of the fact that the neoclassical critique of the ISI model rightly spells out a number of major aspects in which the 'visible hand' of government has failed dramatically, we have to recognize that many 'ifs and buts' still persist and that both at the conceptual and policy level it is by no means obvious – at least not for the present author – that the advice of 'get your macro 'prices' right and let the market mechanism do the rest' is all that we need in development economics.

There are at least three different sources of doubts concerning the simple neoclassical views on these matters.

First, even 'well-behaved cases' – such as Korea or Chile –, frequently quoted by supporters of the liberalization approach, such as Krueger and Balassa (Balassa, 1990) have been seen in quite a different perspective by other authors (A. Amsdem, 1989;

L. Kim, 1990) which have pointed to a much higher degree of government involvement in the economy than what neoclassical economists have reported in their own accounts of the facts.

Consider the case of Chile. Availability of external finance in the mid-1980's — even in the face of a dramatically high external debt ratio — public ownership of its major export commodity — copper — etc. seem to suggest that the explanation of the Chilean economic re-structuring efforts of the 1980's requires a more complex discussion than the one emerging from a simple neoclassical account of the facts. Similarly the rather peculiar relationship which the Korean State managed to establish with its large national conglomerates — the Chaebolds — seems to indicate that the Korean story also has its own idiosyncratic side which is not adequately accounted for by a simple neoclassical description of the facts.

Second, some skeptical Latin American voices have recently argued that ... "the neoclassical approach tends to 'miss' the problems posed by the Smithian and Keynesian tradition. They 'miss' the problem of how to generate more savings and how to ensure that savings be allocated to investment because they think that the market forces are potentially able to simultaneously resolve the classical, Keynesian and neoclassical questions. The problem of increasing savings — the classical or Smithian question — does not exist per se because the interest rate determined by the market can induce the optimal amount of savings. By the same token, the 'animal spirit'/portfolio decision aspect — the Keynesian question — does not arise, because the growth models of the Arrow tradition assume that investment and savings are instantly equalized by the market". (J. M. Fanelli et al., 1990).

Now, it so happens that over the course of the last 15 years the rate of *public* savings and investment has been cut down to nearly one half of their historical value in many LDCs while *private* savings have been transnationalized and are now financing the economic re-structuring process of more mature industrial societies. Lack of credibility — in some cases not restored even after a few years of succesful short term stabilization efforts, as in the case of Bolivia or Uruguay — have prevented the restoration of capital markets and of the capital accumulation process. A 'bottom of the well' equilibrium situation has emerged and it is by no means obvious how to deal with such a new set of circumstances. 'Wait and see' seems to be the only answer the neoclassical model so far has provided for cases of that sort.

In the face of the above Fanelli et al., conclude that the (neoclassical) "policy proposals for structural reform underscore *the need to generate more savings and to reinforce the links between savings and investment in order to restore growth in Latin America*" (op. cit. 1990, pag. 41.).

Third, while the above mentioned sources of failure are 'macro' in nature i.e. they involve economy-wide disequilibrium processes, there is yet another important category of 'market failure' situations which are essentially 'micro' and which the neoclassical model frequently leaves out of consideration as well. Some of these market failure situations – notably those related to the existence of 'public goods', externalities, increasing returns to scale, etc. – clearly provide a strong case for State intervention and valid grounds from which to argue that the 'visible hand' of the Government still has a valuable role to play in development economics.

In particular, many of these issues appear in relation to the generation, diffusion and utilization of technical knowledge and to the functioning of the national system of innovation supporting the process of technical advance in the production of goods and services. There can be little doubt as to the crucial role innovation and technological change play in the building up of international competitiveness and it is precisely here that the role of Governments strengthening the workings of the national system of innovation supporting the process of technical change and promoting a greater degree of technological innovation at the enterprise level can be conceptually defended, even under strict laissez faire rules. Again, the last Annual World Bank Report explicitly recognizes this when it says: "Certain actions involving public goods (admit intervention) because the private sector does not usualy carry them out: spending on basic education, building up infrastructure, etc." (World Bank, 1991).

We shall argue here that there are strong a priori grounds for believing that market signals operate only in a very imperfect manner in the field of knowledge generation and diffusion as well as in the upgrading and development of qualified human resources. As a consequence of that explicit government action is needed if LDCs are to generate the basic technological and human capital infrastructure required for a satisfactory process of growth, technological modernization and re-insertion into world markets. These are the topics that we shall examine in our next section.

2. Market failure in the generation, diffusion and utilization of technical knowledge and the need for an explicit technological policy.

We have so far argued that policy proposals involving short term stabilization efforts, de-regulation of markets, the opening up of the economy to foreign competition, etc. constitute a sine qua non condition for a succesful process of re-insertion into the contemporary international environment. We have also indicated that there are strong grounds a priori to believe that such macropolicy actions might constitute a necessary but not a sufficient policy package if LDCs are succesfully to revitalize their capacity for growth and their international competitiveness.

At the 'macro' level explicit policy actions might be needed in order simultaneously to deal with what Fanelli et al., have called the 'Smithian' and the 'Keynesian' constraints to growth, i.e. the now insufficient volume of domestic savings and the difficulty to ensure that domestic savings are effectively channeled into production investment activities within the local economy. The existence of the 'Smithian' and 'Keynesian' constraints to growth induced Fanelli et al., to argue that the agenda of public actions required in the near future probably needs to incorporate far more questions and issues than what neoclassical authors have so far considered necessary. Stabilization with growth — which means simultaneously closing up the fiscal and external gaps plus the restoration of the capital accumulation process — will probably require more than just minimal actions on the part of local governments as well as new attitudes on the part of DCs governments, financial institutions and international/regional organizations such as the IDB, World Bank, etc. Further de-regulation and opening up of the economy to foreign competition, new forms of external financing, a lower degree of protectionism in raw material markets on the part of DCs, a more open attitude of industrialized nations concerning the diffusion of technology and intellectual property rights etc. belong in this area. Many of these issues are presently being discussed in relation to the Uruguay Round or the Brady Initiative, but we are still a long way off from having achieved significant progress along this front.

Macro/micro policy oriented research seems to be strongly needed in this field.

Leaving for the time being the 'macro' policy debate on stabilization and growth let us concentrate on 'micro' issues related to how to strengthen domestic technological capabilities and the functioning of the national system of innovation supporting the process of technical change in industry, agriculture, etc. In other words, let us now concentrate on the issue of how to develop and consolidate a 'generic' technological infrastructure, capable of supporting the modernization of the production structure of the economy and the transition to the world of 'flexible automation', biotechnologies, telecommunications, new materials, etc. which is gradually gaining ground in mature industrial societies.

A number of structural features prevailing in the markets for technical knowledge and information as well as in the field of education and human capital creation -such as imperfect appropiability of benefits, externalities, incomplete specification of production functions, scale economies in the generation and utilization of knowledge,etc. — suggest that institutions other than the price mechanism might be needed in this field if peripheral countries are gradually to build up the kind of 'generic' technological infrastructure — and the new company attitudes towards innovation and technical change as well as towards human capital upgrading - they presently need to meet the challenge of the international market place. The creation and strengthening of a network of institutions, agencies and policies related to the generation and diffusion of technical change, to the re-cycling and upgrading of human resources, to the opening up of new international markets, etc. appear as a sine qua non condition for a dynamic process of technological change and modernization and for the consolidation of new patterns of insertion into world markets for goods and services. Universities, public research agencies, producers of capital goods, trading companies, Banks, Ministries of Industry and Trade, of Education, Secretaries of Science and Technology, etc. need to be seen as individual parts of a complex network of actors whose coherence appears as crucial if peripheral countries are to regain international competitiveness and capability for self-substained growth. In addition to the above, a new set of incentives seems to be required in order to revitalize 'animal spirits' and entreprenurial attitudes after long years of macroeconomic instability and income-seeking behaviour.

Major changes in the domestic socio-economic and institutional environment seem to be required for this to take place. On the one hand, the building up of new domestic technological and managerial capabilities appears as a sine qua non condition for any further improvement in productivity and international competitiveness. On the other hand, this by itself might not be enough if it is not supplemented with the right kind of economic incentives and institutions which would ensure that the re-structuring process is accompanied by a new export-oriented mentality capable of inducing local entreprenurs to explore new and imaginative ways of entering the international market place. Let us consider the above-mentioned aspects in further detail, beginning with the issue of how to develop a stronger domestic technological and human capital infrastructure.

2.1. The strengthening of the domestic technological, managerial and human capital infrastructure

A first major issue related to the achievement of better international competitiveness surely has to do with the creation and upgrading of human capital and with the enhancement of domestic technological and managerial capabilities. Let us examine this broad topic in some more detail.

2.1.1. The creation and upgrading of human capital

Notwithstanding the fact that all kinds of education seem to be needed for industrial progress, a greater emphasis on science and engineering training appears as a sine qua non condition for coping with fast moving and complex new technologies as the ones involved in the transition from electromechanical to electronic production processes and product designs. Micro aspects related to the organization of work on the shop floor as well as industrial organization issues of a sectorial and macro level are hereby involved and demand urgent consideration. A different type of information management, new forms of telecommunications, new patterns of industrial relations, etc. are here at stake and in all of these spheres managers, engineers and technicians as well as plant workers need to learnt new skills and patterns of interaction.

How significant secondary and tertiary enrolment ratios are

appears as an important issue, but also such aspects as the technical orientation of students, the length of training, the quality of teaching, etc. appear as major aspects educational authorities should look into. These are all topics about which we still know very little and which demand urgent new research if public policies are to proceed on a strong footing on this front. The Korean and Taiwanese experience in this territory is quite remarkable and many economists have in recent years suggested that their policies in this respect are the main explanatory factor of their successful economic performance of the last two decades. (Lall, 1990).

Urgent domestic action – and international collaboration – in the building up of a 'generic' human capital infrastructure is clearly a first priority in the present agenda of public action. Complementary to such public policy efforts intra-firm training programmes are also required in order to facilitate:

a. The transition from electromechanical to electronic skills and techniques.

This involves the recycling of engineers, machine-tool operators, etc.already in the labour force as well as a complete re-thinking of the curricula new generations of technicians, workers and engineers are taught at universities, secondary, vocational and technical schools. The curricula in such aspects as mathematics, trigonometrics, computer sciences, etc. have to be strengthened and modernized. 'Custom-made'product design, flexible manufacturing production organization techniques, universal standards and norms, etc. appear as some of the crucial aspects with which new generations of engineers and technicians will have to be familiarized in their training. Much of this is in the nature of a 'public good' where public expenditure is widely justified in view of its high expected social rate of return.

b. The recycling of industrial management

Strategic planning, 'Kan Ban', 'just in time' and 'total quality' production organization techniques, as well as the use of more 'roundaboutness' in the production process, new forms of global sourcing, etc. appear among the new skills modern industrial managment has to handle in a market place which is rapidly evolving towards 'custom-made' products and world-wide production systems. (Kliksberg, 1991). De-centralization of production and global sourcing appear as some of the new conceptual tools the oncoming generation of managers will have to learn to use under present circumstances.

The dramatic transition many large multinational firms – like Ford, Fiat or Olivetti – had to go through in recent years in order to regain international competitiveness, and the high price – both in terms of personnel turnover and management re-structuring – which all of these firms had to pay in order to master newly emerging electronic-based production planning and organization techniques indicates that this is by no means a marginal issue. A network of public and private institutions needs to be created to facilitate this transition. Experimental research on this front 'trying out' different approaches to see what works, and how, as well as joint efforts between the Public and the Private Sector seem to be required on this front.

c. Flexible automation and trade union participation on the shop floor

The successful adoption of many of the new production organization techniques – such as 'just in time' or 'total quality' arrangements on the shop floor – requires institutionalized procedures for trade union participation in production decisions as well as a complete new approach towards 'on the job' training. It also demands a major transformation in trade unions attitudes towards plant operation and the flexibilization of labour contracts. Much of this is presently happening at the enterprise level (K. Middlebrook, 1991), but we still lack real understanding concerning many of the new micro/macro issues hereby involved. As in previous cases more research on these topics seems to be urgently needed.

The demand for a massive effort on the educational front and in the building up of human resources comes at a time in which Public Social Expenditure is contracting quite drastically in most LDCs as a result of structural adjustment programmes whose main priority is that of reducing – or eliminating altogether – the Public Sector deficit regardless of the long term impact such a policy option is going to have upon the 'social sectors' of the economy – health, education, etc. – and of the likely negative consequences upon the 'sources of economic growth'.

According to recent World Bank statistics (World Bank, 1991) a large number of Latin American countries registered a declining share of Government expenditure over GDP for health and education between 1980 and 1985. The impact these policies are going to have upon total factor productivity growth and international competitiveness in the years to come has not as yet been seriously examined and there are strong grounds a priori to believe that it is going to be far from negligible.

The importance of foreign collaboration in all of the abovementioned areas should be stressed at this point of the argument. Former local expatriates – now permanently established in the academic and professional communities of more mature industrial societies – as well as professional senior citizens and educational agencies from DCs could be called upon in order to assist LDCs in the massive educational building up effort they now require if they are to meet the challenge of the international market place.

The development of human capital along the lines suggested in our previous paragraphs appears as a necessary but not as a sufficient condition for the gradual revitalization of international competitiveness. Additional actions aimed at strengthening firm-specific administrative and technological capabilities and country-wide export orientation and international marketing penetration might be needed as well, and will be examined later on in this paper when dealing with the creation of new institutions and incentives. Government intervention seems to be widely justified in this territory in view of the 'public good' nature of the 'generic' industrial organization infrastructure hereby required.

In many of these aspects we still lack basic understanding as to the best way to proceed and experimental research trying to explore what works and what does not work might be highly valuable for further public policy design and implementation. In spite of the already acknowledged long history of 'government failure' during the ISI process imaginative new ways of intervention will have to be explored on this front given our a priori knowledge of the highly imperfect behaviour of markets when 'public goods' are involved.

2.1.2. The generation and diffusion of new technical knowledge and information.

Close to the previously discussed topic of how to create and upgrade the human capital infrastructure of peripheral nations we find a set of issues concerned with the size and quality of the already available R&D infrastructure. Let us now briefly examine some of the questions hereby involved.

a. R&D efforts

Imperfect appropiability of results, increasing returns to the generation and utilization of scientific and technical knowledge, etc. indicate that we can a priori expect markets to behave in an imperfect manner in relation to the allocation of resources to R&D activities. The role of public sector spending in R&D can therefore be justified even under strict laissez faire rules. On the other hand, much of the public sector requirements in areas such as transport facilities — including roads, port and shipping infrastructure, etc — telecommunications, energy, health, etc. demand 'made to order' equipment and technologies which can not be easily obtained 'off the shelf' in the international market. 'Tailor-made' solutions demand a great deal of highly idiosyncratic knowledge-generation efforts which have to be made locally.

The case for public support of R&D activities and risk-sharing and subcontracting with the private sector in the above-mentioned fields seems therefore particularly strong. The experience of mature industrial societies in this respect is highly illuminating, if we are to judge by the role played by NASA, The Ministries of Agriculture or Health, the Department of Defense, etc. in the US, or by the Ministry of Industry and Trade in the UK and MITI in Japan, to name just a few examples.

Having said the above, it is important to understand that many LDCs in the Latin American Region do presently spend somewhere in the order of 0.5% to 0.7% of GDP financing R&D activities. Around 2/3 of such expenditure is absorbed by research and development efforts carried out by public laboratories, universities, etc.

A great deal of institutional slack, inadequate selection of research priorities, lack of ex post peer evaluation efforts, etc. underlie much of what is presently happening along this front. A major 'institutional engineering' effort needs to be undertaken in this field before further resources are spent in domestic R&D activities, but there is no doubt as to the fact that the domestic effort on the R&D front needs to be significantly expanded if these countries are to meet the challenge of creating the new social and technological infrastructure they nowadays require. Only after a serious effort is carried out in re-organizing and improving the cost efficiency of the existing R&D network and infrastructure should resources be significantly increased on this front.

b. Diffusion of technology

It is important to understand that from the point of view of total factor productivity growth and international competitiveness the technological upgrading of small and medium size enterprises appears as a major issue requiring consideration. Many small and medium size family firms can be thought of as operating well behind prevailing average technological practices and their gradual upgrading as far as production planning and organization, product design capabilities, etc. are concerned should be given high priority within the national agenda. Also in this respect a fair amount of 'institutional engineering' efforts and government intervention actions seem unavoidable, given the 'public good' nature of the 'generic' technological assets hereby involved.

Recent policy actions by the British Ministry of Industry and Trade on what we could call 'Industrial Extensionism' point to the general direction of the policy prescription we have in mind in this case. In this respect a widely circulated paper from the above mentioned Ministry tells British small and medium size firms that. . . . "The (Ministry's) Advisory Service will undertake a feasibility study lasting up to 15 man-days with the cost split equally between you — the firm — and them. Alternatively 50% support is also available from DOI (Department of Industry) if you employ an independent authorized consultant." And it continues to mention that. . . "Another, very valuable source of information and advice, is the British Robot Association. It will put you in touch with manufacturers experienced in your type of application, suggest further reading materials, etc." (Department of Industry, 1982).

The above provides a clear example as to how a central government agency could explicitly intervene in favor of a faster process of technological diffusion and productivity improvement, particularly so among small and medium size enterprises which might be thought to operate with imperfect information about alternative opportunities and possible courses of action. This particular type of intervention has to be seen as part of a broader set of institutional interactions loosely defining what we consider a 'generic' technological policy to be. Obviously, both public and private agencies have important roles to play in networks of this sort.

We have so far examined public actions related both to the creation and upgrading of human capital and to the generation and diffusion of new technical knowledge and information. Such actions might be important for the enhancement of international competitiveness, but they might not be sufficient under present circumstances. In our next section we shall examine various additional incentives and institutions which might be called upon in order to support the new export orientation which is presently required on the part of the domestic entreprenurial community.

3. 'Institutional engineering' efforts.

Many of the above mentioned spheres of public policy action clearly demand institutions — both public and private — capable of interacting in new and creative ways. It would be wrong to expect that the 'invisible hand' of the market will per se induce the erection and strengthening of the kind of institutional networks hereby needed. Exploratory programmes between Public and Private Agencies — entrepreneur associations, groups of firms, Universities, Public R&D laboratories, etc. — have to be set in motion trying to develop the kind of scientific and technological infrastructure most LDCs now require in order to attain a faster process of modernization as well as a less painful transition to electronic-based technologies, telecommunications, etc.

It is important to understand that it is the 'public good' nature of the technological assets hereby involved that calls for collective action and exploitation of the 'generic' part of such assets. Contemporary writers think of such collaborative efforts as 'pre-competitive' research and they point out to the 'common pool' aspect of the social organization model which underlies their functioning (Stiglitz, 1987). Price signals seem to be particularly inefficient in situations of this sort and it is precisely such a feature that calls for public intervention.

It should be noted, however, that actions of this sort on educational and technological matters, important as they are, might not be enough for a succesful revitalization of international competitiveness under present circumstances. Given the low state of 'animal spirits' the domestic business community presently exhibits in many LDCs and the a-critical effort most of these countries are nowadays carrying out in the de-regulation of markets and in the opening up of the economy to foreign competition, further actions might be needed on the part of the Public Sector if the present transition period towards decentralized market functioning is going to bring about the expected positive social returns.

We find it reasonable to argue that external collaboration form DCs and new institutions and mechanisms of interaction between Public and Private agents might be needed during the abovementioned transition period to a much less regulated model of production organization. Such institutions should focus on aspects such as the following ones:

a. The development of international competitiveness.
b. Equity deterioration and its impact upon governance and the 'sources of economic growth'.
c. Anti-dumping protectionism in the face of a strong foreign competitive presence in the domestic environment, etc.

Consider the above mentioned topics in some detail.

A broad set of issues — some apparently as insignificant as organizing the right kind of consular and marketing information services in support of domestic exporting companies, others as major and fundamental as having adequate port and shipping facilities — might be listed in the Agenda of possible public actions carried out with the purpose of enhancing international competitiveness. As in the case of education and technological generation and diffusion there are many 'public goods' hereby involved and it is precisely this which justifies explicit government intervention on this front.

Equity aspects — and their relationship with productivity growth, on the one hand, and with issues of political governance, on the other, — appear next in the list of topics demanding urgent consideration and explicit government action. A falling rate of Public Social Expenditure in areas such as Health or Education might prove to be highly detrimental in the years to come from the point of view of production organization, quality standards and, ultimately, international competitiveness. On the other hand, a higher unemployment rate and the transfer of human resources to the informal sector of the economy, as well as the deterioration of the average health standards of the population — aspects which might well result from the ongoing industrial re-structuring process – might bring about a widespread feeling of illegitimacy and call into question an otherwise highly needed structural adjustment process. Unemployment subsidies and institutions capable of mitigating the hardship of the transition period as far as health, social security, etc. considerations are involved might be justified in order to consolidate the expected benefits of the structural adjustment efforts, as well as to avoid extreme forms of social conflict.

Finally, a few remarks on anti-dumping protection. Given the highly a-critical way in which the opening up of the economy to foreign competition is now taking place, we find it reasonable to hoist a cautionary signal. It would be useful to remember that the experience of the most successful NICs has not been that of massively exposing their manufacturing firms to foreign competition during the early stages of their development process. That is certainly the more common reading of the Korean and Taiwanese experience. It is no doubt true that the 'infant industry' argument has been grossly overplayed in many peripheral countries during the ISI period and that this has made both economists and ordinary citizens highly critical of protectionism and inward-orientedness. It is also true, however, that learning takes time and money and that the risk of dumping activities on the part of foreign suppliers should not be minimized. An a-critical opening up of the economy to foreign restrictive practices might be instrumental for an eventual failure of the whole of the industrial re-structuring effort. Antimonopoly and antidumping legislation and careful custom rules and procedures seem to be needed as part and parcel of the present institutional re-structuring efforts.

So much for some of the 'institutional' actions which might be needed in support of structural adjustment programmes of the sort now being applied by many peripheral countries. One final issue we find important to discuss is that of national versus supranational levels of intervention. To this last topic we now turn.

4. National and supranational levels of intervention.

There are strong indications that the world economy is now gradually entering into a stage of transnationalization and globalization, particularly so as far as production and trade are concerned. National development strategies – though still very mildly influenced by these trends – will eventually come to incorporate in a more explicit way the opportunities and restrictions resulting from the process of regional and subregional integration now under way.

Integration programmes such as those of Mercosur, Junac, the Free Trade Agreement between the US, Canada and Mexico, etc. are examples of the process of globalization we are referring to. The traditional meaning of national frontiers is bound to lose sense in the years to come and institutions of a supranational level will gradually have an increasing impact upon the behaviour of the local economic agents.

The impact of the globalization process needs to be discussed both at the micro level – in relation to new types of enterprise strategies – as well as at the macro level in connection with national development strategies. Neither of these spheres has been significantly explored so far and demand major research efforts in the years to come.

At the macro level integration programmes – such as Mercosur, for example – involve the establishment of a common external tariff and a commercial policy regarding third countries (or groups of countries), as well as the coordination and harmonization of macroeconomic, fiscal, monetary, exchange, agricultural, industrial, etc. policies. The task of coordination and harmonization is by no means an easy one as the experience of the EEC clearly shows. Ad hoc research and technical information concerning each one of the above-mentioned fields is required and technical groups exploring the oncoming new issues have to be put together before any serious progress could be attained in the negotiation itself. This is precisely where both Argentina and Brazil presently stand as far as their future participation in Mercosur is concerned. Consider, for example, the discussion between the Mercosur countries in relation to the establishment of a common external duty and a tariff structure.

In spite of the fact that both the average and the interindustry variance of import duties have fallen in four of the above-mentioned countries during the course of the last decade, it is nevertheless true that significant differences still persist and will have to be ironed out before the actual starting of Mercosur in 1994. Argentina operates with an average external duty of 12,7% while the other three countries presently exhibit an average external duty of 23,7%, 16% and 28% respectively (Conexion, 1991).

Representatives of these four countries are presently working on the design of a common external tariff structure but differences in industrial structural and productivity levels and the paucity of the available information make this specific task a highly difficult one. Still a major 'institutional engineering' effort remains to be made on this front even before other equally complex issues concerning monetary, exchange, etc. policies begin to be examined. The macroeconomic coordination and harmonization required for the integration process is far from easy and will demand a great deal of economic research, 'learning' and political will in the years ahead. A number of new institutions of a supranational level will have to be designed and put into operation and a 'learning by doing' process is likely to obtain pari pasu with the economic integration itself.

Of a different nature appear to be the supranational institutional efforts needed in relation to the training and upgrading of human resources. The common perception of fragility in areas such as Information Technology or Biotechnology has in recent years induced Argentina and Brazil jointly to tackle the question of human capital development through the creation of the Latin American School of Informatics Technology and the Argentine–Brazilian Center for Biotechnologies (CABBIO), both incorporated within the framework of Mercosur. In spite of the fact that both these experiences are recent and rather small in terms of expenditure they seem to be pinpointing the type of collaborative efforts that could be explored in the future in the field of human capital upgrading.

Finally, we also need to consider micro aspects related to changes in individual firm behaviour triggered off by regional integration processes. Technical cooperation agreements between companies – such as those that have flourished among firms in the Pacific Region, between US, Japanese, Korean, etc. enterprises – will probably emerge in due course in other regional groupings such as Mercosur or the Free Trade Area between Canada, the US and Mexico.

The question of Intellectual Property Rights and the strengthening of the Patent System appears as a major issue in this field and one in which a great deal of institutional change is presently taking place under the pressure of the US Secretary of Trade. Countries as different as Spain, Greece, Mexico or Argentina are currently introducing a more stringent patent legislation than the one they had during the ISI period, with the expectation that such policy action will greatly improve the country's institutional credibility and the reception of foreign manufacturing investment and its associated technological component. It goes without saying that the evidence in support of such expectation is rather thin and that this is certainly an area in which further research seems to be needed in the years ahead.

BIBLIOGRAPHY

D. Helm: *The economic Borders of the State*. Oxford University Press, 1989.

J. M. Fanelli, R. Frenkel and G. Rozenwurcel: Growth and Structural reform in Latin America. Where we stand. *Documento CEDES*, Buenos Aires, 1990.

R. Nelson: Institutions supporting technical change in the United States. Chapter 15, In J. Dosi et al., *Technical change and Economic Theory*. London, Pinter, 1988.

S. Fisher: "Comment to Williamson's paper in J. Williams *Latin American adjustment. How much has happened?*. Institute of International Economics, Washington, 1990.

B. Balassa: Policy choices in the newly industrializing countries. *World Bank Working Papers* Development Economics, May 1990.

A. Amsdem: *Asia's next Giant. South Korea and late industrialization*. Oxford University Press, 1989.

J. Stiglitz: On the microeconomics of technical progress. In (J.Katz, Ed.) *Technology generation in Latin American Manufacturing Industries*. MacMillan Press, London, 1987.

Department of Industry. *A human guide to Robots*. Ministry of Industry and Trade, London, 1982.

S. Lall: Building industrial Competitiveness in LDCs. OECD, Paris, 1990.

N. Bercovich and J. Katz. *Biotecnologia y Economia Politica. Estudios del caso Argentino*. CEAL/CEPAL, Buenos Aires, 1990.

L. Kim: National system of industrial innovation. Dynamics of capability building in Korea. Mimeo, January 1991.

World Bank: *The challenge of Development*. World Bank Report 1991.

K. Middlebrook. The politics of Industrial Re-structuring. *Comparative Politics*, April 1991.

B. Kliksberg. Dilemas en la formacion de ejecutivos. *Alta Gerencia*. Buenos Aires, Octobre 1991.

Conexion. Revista Latinoamericana de Integracion. Fundacion Banco de Boston, Buenos Aires, September 1991.

International Process and Forms of Market Penetration: a Dynamic Proposal

José Antonio Alonso

The reality of international markets has undergone important transformations in the last two decades. The growing level of interrelationship existing among national economies, the prominent role acquired by more dynamic sources of competitive advantage, the obligatory use of more complex mechanisms of competition or the alterations occurring in the forms of organisation of business activities are some of the most outstanding changes. This is a broad and intensive mutation affecting the company and its environment. As a consequence, new criteria, approaches and instruments have to be applied to the analysis of those emerging realities, to gain a greater insight into their meaning.

Those alterations have had direct repercussions on the ways in which the company internationalisation process is presented. There are three most important changes to highlight:

- First, the lead role acquired in international markets by small and medium-sized companies, which, through very different methods have extended their range of activity beyond national frontiers, showing that this possibility is not just reserved for multinational units.
- Second, the proliferation of new institutional formulas of international projection. The old predominance of the parent-subsidiary relationship which governed the internationalisation

process in the fifties and sixties has given way to a wide variety of options, of new mixed and contractual formulas which make for a more agile, flexible display of competitive capacities in changing contexts – Davidson and McFetridge (1985) or McKiernam (1992).

- Finally, and in accord with the above-mentioned changes, the internationalisation process has ceased to be seen as a lone adventure for the company, and is, more and more, a case of becoming part of a network of intercompany agreements which transcend frontiers – Turnbull and Valla (1986) or Forsgren (1989). The direct paths to international projection have been replaced by new methods of cooperation, so that the choice of partners, the scope of agreements and contractual formulas have become key aspects in companies' international strategy.

The above-mentioned alterations are sufficiently important to promote a change in the way the internationalisation process is understood. It is no longer possible to associate such a process, exclusively, with operations of an investment nature – the setting up of subsidiaries; nor to restrict it to formulas for active projection abroad. Instead, it must be interpreted, in a broad sense, as that process through which the company establishes its links, more or less stable, with international markets, in whatever direction, at whatever level, and under whatever formula they may be presented.[1] Internationalisation begins at the moment when the overseas market becomes a compulsory reference point for the firm's strategic decisions: covering a wide band of possible activities ranging from active exporting to overseas investment and including all the intermediate mixed and contractual formulas.[2]

Understood thus, internationalisation must be seen as a complex process, admitting of diverse institutional formulas, depending upon the level of commitment acquired by the company; formulas and levels of commitment which are likely to change

[1] This meaning coincides with the one suggested by Welch and Luostarinen (1988), who associate internationalisation with the "process of the company's growing involvement in international operations"; and comment on the need to consider the two directions – inward and outward – of the relationship, page 36.

[2] The analysis of the internationalisation process must necessarily begin with formulas of exporting projection; since, more and more, the latter involve the commitment of company assets in foreign markets. A more lengthy development of this view can be found in Alonso (1993).

with time, as the company establishes its presence on the foreign stage. This changing and ever-more complex reality has not always been adequately reflected in the existing doctrine of international business.

1. THEORIES OF DIRECT INVESTMENT

1.1. Basic approaches

Even when it cannot be said that there is a rounded theory on the internationalisation process, the main doctrinal contributions centre their explanation on factors related to the characteristics of companies and on imperfections of the markets in which they operate.

These are the factors mentioned in Hymer's interpretation (1976), upon which is based a large part of the most persuasive contributions on direct investment abroad. In its basic version, Hymer's hypothesis can be expressed as follows: the firm which moves abroad must have some type of advantage, of a quasi-monopolistic nature, to enable it to compete with local firms, who are supposedly more established and have a better knowledge of their respective markets. Such advantages may have diverse origins — technological, organisational or commercial — but for them to give rise to direct investment, they must be specific to the investing company and easily transferable beyond national borders. They must also be of sufficient magnitude and durability to offset the competitive erosion of local firms.

The basis of direct overseas investment appears, in this case, related to the firm's ability to internalise and profit from certain imperfections in the market. Hymer centred his attention on those imperfections of a "structural" nature, extending the concept of entry barriers to an international context: the specific advantages of the multinational appear to be linked to the exercise of market power and thus reveal the characteristics of a monopolistic or monopsonic advantage.

Nevertheless, as Dunning and Rugman (1985) noticed, such a condition is not necessary to explain the existence of multinationals: they can spring from "natural" market imperfections, that is, those related to the market's inability to carry out — or to do so efficiently — certain transactions.[3] It is on an analysis of this type of imperfection that the main developments subsequent to Hymer have been centred.

Consequently, the two most recognised approaches give a leading role to the analysis of the transaction costs which the company incurs when it moves assets beyond national frontiers. In one case — the internalisation theory, to build on them, and on locational costs, the explanation of the investing phenomenon; in the other — the eclectic approach, to integrate them into a wider consideration of the decision to go international.

The first hypothesis — the internalisation theory — means extending to the international arena the enterprise contractual theory, the origin of which dates back to Coase (1937).[4] The central idea of this approach is that the firm, as an organisational structure, is born to integrate under a hierarchical principle those transactions that the market carries out in an inefficient or costly way. Buckley and Casson (1976) observed that a large part of specific intermediate goods transactions, particularly intangible assets — knowhow, technology, managing and marketing ability — showed these characteristics, so that they were inefficiently carried out through the market: thus the firm attempts to integrate these operations under the hierarchy of its organisation.[5] If these transactions were carried out beyond national frontiers the dynamic of internalisation described above would lead to the company's growing international expansion. The process will continue as long as the transaction costs which are avoided are

[3] Though the two types of imperfections may be related, the distinction is important: in the first case, the multinational, when market imperfections become endogenous, can strengthen the existing levels of inefficiency; in the second case, the firm tries to elude some limitations of the market, by seeking in organisation a more efficient alternative for certain transactions. See Casson (1987).

[4] The application of this approach to the multinational was initially carried out by Buckley and Casson (1976), and later developed by such authors as Casson (1979, 1982, 1987), Buckley and Casson (1985), Caves (1982), Rugman (1981,1986), Teece (1981 and 1985) or Hennart (1977, 1982, 1986) among others.

[5] This is a question of operations with high transaction costs deriving from the difficulty of finding a suitable price, of defining the contractual commitments of the parties, of making sure they are carried out or evaluating the risk if they are not.

higher than those deriving from the organisational integration of such transactions.[6]

So, from the point of view of this theory, the internationalisation process is based on two fundamental axioms: "(1) Firms choose the least cost location for each activity they perform, and (2) firms grow by internalising markets up to the point where the benefits of further internalization are outweighed by the costs"[7] This hypothesis was born with the idea of becoming a general theory of foreign investment; there is no aspect which may influence internationalisation – or affect the market structures or the characteristics of the firm – which cannot be evaluated from the viewpoint of location and/or transaction costs. So, most of the other hypotheses could be integrated within this interpretation – Rugman (1980). However, that same generality is a drawback when we wish to give the theory an empirical content.[8] In fact, its greatest interpretative use is to be seen in the case of vertically integrated industries, which are technology and/or knowhow-intensive, and with strong demands for customization and pre- and post-sales services.

The second attempt to construct a general theory of the multinational company stems from a more pragmatic option: the one resulting from an aggregate of the different elements considered in the previously existing partial approaches.[9] This proposal, which is voluntarily integrating, has been described by its promoter, Dunning (1979) as an *eclectic approach*. Specifically, there are three factors deemed necessary to explain the ability and willingness of the company to become international:

a) The firm must have a specific advantage, generally linked to intangible assets, which, at least for a time is not available to local competitors.
b) Assuming the above, the firm will have to decide whether to

[6] As Hennart (1986) points out: "Whether firms displace markets depends on their ability to reduce internal organization cost below market transaction costs", page 801.

[7] Buckley (1988), pages 181 and 182.

[8] Buckley (1988) is aware of these difficulties, so he suggests an indirect path, by means of partial hypotheses, to test the theory.

[9] Dunning (1979) sums it up thus: "The industrial organisation approach does not explain where the specific advantages of the company will be exploited, the location approach does not explain how foreign firms can compete with local firms in their own markets", page 273.

opt for internalising those advantages, by profiting from them in the new markets — through exports or investment— or whether to cede them to other firms already located in those markets through a contract or licence.

c) Given the above conditions, if the firm is to opt for an investment formula, it must be profitable to exploit those advantages along with some location factor belonging to the end delivery market, since, otherwise,

it would opt for exporting instead of investment.

Thus, the eclectic approach brings together in just one proposal the firm's specific advantages, the advantages of internalisation and those stemming from the cost conditions of the receiving market.[10] This integration effort even when it may have inspired the applied work, has given rise to new conceptual problems, stemming from the debatable theoretical justification for the factor segregation carried out. Particularly debatable is the distinction between firm-specific advantages and advantages derived from internalisation: the process of generation and acquisition of the former can hardly be conceived of without considering the internalisation dynamic which causes them and integrates them in the heart of the firm.[11] These imprecisions, along with their deliberate pragmatism, explain why the eclectic approach is considered by some, rather than as a rounded theory, as a paradigm — Cantwell (1988) — or, more critically, as a mere taxonomy of factors promoting foreign investment — Itaki (1991).

1.2. Some limitations

Despite the undoubted capacity for suggestion of the two approaches we have referred to, there are factors which make it difficult to fit them in with the complex nature shown at present

---

[10] As Dunning (1988) mentions: "It is then the juxtaposition of the ownership-specific advantages of firms contemplating foreign production, or an increase in foreign production, the propensity to internalise the cross-border markets for these, and the attractions of a foreign location for production which is the gist of the eclectic paradigm of international production", page 5.

[11] This is an element which differentiates the two approaches mentioned. For the internalisation theory, considering these two factors in a differentiated way means double accounting,Buckley (1988), page 183; whilst, on the contrary, the promoter of the eclectic theory considers such a distinction as not only useful but also logically right, Dunning (1988) page 3.

by internationalisation processes. There are three basic aspects to be stressed:

- First, they are theories strongly biased towards explaining direct investment overseas, and devote less attention to specific questions of other alternative methods of international projection. Thus, subsequent developments are needed to deal with the diversity of formulas through which the internationalisation process is seen at the present time.
- Second, they are theories of a predominantly static nature: they investigate the reasons for investment, but say little about how this process is developed over time. There is clear evidence, however, that a large part of the capacities required for internationalisation are acquired by the firm through a learning process, cumulative in nature, so that the time dimension has extraordinary importance. This had already been noticed some time ago by Horst (1972), and had been recently registered by Buckley (1988).[12]
- Finally, his insistence on the specific advantages of the firm and/or on the vertical integration of operations makes these theories particularly suitable for explaining the behaviour of large units, well established internationally, but says little about the formulas of cooperation between firms to which small and medium-sized firms often have recourse.

To sum up, we are dealing with static approaches which have as their favourite theme large-sized companies, well established in international markets. Thus, to study the sequence followed by small and medium-sized firms it is useful to consider the contribution made from a different tradition: the *theory of the phases of development.*

2. THE INTERNATIONALISATION PROCESS

2.1. The phases of development

The study of a series of European multinationals-particularly Nordic ones- led some authors, followers of the Uppsala school, to

[12] This author, in his recent revision of the theory, concludes that the "introduction of dynamic elements is a matter of urgency" though recognising that it is "a difficult task", page 191.

attribute to the internationalisation process a fundamentally evolutionary nature: the firm rises to higher levels of international commitment, after becoming established and accumulating experience in the previous stages.[13] Subsequently, this gradualist view was enriched by the analysis of the international experience of companies originating in other geographical areas and countries.[14]

This hypothesis finds its basis in a behavioral conception of the firm: to the latter is attributed the nature of an active agent, possessing imperfect information, drawing up strategies, in an uncertain environment on the basis of its own capacities and the possibilities offered by the medium it is operating in.[15] In these conditions, the internationalisation process adopts a gradual sequence, stemming from the effect that learning and the level of international commitment has in reducing the uncertainty with which the firm operates in foreign markets. The firm travels through stages of an increasing level of international commitment as it gradually acquires, assimilates and uses the knowledge on foreign markets and operations. As Welsh and Luostarinen (1988) point out: "The learning-by-doing process explains much in the evolutionary patterns of internationalisation revealed in research."[16] The accumulated experience permits a more suitable perception of the opportunities and risks, by reducing the effects generated by the firm's unfamiliarity with the conditions of its environment.[17]

---

[13] The first studies which reflect on this evolutionary sequence of internationalisation are those by Johanson and Wiedersheim-Paul (1975), Johanson and Vahlne (1977) and Luostarinen (1979).

[14] Particularly, study has been made of American, European and Australian firms. See, among others, Bilkey and Tesar (1977), Welch and Wiedersheim-Paul (1980), Cavusgil (1980 and 1984), Piercy (1981), Denis and Depelteau (1985), Juul and Walters (1987) or Hornell and Vahlne (1982).

[15] In line with the tradition developed by Cyert and March (1963) or Aharoni (1966).

[16] Welch and Luostarinen (1988), page 166. Like Penrose (1959), two possible types of learning are distinguished: one of an objective nature, which is — or may be-easily codifiable and transferable; and the other of a more tacit and idiosyncratic nature, linked to experience, which can only be acquired through a process of practical learning. It is the latter which conditions the gradual sequence of the internationalisation process.

[17] As Johanson and Wierdersheim-Paul (1975) point out: "We also assume that the most important obstacles to internationalisation are lack of knowledge and resources. These obstacles are reduced through incremental decision-making and

The sequence described has its reflection in the organisational field: the growing level of international commitment is seen in the institutional formulas through which the firm travels as it progresses in its accumulated experience. It begins by selling abroad through independent representatives before setting up a sales subsidiary, and it usually has its own marketing network and sales subsidiaries before deciding to install a production subsidiary.[18] In turn, these organisational forms are associated with dissimilar levels of international commitment and risk, owing to the different asset levels involved in each case. So the firm, to avoid uncertainty as much as possible, tries to move between neighbouring options in its level of international commitment, giving each of its decisions a preferentially incremental nature.

And while advancing in the level of international commitment, the type of operation through which the firm is projected abroad becomes more complex. At the beginning, activity is normally limited to merely having the product available for export; later on, this action is accompanied by the provision of commercial and technical services which broaden the definition of the goods being offered, and, finally, there is the offer of complete systems and packages to deal with needs or solve problems — Luostarinen (1979). So the process brings more depth and diversity to the company's operational methods in the international field.

From the gradual nature of the process there also derives a consequence involving the choice of the preferred areas of geographical projection. In trying to avoid risks and uncertainty as much as possible, the firm will tend to project itself initially towards those markets which it knows best, the nearest in geographical and cultural terms, that is, those from which it is least "psychologically distant." Under this latter heading a whole group of differentiating factors is grouped — language, educational levels, business habits, market climates, institutional frameworks and degrees of industrial development — which affect the levels of certainty with which one country's company operates in another.[19]

---

learning about foreign markets and operations", page 306.

[18] As Johanson and Vahlne (1977) comment: "Sales subsidiaries are preceded in virtually all cases by selling via an agent; similarly, local production is generally preceded by sales subsidiaries", page 24.

[19] Although the concept has precedents, the first to use it with regard to the dynamic of internationalisation was Wiedersheim-Paul (1972). See also Johanson and Wiedersheim-Paul (1975), page 307.

The prescriptions of this approach have their most notable exceptions in one of the three following cases. In the first place, when the firm has enough resources to lessen the relative evaluation of risk involved in the international commitment taken on. It is the case of a large company, for which a decision to go international supposes a smaller relative effort than for a firm of lesser size. Secondly, when the markets are highly stable, and/or homogeneous, which makes it easier for the firm to reduce the risk stemming from operating in the international environment. And, finally, when the company is strongly established in international markets, which enables it to put into the new projects the experience acquired in previous markets.

2.2. Limitations of the approach

The theory of phases of development offers an interpretation of the process which is particularly useful for referring to the international experience of small and medium-sized firms; or for those who are at the early stages of the internationalisation process, Forsgren (1989). It is easier for the large firm or the highly internationalised one to omit the suggested gradualism; but it is not the same with one lacking international experience or with limited resources.

Otherwise, this approach provides several new aspects regarding preceding theories[20] There are three to be highlighted here: first, their insistence on the dynamic of the internationalisation process, not taken into consideration in the alternative proposals; second, the complete, integrated consideration of the different formulas – exporting, licence and investment – which a company has for entering markets, by presenting them as not strictly alternative options, but sequentially complementary ones; and, third, the attention given to the role played by the perception of risks and opportunities in business decisions.[21] All these aspects are important bearing in mind the changes registered in the different ways of entry into foreign markets, and the proliferation of mixed

---

[20] A presentation of these aspects can be found in Johanson and Vahlne (1990) and Alonso (1993).

[21] In the first two notes this approach coincides with Vernon's proposal about the product life cycle. But, in this latter case, the internationalising dynamic is made to rest on objective factors – the technological life of the product, and not on the capacities and aptitudes of the firm's management.

formulas, of a contractual nature, used by companies in recent times.

Now, having pointed out its contributions, reference must also be made to two of its deficiencies. The first one refers to the rather unclear nature of the proposed relationships, which hinders its transfer to operative variables. Johanson and Vahlne (1977) tried to clarify the model via a definition of the variables involved and the sense of the proposed causality. In this way, they made a distinction between state and change aspects of internationalisation. Among the former are accumulated knowledge of foreign operations and the commitment acquired with the market (measured by the volume and degree of irreversibility of the resources committed). Among the changing aspects are decisions adopted on the resources that they wish to commit abroad and the dynamic of current activities (Fig. 1). Thus, the levels of knowledge and commitment acquired in international markets affect company decisions and forms of behaviour; and these, in turn, influence the levels of knowledge and international commitment.

Despite this attempt at clarification, numerous theoretical problems persist in the model. In the first place, it was impossible to avoid a certain circularity in the proposal: the results of a cycle are constituted in inputs of the next cycle. The centre of the

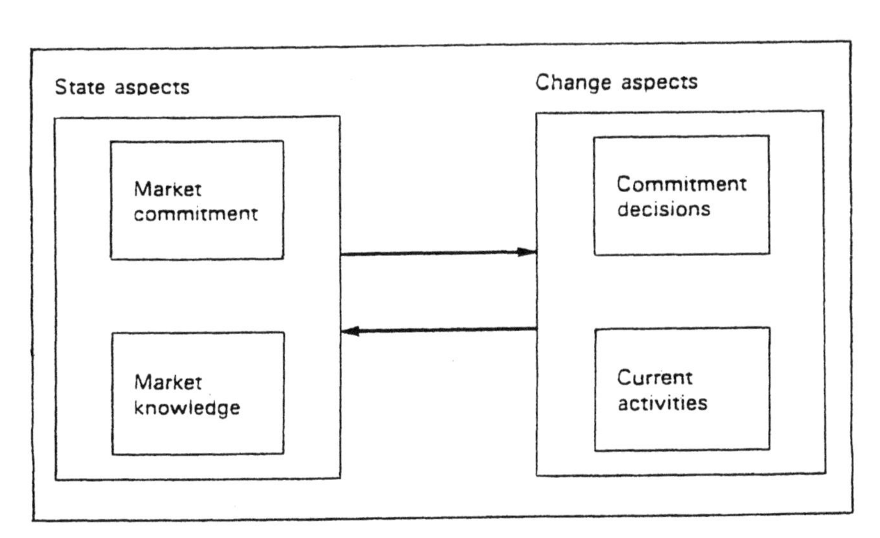

Figure 1 The Internationalisation process
Source: Johanson Y Vahlne (1977)

explanation is based on the bidirectional relationship postulated between the growing knowledge of the markets and the greater international commitment. Nonetheless, both variables are related to the resources displaced to those markets, so there remains a factor which to a certain extent is tautological in the proposal.[22] And, along with that there is still no revelation of the reasons to explain that a firm changes its level of international commitment or the preferred way of international projection. The evolutionary direction of the process is argued but there are no criteria to explain the transition from one phase to another.

Otherwise, a precise definition is lacking of the stages suggested, the object of a highly varied classification, according to the authors.[23] It also lacks an agreed procedure for estimating the level of the company's international commitment, linked in some cases with ways of penetrating markets, Johanson and Vahlne (1977), and in others with some expressive measurement of the business figures in overseas markets, Cavusgil (1984). Thus, there exists a capacity for suggestion in the model which exceeds the analytical precision with which it is constructed: It is the "deceptive allure of development models" which Stubbart (1992) observed.[24]

The second limitation derives from its excessively linear view of the internationalisation process, which is hardly compatible with the complexity of the present-day world and with the diversity of opinions faced by the company. In fact, when the prescriptions of the theory of development phases are taken to extremes, the proposed stages come to be seen as a sort of obligatory sequence, the best path along which the international life of the firm has to run. The theory thus creates its own normative derivations, and bases itself, in its simplest, most radical form on a deterministic proposal, in which there is hardly room for individual firm-specific elements, or for the contingent factors making up the environ-

[22] See in this respect Andersen (1993). Perhaps the attempt to avoid this circularity is what makes Johanson and Vahlne reduce the explanatory variables to just one: the knowledge acquired by the firm, page 17.

[23] See, for example, the different proposition of Wiedersheim-Paul et al. (1978), Pavord and Bogart (1975), Cavusgil (1980) and (1984), Bilkey and Tesar (1977), Johanson and Wierdersheim-Paul (1975) or Czinkota (1982).

[24] To this characteristic another from its critics should be added: "In conclusion, it can be said that the stages theory has merit in its use as a framework for classification purposes rather than for an understanding of the internationalization process itself", Turnbull (1987), page 37.

ment. Both components turn out to be, nevertheless, of proven importance in determining company strategy, Reid (1983) and Turnbull (1987).[25]

This determinism and the lack of a theoretical definition of the proposal have affected the ability to test it, and there is no unanimity about it. Despite the fact that the evidence largely points to the importance of the time sequence in the internationalisation process, there is no lack of critical comment on the sequence of stages, Turnbull (1987) or Ayal and Raben (1987), or of the market's dynamic of choice proposed, Sullivan and Bauerschmidt (1990) or Papadopoulos and Denis (1988). The difficulty in transferring the model to operative variables and to clear causal relationships, the debatable link between proven relationships and the theory's prescriptions and the recourse to testing formulas which are not always adequate – based on the cross-section analysis of company samples, makes it difficult for the confirmatory results to be obtained free of error in order to validate the model.[26]

Nevertheless, these criticisms do not totally invalidate the theory; instead, they express the reservations with which some of its applications should be regarded. In fact, Johanson and Vahlne (1990) insist that both the suggested stages and the psychological difference are mere manifestations of the model, indicators with which the latter attempts to become operative, and that other different patterns and indicators cannot be excluded.[27] The warning is relevant, but it should not be ignored that a great deal of the confusion has been originated by the selfsame defenders of the model, in not separating their basic propositions from what are their possible applications. What is left of the proposal once we question the stages in which the suggested process materialises? Or what effect does psychological proximity of the markets have when

[25] It is the weight of these factors that justifies the presence in the markets both of opportunist behaviour, according to changing market conditions, and planned behaviour, attempting to forecast the trend in the environment. See Millington and Bayliss (1990).

[26] See, regarding this, Alonso (1993) or Andersen (1993)

[27] Johanson and Vahlne (1990), page 13. As these same authors comment, referring to the determinism of the proposal: "This argument is quite plausible but should perhaps not be primarily an argument against the process model – unless it is directed at the manifestations of the model – but rather an argument for development and differentiation of the model", page 14.

the sequence of geographical expansion breaks its supposed gradualism? If what one wishes is to rescue the model's capacity for suggestion it will have to be submitted to a necessary reconsideration: it will have to be presented from new bases, avoiding its original limitations and rigidities.

3 INNOVATING IN THE NETWORK

The suggested revision has to affect, at least, the existing concept on two complementary aspects: the factors governing the company's international dynamic and the nature of the markets on which the latter is projected.

3.1 Internationalisation as innovation

The flexibilisation process as suggested involves, in the first place, abandoning the supposedly obligatory character of the stages proposed. The present level of interpenetration and homogeneity of the markets makes it less necessary for the firm to have the slow build up of experience suggested by the theory. To a large extent the growing globalisation of markets is translated into a progressive reduction of the psychological distance, at least in the developed world. And, in a complementary fashion, the more dynamic climate of competition leads the firm to seek more immediate and flexible mechanisms for occupying the markets. This is a trend which particularly affects highly product-innovative industries, since it forces them to profit from their technological effort in the shortest possible time. Thus, new methods of foreign penetration are born, as a consequence of the development of innovative formulas of a mixed, contractual nature; while the sequence followed by the firm in its international projection becomes more flexible and shorter, Hedlund and Kverneland (1984), Young (1987), Lindqvist (1988) Nordström (1990) or Forsgren (1989).

Now, if there is a modification of the forms by which the internationalisation process is presented, there still remains, the logic of its gradual and basically irreversible sequence. It is led to that by the contradictory dynamic of the factors sustaining the process of company expansion. In fact, the cumulative dynamic followed by certain assets, on which the development of the firm is based- technological capacities or experience and level of business knowledge,- comes into conflict with forces resistant to change — organisational routines and risk perception — giving the resulting process its discrete sequence, of progression through successive stages of stability and change (Figure 2). This process takes place in a changing environment, in which opportunities and risks emerge in a way which can only partially be forecast by the firm. Thus, in the firm's behaviour, factors subject to different dynamics have their influence, with a combination of cumulative sequence, chance and inertial resistance; all within a specific framework, governed by conditions of competition in the industry.[28]

This view makes internationalisation similar to the process followed by the firm in other areas of activity. The analogy which can be established with the process of generation and assimilation of technological capacities is particularly inspiring.[29] In fact, increasing the level of international commitment means for the firm taking an innovatory decision, so it is not odd if both processes have some traits in common.[30] Three are of special importance for what we wish to argue here.

- First, in both cases we are dealing with creative decisions adopted in accordance with the conditions imposed by the market and with the possibilities, always restricted, of an organisation acting in uncertain conditions. Neither the development of technological capacities nor the increase in the international commitment are, in their essence, spontaneous processes: they need deliberate decisions. And they are decisions adopted in conditions of uncertainty: there is no complete knowledge of the results deriving from the chosen option. Consequently, as is underlined by the specialised studies, the attitude of the decision-makers have a central role in promoting the process.

---

[28] The characteristics of the market condition the firm's internationalisation: the demands of the internationalisation process are not the same in a sector highly fragmented internationally, such as textiles, as in one which is highly oligopolised, such as the car industry. And these dissimilar characteristics influence the time sequence through which the international learning process of the firm develops.

[29] Alonso (1993)

[30] From a different viewpoint, this analogy had been explored by Simmonds and Smith (1968) and Lee and Brasch (1978), to determine the spontaneous or induced nature of exporting activity.

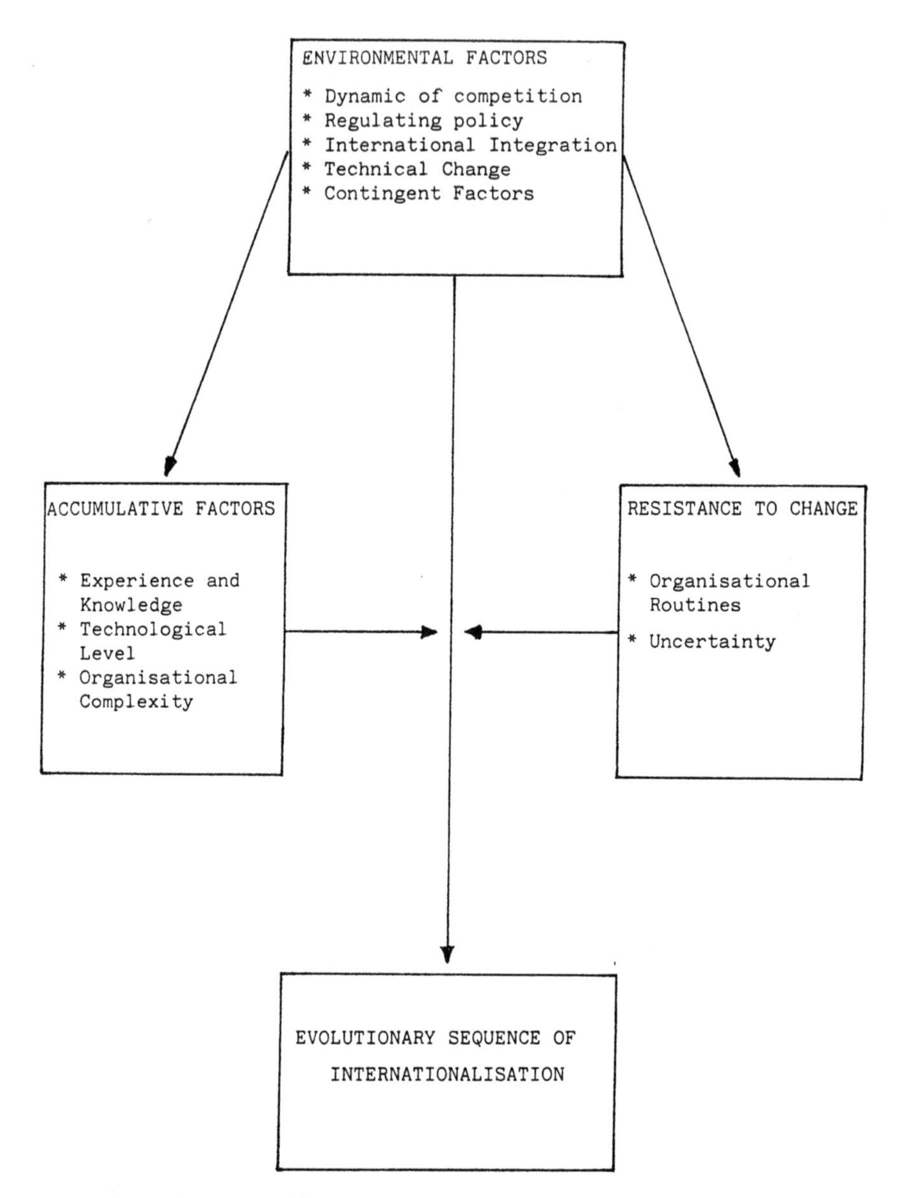

Figure 2 Factors in the Internationalisation Process

• Second, and even when a deterministic approach is not accepted, it is necessary to recognise that in both processes factors intervene which are governed by a manifestly cumulative sequence. Since the two processes benefit from the time dynamic characteristic of learning processes: it will be easier for the firm to achieve growing levels of international commitment as it starts from higher internationalisation levels.

- And, finally, both processes are far from following both a determinist route – as could be derived from a simplifying view of its cumulative nature, and from a completely chance or uncertain one — which could be the result of the deliberate character of the supporting decisions. The latter, with the degrees of freedom that may be desired, operate against a background of options conditioned by the past sequence followed by the firm. One could thus talk of a type of internationalising route along which the firm travels; a type of path which opens out in successive ramifications in time, with routes which are neither completely foreseeable nor absolutely random. Thus, the framework of options in each one of them is limited, in accordance with the accumulated experience and the previously travelled path.

From the whole of these traits perhaps a more complex view of the internationalisation process is obtained, in which the latter appears as an open path, though conditioned by previous experience. From a dynamic viewpoint, we are dealing with a process which is rather autogenous, since it is based on the capacities and strengths corresponding to the firm — in relation to the environment; and predominantly irreversible, not so much because of the institutional formulas chosen in each case as because of the sequence of levels of international commitment which the latter involve.

3.2. The market as a complex network

So far, the internationalisation process has been considered as a path which the firm takes alone, according to its assets and competing with rival agents. In this approach the revised theories, explicitly or implicitly, coincide: so, they insist on the firm's specific advantages, as the leading figure in the internationalisation process. Behind this concept is a highly mythical view of the market: the latter is conceived as an empty space, a sort of *locus logico* where independent agents interact and confront each other. Opposed to this image applied research has underlined the role that stable interfirm relations have in the development of competitive action. Networks of relationships, commitments and inter-firm agreements coexist in the market, and these are maintained in a markedly lasting manner beyond the time when a specific transaction takes place, Häkansson (1982), Turnbull and Valla (1986) or Forsgren (1989). The reality of the market is more akin to a system of nets, linked at different levels, than an atomised space.

Admitting the presence of agreements and commitments between firms does not imply questioning the crowd dynamic of the market, but, rather, perhaps, changing its logic: confrontation is not produced so much between independent units as between networks of firms, between interrelated groups. In fact, in a market several subsystems compete, each of them made up of a group of firms linked through shared commitments. The same firm may belong circumstantially to more than one subsystem, but the latter differ radically among themselves in the basic nucleus of participating firms, and through the relationships and hierarchies established in their midst.

This image is in accord with the behaviour of the firm in the markets. In fact, for the development of their functions the firm establishes relationships with a broad group of independent agents: input suppliers, those providing technical assistance, advisers and experts, privileged customers and units collaborating in specific areas. The firm attempts to stabilise the framework of these basic relationships, with the aim of achieving the maximum certainty and conformity in its commitments. Stability will be even more necessary according to how specific, frequent and irreplaceable the transaction is. Some of them may become integrated in the firm's hierarchy; but many others will continue to be entrusted to independent agents. Now, this does not mean that the firm must build ex-novo the relationships with each new transaction; nor that its decision is limited to a sole parameter – an occasional price advantage from a supplier, according to the naive view of the market suggested by economic theory. Rather, the firm tries to make a careful selection of its collaborators, taking into account, as well as price, other equally important aspects, such as quality, suitability and opportunity of the service, or the willingness, trust and understanding shown by the partner. Thus, loyalties and commitments are created between firms; and stable relationships are established, founded mainly on shared demands and confidence.

The formulas for company cooperation referred to are located in this huge space which exists between the free market and the organisational hierarchy, Jacquemin (1989). The agreements signed, however formal or informal they may be, allow the units involved greater independence and more equal relationships than those stemming from incorporating their relationships within a company unit; at the same time they provide the transactions with greater stability than could be obtained from their free contracting in the market, by avoiding, more efficiently, possible opportunist behaviour. Therefore, in a very generic fashion, a firm will seek formulas of cooperation when the transaction costs involved in the agreement are lower both than those deriving from setting up an integrated company — internalisation costs — and those stemming from leaving those transactions to the complete free will of the market.

The range of relationships of this type used by the firm in the markets is very wide. In some cases they are formalised relationships, on a contractual basis, while in others they are simple implicit agreements, verbal commitments or merely repeated routines; some are exclusively binding on agents, others, however, allow the parties broad margins of independence; in some cases it is an assymetrical relationship, in others, however, a link between equals. And if the nature of the relationships is diverse, the importance acquired by the latter for the agents is also variable — depending on the quality and frequency of the transaction; the type of link they offer — technological, commercial, legal or merely personal, and the function of the firm concerned — financing, supplying, technology, marketing... . On the whole it is a complete network of hierarchical relationships into which the firm is integrated.

So, when a firm tries to enter a new market it has to set up the necessary network of commitments to establish its activity. Constructing this network is not, however, a simple task. The existing agreements are not immediately visible to a unit not connected to them. Experience is required to check the willingness of agents and the quality of their services. The more different and unknown the market, greater are the difficulties. The firm, consequently, sets up its network of commitments gradually, as its experience and degree of establishment in the market increases.

Through this sequential process of trial and error, the company selects its partners, the scope of its agreements and the contractual formulas which are needed. On the solidity and quality of this network to a great extent will depend the possibilities for action of the firm, Porter and Fuller (1988) or Jacquemin (1990).

The view of markets presented substantially modifies the concept of internationalisation. This can no longer be seen as a solitary path, but as the result of the firm's integration in a system of relationships extending beyond national frontiers. The big challenge for the firm is the successful building of the network of commitments which will best enable it to establish and reinforce its international presence. Thus it is recognised that a firm's competitive capacities do not just depend upon its assets, but also upon the type of relationships it is able to establish with its environment.[31] And, correspondingly, internationalisation is identified with a strategic management process of interdependences, Johanson and Vahlne (1990).

The function assigned to each of these networks of agreements will crucially depend upon the firm's capacities and resources and the level of international integration shown by the market. It is reasonable to suppose that the fewer the assets, the greater will be the leading role acquired in its international strategy by the system of agreements which the firm establishes with its environment. And, meanwhile, the more internationalised are the networks which make up a market, the easier it will be to externalise part of its transactions, without the firm losing control of its intangible assets, Johanson and Mattsson (1988). On the contrary, the internalisation path will be based in a more autonomous way on its own assets as these are greater and the level of market integration is lower. The latter is the framework to which, implicitly, the theories revised in the two previous sections refer-internalisation, the eclectic theory and the Uppsala proposal.[32]

---

[31] As Perlmutter and Heenan remind us, quoting Thomas the biologist, "the survival of the best adapted does not mean that in nature teeth and claws prevail (. . .), it does not mean that only the strongest, wiliest or the most dominant are the winners. According to Thomas, the best adapted (the survivors) are those who cooperate with other living formulas", page 58.

[32] The case which most comfortably fits the Uppsala theory would be that of the firm which begins its internationalisation process in a market which is not very integrated internationally: an "early starter", in Johanson and Mattssons' (1988) terms. Moreover, the internalisation theory and the eclectic approach best express

Concurring with the above, internationalisation acquires greater complexity: it involves not only an intraorganisational commitment, but also an interorganisational one; and it no longer, necessarily, follows a linear sequence, but a multiple, ramified one, with varied options of international presence being manifested. Specifically, different functions of the same firm can be implicated, each of them in a different formula of international commitment. Thus, for example, the same firm may keep its input suppliers in the domestic market, guarantee its technological supplies through its share in a mixed company abroad, have an international management contract and market its products by means of a piggyback system. The possibilities of combining institutional formulas in the same firm are multiple; just as the levels of international commitment which each one involves are different.

Nevertheless, the fact that the formulas for international commitment are varied does not mean that the firm does not have available a general strategy which gives coherence to the diverse options and commitments partially adopted. All of them are integrated in a broader project, which is what defines international strategy. But, the latter is not expressed in a sole institutional formula, but in a complex of integrated formulas, according to the systems of agreements the firm initiates. The evolutionary nature of the internationalisation process is maintained, and this is manifested not just in the sequence following the generation of its own capacities within the firm, but, also, in how dynamically the network of international relationships is displayed.

4. AN APPLICATION OF TRANSACTION COSTS

4.1. Previous assumptions

A balance sheet of what has been put forward so far reveals a situation which is largely unsatisfactory. We have a fruitful hypothesis of internationalisation — the theory of internalisation and/or the eclectic theory, but predominantly static and restricted in the scope of its favourite field of attention; and, also, there exists a proposal with a dynamic content — the theory of

---

the case of a firm well established in an equally fragmented market: a "lonely international". There is, therefore, a lack of a further development of the internationalisation theory in integrated environments.

development phases, which rightly points out the role of experience in company decision-making, but lacks an adequate analytical structure to eliminate some of its original indeterminate areas. Both, however, project an excessively linear image of the internationalisation process: they do not consider either the complex range of options offered simultaneously in a firm, nor the interorganisational nature the process involves.

The present section starts from the need to find a theoretical space to recover the most fruitful aspects of the different interpretations commented on. More specifically, its aim is to contribute to the necessary construction of an approach from which to investigate the factors influencing the choice of ways of projecting the firm in foreign markets. The level at which the argument takes place is still highly abstract, but it enables some conclusions of interest to be obtained, by applying for this purpose, a dynamic version of the analysis of transaction costs.

Before taking our task any further one must warn that in no way are we claiming to hide the differences which may exist among the proposals referred to. Quite the contrary, it is recognised that such differences exist, both in the assumptions and in some of their respective prescriptions. Perhaps the most important discrepancy, in terms of what we are considering here, affects the concept one has of the firm. Both in the internalisation theory and the eclectic one it is recognised that the firm is an agent operating with awareness of the effects deriving from its choice; it is, therefore, a rationalising agent which adopts a maximising form of behaviour, even when operating in conditions of slight uncertainty. On the contrary, in the case of the evolution theory, the firm is supposed to operate in an uncertain world, where it is unaware of the effect of its decisions, so an important role is reserved for the dynamic of choice and learning with regard to the medium. Undoubtedly, this different concept has marked implications in the makeup of the respective theories.

For the present essay a relatively admitted eclectic position will be adopted for the purpose: in the medium term the market ends up by penalising non-maximising behaviour.[33] Thus, even if it is

[33] In reality, this position, suggested by Williamson (1975), means a covert acceptance of the substantial rationality of agents. It is accepted that the rational way in which agents operate is purely procedural, but a principle is introduced in an intelligent way and with nuances, — the crowd — which, finally, leads the

a simplification, it can be assumed that the firm will seek to maximise its performance — or minimise its costs — in an uncertain environment — maximisation subject to risk; but, according to the theory of development phases, it is accepted that previous accumulated experience involves a reduction of the risk level with which such decisions are adopted.

The choice of transaction costs as the starting point is not arbitrary, if we bear in mind, first, that that theory offers a stimulating conceptual framework to explain the firm's organisation processes; and, secondly, it provides a theóretical field in which it is possible to have a dialogue — though not full agreement — among the different contributions mentioned.

In fact, the transition costs theory has provided a useful approach for the analysis of the criteria backing a particular form of the firm's overseas projection, Anderson and Gatignon (1986), Reid (1983), Klein (1989), Hennart (1989), Hill and Kim (1988) or Hill, Hwang and Kim (1990). Though the analysis has been maintained on a highly general plane, it offered a set of valuable propositions which could be empirically tested. Generally, the works start by discriminating between different forms of overseas projection — preferably two — to discuss and, subsequently, estimate the factors leading the firm to decide between them. Thus, has been investigated the option between licence and subsidiary by Davidson and McFetridge (1985); between subsidiary and joint venture by Hennart (1988) or Kogut and Sinh (1988); or between integrated and independent commercial networks — Anderson and Cughlan (1987), Heide and John (1988), Klein (1989) or Klein, Frazier and Roth (1990).

Despite this effort, little advance has been made in the dynamic consideration of the problem: most of the above-mentioned works restrict themselves to a static application of transaction costs.[34] The internationalisation process, however, requires a suitable theoretical framework to register the dynamic factors which constitute it. Such a purpose was to be found, as Buckley (1988) reminds us, in the origins of the internalisation theory, since with it an attempt was made to build a dynamic model of company growth. Nevertheless, in practice, that claim was forgotten, since

---

former to act as if operating with completely rational criteria. *See* Brosseau (1993), page 20.

[34] An exception is, in this line, the work by Hill and Kim (1988).

the capacities that are the object of internalisation were considered as given, the problem was restricted to deciding the most efficient form of transaction for previously existing assets. In opposition to this concept, it is worth repeating that internationalisation is not just a way of exploiting an already existing advantage, but also – and, perhaps, rather, a way to acquire an advantage, to create new resources and capacities in the firm.[35] Therefore it is necessary to insist on a dynamic application of transaction costs. So, in fact, in time there is a change in the assets on which company expansion is based, just as, logically, there is a change in the costs related to a transaction as the firm becomes established and accumulates experience in a particular market.

It may be considered, for this essay's purposes, that the assets which the firm's international action are based on are related in a generic way with some intangible resource, whether linked to production technology and/or marketing technology.[36] The latter will be an important aspect when deciding between having independent or integrated channels of distribution overseas. The choice will depend upon the effect it may have for preserving and developing the indicated asset – which is related to the reputation of the brand or the corporate image, for example – to externalise commercial activities in the end market. Where the advantage is based on production technology, the firm faces the possibility of externalising the transactions related to those assets – by means of a licence – or of its integration in the firm's organisational hierarchy – through direct overseas investment.

To progress in the analysis, in this case we will start from previous simplifying assumptions which may have been relaxed in subsequent developments. Basically they are the following:

- First, in the internationalisation process there is involvement both of the advantages related to choice of the most efficient form of transaction – in its extreme version, internalisation vs externalisation,– and those deriving from the most suitable location of activities, and which basically affect production and transport

[35] As Itaki (1991) mentions: "the internalization and integration generate an advantage and the advantage promotes further internalization and integration", page 448.

[36] It is common to consider, in an additional manner, a possible advantage in management technology. Here, however, that possibility will not be considered.

costs.[37] With the aim of avoiding the distortion that these latter factors may generate, there will only be a comparison of options in the same location conditions. And, therefore, exporting will be treated separately, on the one hand, with its different possible marketing channels; and licence and investment on the other, with its different levels of activity internalisation. In this way, productive conditions — factor costs and transport — are guaranteed to be similar between the options studied.[38]

• Secondly, in this version demand-related aspects will not be considered. That is, it will be supposed that consumers are indifferent to how the products reach the market. Thus they will not discriminate among imported products on the basis of the chosen distribution channel; and they will continue to show such behaviour whatever may be the origin of the producer firm's capital. Likewise, we will not take into account income deriving from the respective options, and which will change with the strategic possibilities which each of them will give the firm. The exclusion of this aspect is due to mere reasons of exposition, since it must be understood that the option finally taken by the firm has to be the result of simultaneous consideration not just of costs, but also of the profitability associated with each of the options.[39]

• Finally, and bearing in mind how imperfect is the market for the transaction of intangible assets — technological, management or marketing ones, the firm will attempt to find the channel which will allow it a greater guarantee for sustaining and developing its advantage. This will make it pursue the most complete forms of integration possible in international scenarios. A conclusion derived from the cumulative nature of assets — capacities and resources — on which the firm's international expansion is based: when an asset is cumulative the market is not the best medium for organising its transactions. The advantages of integrated formulas — including those of a strategic nature — are so high that open formulas will only be made use of when organisational costs are high — or when the integration capacity of the activities within the firm are low — and/or when market conditions involve a low risk

[37] Even when these are differentiated, location and transaction costs are related.

[38] See Hennart (1989).

[39] And, therefore, the search for income associated with market power may be one of the aims justifying the option via more integrated formulas of international projection.

for sustaining and promoting the advantage.[40] In short, when internalisation costs are high and more than transaction costs.

This last assumption gives rise to a first proposition:

> H1: In moving into international markets, the firm will seek to find the most integrated formulas allowed it by its resources and the market situation. And it will only resort to externalising part of its transactions when integration costs are high and the specific nature of its assets is low.

This hypothesis means admitting that when internalisation costs are reduced, firms prefer integrated formulas, even despite the low specific nature of their assets and, therefore, their reduced transaction costs. A different situation arises when internalisation costs are high, in which case only firms with highly specified assets – and, therefore, high transaction costs – will opt for integrated formulas.[41]

The state of the environment similarly conditions the perception of risk accompanying the externalisation of company activities. One should suppose that the denser the network of intercompany agreements in the market, the easier it will be for the firm to allow the externalisation of part of its activities. This gives rise to a new conclusion:

> H2: The more internationally integrated the market and the denser and more structured the network of interfirm agreements in its midst, the greater will be the firm's propensity to use open forms of organisation in overseas markets. And, inversely, the more fragmented the market, the greater will be the recourse by the firm to integrated formulas of international presence.

To carry out the analysis, two extreme options were considered

[40] This assumption is the opposite of the one normally used in analysing transaction costs. In general, it is usually considered that the firm will entrust its transactions to the market, except if transaction costs are very high. Nevertheless, it seems more realistic to start from the opposite principle: the firm will try to control the whole process, except when it is too costly. That is, faced with the conventional maxim that: "in the beginning was the market", we will start, on this occasion, from the alternative and equally debatable assumption: "in the beginning was the organisation". For a reference to the arbitrary nature of the conventional assumption, see Williamson (1975), page 37. In the same line, see Krishna Erramilli and Rao (1993) and Gatignon and Anderson (1988).

[41] This position coincides with that argued by Krishna Erramilli and Rao (1993).

in each of the chosen forms of international projection.[42] And, thus, if the firm chooses to maintain production in the domestic market, the relevant decision affects the degree of control it wishes to exercise over its marketing activities abroad. The two options considered will be: the use of outside ways or the firm's direct involvement in marketing activities. Furthermore, if it decides to produce in the end market, the two basic options will be: to transfer the advantage to another firm, via a licence, or to create its own subsidiary in the end market.

4.2 Basic development

When the firm decides the organisational form in which to attempt to project itself in the international market it faces two types of cost with opposing sign. When choosing a formula integrated in the firm's hierarchy, it will avoid transaction costs related to free contracting of market exchanges; but, in return, it will incur different types of costs linked to the internalisation of these tasks.

Moreover, and in accordance with an accepted distinction, transaction costs may be of two types: those related to information seeking, choice of spokesmen and negotiating the terms of the contract *ex-ante costs*; and those related to the risks deriving from not fulfilling the contract *ex-post* costs.[43] The firm will attempt to integrate a particular operation in its organisational hierarchy as long as savings in transaction costs — ex-ante and post-ante — are higher than internalisation costs involved in this decision.[44]

These decisions may be represented by a graph.[45] As has been described, transaction costs are the result of the total negotiation costs, Ta, and costs related to the possible non-fulfilment of the contract, Tp:

$$TTC = Ta + Tp$$

[42] The necessary recourse to dichotomic forms of reasoning constitutes a limitation in the operative development of the transaction costs analysis. Nonetheless, given the tentative nature of this essay, this procedure will not be questioned. See Williamson (1985), page 203 or Heide and John (1988).

[43] See, among others, Hennart (1982) or Hill and Kim (1993).

[44] As Buckley (1990) points out, "the firm grows by replacing or creating adjacent markets in accordance with the positive balance between the benefits of internalisation and the costs deriving from the decision", page 660. *See, also,* Hill, Hwang and Kim (1990).

[45] The form of presentation is based upon Hill and Kim (1993).

Both aspects are, however, related.

In fact, the ex-post costs will depend on the likelihood of opportunist behaviour arising, affecting the firm's advantage — the "dissipation problem" which Rugman notes. So,

$$Tp = p(v)$$

The shape of the curve will depend upon the nature of the assets on which the firm's advantage is founded, v. In turn, the likelihood of opportunist behaviour, p, will depend on the previous effort made in defining the contract, so that as Ta increases Tp must diminish. The shape of the curve Tp will be rising - the greater the likelihood, the greater the costs, though with reduced earnings, stating that the greater increases in losses are registered in the first margins of likelihood of opportunist behaviour (Figure 3).

Moreover, ex-ante costs will have the shape of a negative-slope curve: as the costs involved in drawing up the contract grow, the likelihood of opportunist behaviour declines. Nevertheless, this aim is achieved with decreasing earnings: each time greater ex-ante costs are incurred to achieve reductions in the likelihood of opportunist behaviour. The curve is, therefore, asyntotic on the vertical axis: however much negotiation costs rise, they will never completely eliminate the likelihood of opportunist behaviour, given the conditions of uncertainty and limited rationality in which the firm operates.

What is more, when the firm decides to internalise a particular activity, it incurs costs, which are the result of submitting the transaction to an organisational hierarchy. This occurs when a firm integrates under its organisation the tasks of distribution and marketing in the overseas market — its own networks; or when it decides to create a subsidiary, instead of transferring the technological advantage through a patent to another firm. Thus, there will be internalisation costs, IC:

$$IC = CM + CTr + CC + CF$$

where CM are the costs of learning about the new market in which they are setting up; CTr the costs of transferring company knowhow, whether in the technological field, or the commercial; CC the costs of controlling the new activities integrated in the firm; and CF the flexibility costs deriving from the chosen option, which are in inverse relation to the reversibility or capacity for change, at low cost, of the investment made.

So, the firm will show a tendency to externalise part of its

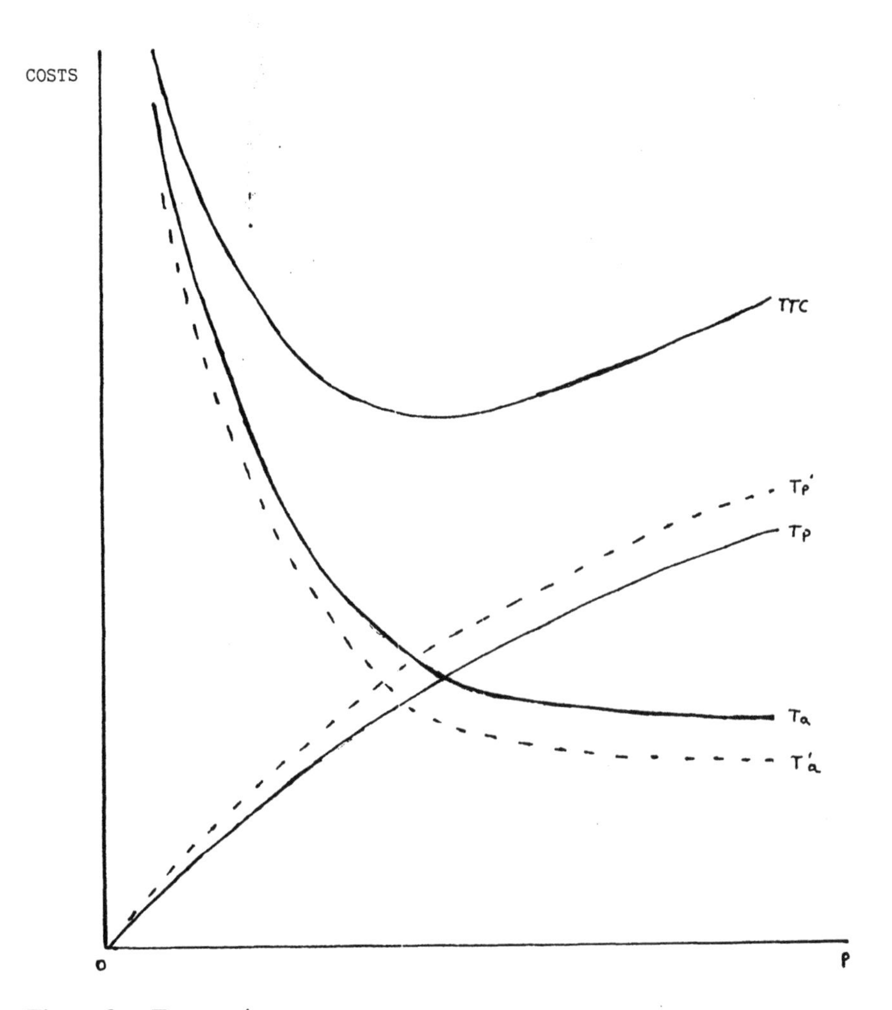

Figure 3 Transaction costs

activities when:

$$Ta + Tp < CM + CTr + CC + CF$$

In evaluating these components, a possible difference arises between the advantage based on production technology and the one determining marketing technology, since control costs are higher in the latter case.[46] In fact, the very nature of technological assets involves the firm in certain operational demands which it

[46] This is more carefully reasoned by Hill and Kim (1993).

tries to profit from; the same thing does not apply with marketing assets, which to a great extent require systems of control less susceptible to being objective, and much more personalised, since they affect human relationships, messages and means of communication. This means higher control costs and, in general, higher costs of internalisation. The firm which bases its advantages on a highly specific marketing asset may choose to take on these higher costs, with the aim of guarateeing durability and development of the transferred assets -brand, trade-mark, reputation, etc. However, if the asset is not highly specific, the costs of internalisation will act as a dissuasive element for the integration process.

So it is possible to draw an additional conclusion

H3: In equal conditions formulas with greater control will be used in a higher proportion when the firm's advantage is based on technological factors than when it is based on marketing-related assets. This means that use of more open control factors is more frequent in the move to export-based internationalisation than when it involves the movement of production capacity — based on technological resources — to the end market.

In determining negotiation costs, a key role belongs to management's willingness in the face of risk. An increase in the capacity for risk acceptance gives rise to movement towards the curve's point of origin — Ta to Ta′: which expresses that, to achieve a similar likelihood of opportunist behaviour, lower negotiation costs are needed. Likewise, in determining the Tp curve, as we have said, the nature of the assets in play in the transaction is crucial: the more exclusive the assets are, the more the curve is displaced upwards — Tp to Tp′— to express the higher losses that could stem from opportunist behaviour.

From the above two additional conclusions can be drawn, related to the specific nature of the assets involved in the transaction.

H4: The transaction costs are higher when involving specific assets, products or processes, so, in those cases, methods of penetration allowing greater control will tend to be more efficient.

As far as knowledge is concerned, the exclusive nature of the assets seems linked to the difficulty involved in substituting, imitating or transferring them. Intangible, relatively immobile assets, such as skills, tacit awareness, organisational routines, management culture or reputation, among others, usually have these characteristics. In general, idiosyncratic assets, generated through one's own experience and active life in the company, constitute the most difficult assets to externalise. And, to the extent that the firm's advantage is based on these factors, which are related to their organisational and learning capacities, the firm will try to opt for integrated formulas for international projection. However, when the firm bases its advantage on less specific knowledge, which is more public and transferable, it will be easier to choose more open control formulas, except when the integration costs are very low.

> H5: Transaction costs increase when activities require assets in human relations form, since these are always more difficult to codify and transfer. So, in their relationships with the market, the firm which needs high technical skills in its staff, customization or highly intensive pre and post-sales services will opt for more integrated control formulas, Coughlan (1985).

In fact, in these cases, it may be difficult for the firm to set up objective control mechanisms in the international field; thus, they may choose subjective control formulas, linked to authority, by means of integrating transactions in the midst of the firm's organisational hierarchy.

Environmental conditions similarly influence transaction costs. And, therefore:

> H6: Transaction costs are less when the level of knowledge of the market is higher and the degree of uncertainty related to negotiating the transaction is lower; so, open formulas will be more frequent in known, stable environments.

A particular way of reducing the risk is to choose the psychologically closest markets, that is, those most similar and best known. Psychological distance creates information costs and increases the agents' perception of risk and uncertainty. Thus, the previous hypothesis could be expressed in the following way:

> H7: Transaction costs are lower in the case of markets of high psychological proximity, so that, in this case, use of high

control formulas is less necessary.

This last conclusion must, however, be related to another with the opposite effect, which points to higher integration costs deriving from performing in uncertain or changeable environments:

> H8: Internalisation costs — particularly costs related to organisational flexibility — will be increased in unknown or uncertain environments, which will make it easier to choose, in those contexts, less integrated, more agile and flexible formulas.

The presence of the last two conclusions shows up the ambiguity produced by the environmental effect on business decisions. Thus, it may be supposed that the firm which has highly specific assets may attempt to opt for integrated formulas, whatever the degree of environmental uncertainty may be, except when internalisation costs are excessive. In fact, the firm will be able to avoid the most unstable markets, but if it decides to set up in them, it will do so through integrated formulas, to save its assets from the uncertainty of the environment. It will do the same when operating in known, stable environments, where internalisation costs are less. On the contrary, if the firm has a limited supply of specific assets, it may choose more open formulas in uncertain environments, with the purpose of reducing internalisation costs as much as possible; reserving the most integrated formulas for cases of known, stable environments, where organisational flexibility is less needed. The option is not clear, however, when the firm has an intermediate level of specific assets, since environmental uncertainty affects both transaction costs and internalisation costs.

This set of possibilities is not completely in accordance with the prescriptions deriving from the theory of development phases, since it is not clear that, in all cases, a choice has to be made of integrated formulas, as the firm acquires international experience and there is a decrease in the uncertainty with which it operates in the market. Nevertheless, some possible discrepancies are the result of the partial and predominantly static nature of the treatment which has been given up to now, so it is worth continuing with the analysis.

4.3. A dynamic view

For this we must bear in mind the dynamic possibilities of the model. This is because the selfsame components of transaction costs and internalisation costs change over time, though with different implications on the balances indicated.

And therefore, in time, we will see:

- First, and as has been pointed out before, a reduction of the risk perceived by the firm as it increases its international experience in the end market. This means a displacement of the curve Ta towards the origin, as an expression of the reduced costs needed for negotiating agreements.
- And, secondly, a progressive reduction of costs related to internalising activities, since some of their components – familiarisation with the new environment or transfer costs – albeit important in the early stages of the international project, will tend to have reduced significance as the firm becomes established in the new markets.

The resulting effect will crucially depend upon the rate at which these two factors evolve (Figure 4). If internalisation costs are reduced at a greater rate than transaction costs, the firm will maintain its preference for integrated forms of international projection – TTC_0 to TTC_1 and IC_0 to IC_1. In the other case, the firm might consider the option of leaving these transactions to the market, via licences or an agreement with outside marketing channels, due to the neighbourhood increasing of externalisation-IC_0 to $IC_{1'}$. That is to say:

$dTTC/dt > dIC/dt$: favours more integrated formulas
$dTTC/dt < dIC/dt$: favours more open formulas

Once more, the possibility arises of the increase in international experience and the consequent reduction of uncertainty levels leading to more open formulas of international penetration, contravening the prescriptions of the theory of development phases. It does not appear that this trend in time towards regression in the forms of international integration is frequent, Davidson (1982), Gatignon and Anderson (1988) or Erramilli (1991). To understand its exceptional character it is worth bearing in mind some additional dynamic factors.

The first refers to the fact that internalisation of activities itself

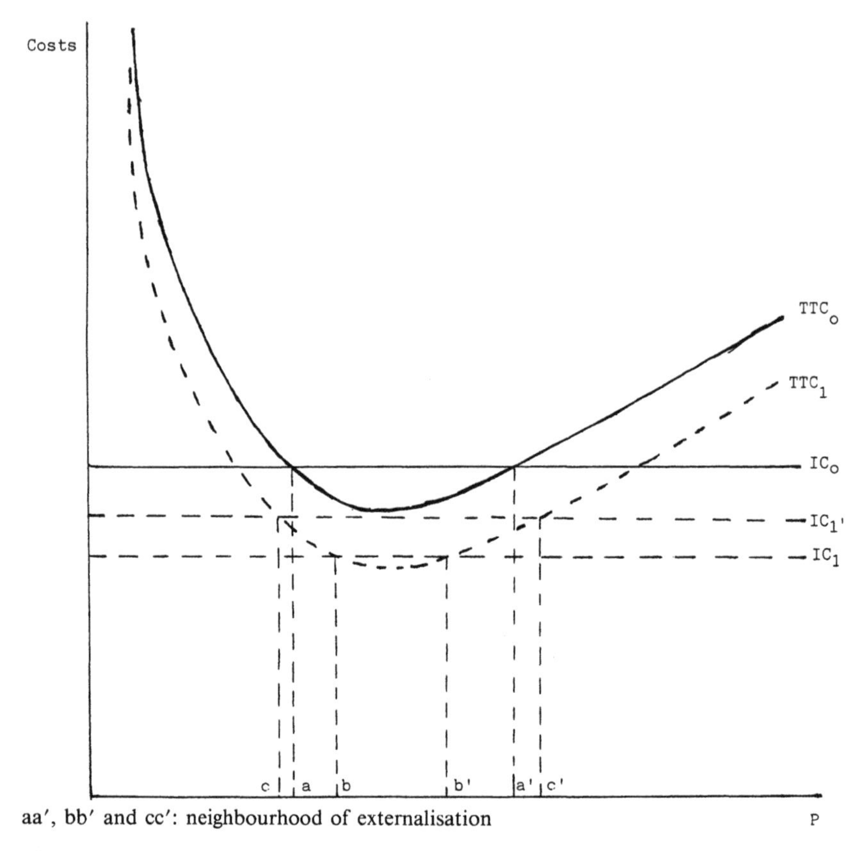

aa′, bb′ and cc′: neighbourhood of externalisation

Figure 4 Transaction Costs

is a source of new business assets, which it is expensive to break up by means of their reverting to the market. And, thus, for example, when a firm sets up its networks for marketing abroad, it promotes the development of new capacities, involving knowledge of the market, the image acquired, human capital generated in these tasks or the organisational and management routines developed. And the same thing happens when investing abroad: the very existence of the subsidiary finally creates new assets which make their subsequent externalisation costly. Expressed another way, decisions, once taken, tend to be confirmed over time; which, indirectly, points to the cost of an unsuitable decision. This trend is revealed as an upward displacement of the Tp curve, as an expression of the higher losses which would be generated from opportunist behaviour. This trend towards reinforcing internationalisation process will be even more noticeable to the extent that in time the assets on which the firm's international action is based become more accumulative. From these considerations an additional conclusion can be drawn:

> H9: With all other conditions equal, it is easier for the firm to move towards growing levels of internalisation than to follow the opposite process; the former will take place more easily in the case of the devaluation over time of the firm's assets and/or a reduction of market uncertainties.

This conclusion is in accord with the cumulative nature which international experience is supposed to have, a basic asset which the firm's overseas projection is based on. The market has the form of an imperfect medium for organising transactions involving this type of asset, cumulative and idiosyncratic in character; so the firm will attempt to capitalise internally on the promotion of those capacities, especially when they are important for competitive advantage. Setting up in the international market will require bearing in mind the cumulative and dynamic nature of management, technological and marketing capacities originating in the firm's own sequence of activity.

The second dynamic factor, already mentioned, refers to the deterioration caused by time to the firm's assets. In this case, it is convenient to distinguish, however, between technological assets and marketing-related ones.

a) Technological assets

Let us suppose that the firm bases its advantage on technological assets, so that it tries to decide between the option of externalising these assets in the new market, through the concession of a licence, or of keeping them integrated under the firm's organisational structure, through the creation of a subsidiary. The march of time will have an erosive effect on the firm's technological advantage, as new innovations are registered by rival units. This will be reflected in the falling trend of the Tp curve as we move on in time. Such a process opens up the possibility of the firm opting for less integrated internationalisation formulas. This gives rise to a new conclusion:

H10: The more mature the product or process technology, the less necessary it is for the firm to use forms of control to project itself towards international markets.

In fact, as technology becomes more public, explicit and mature, the easier it will be for the firm to find formulas for its transfer — by externalising the transaction, either through a licence or by means of transferring its goods to physical form, through exports.

In terms of time it can be said that deterioration of technological advantage will be less when it is based on tacit knowledge, which is difficult to transfer or copy. Thus, the falling trend of transaction costs over time will be reduced. From which we can deduce:

H11: Penetration methods using greater control are more efficient for assets, products or processes which are not very structured or hardly understood; those based on tacit knowledge and difficult to codify or transfer.

Now, in face of the deterioration caused by time, the firm may initiate an active R&D program geared to renovating and broadening its technological assets. The promotion of new resources will have the opposite effect to the one mentioned above. The outcome will crucially depend on the firm's capacity for unleashing its technological resources, compared to the deterioration produced in them by dissemination mechanisms. Technological innovation will have the effect of increasing transaction costs, by interrupting their falling trend over time. And, in parallel fashion, these innovations raise internalisation costs derived from the process of adjustment to the new procedures generated — IC to IC′.

Nonetheless, this latter effect has to be slight, since a large part of internalisation costs remain unchanged. So the innovation process is expected to have more effect on transaction than internalisation costs, favouring the transition towards greater control formulas (Figure 5).

b) Marketing-related assets

If the advantage is based on marketing technology the asset deterioration will probably not take place at the same rate. Even more, it seems reasonable to assume that, as the firm's presence in the markets increases, the greater will be the firm's marketing

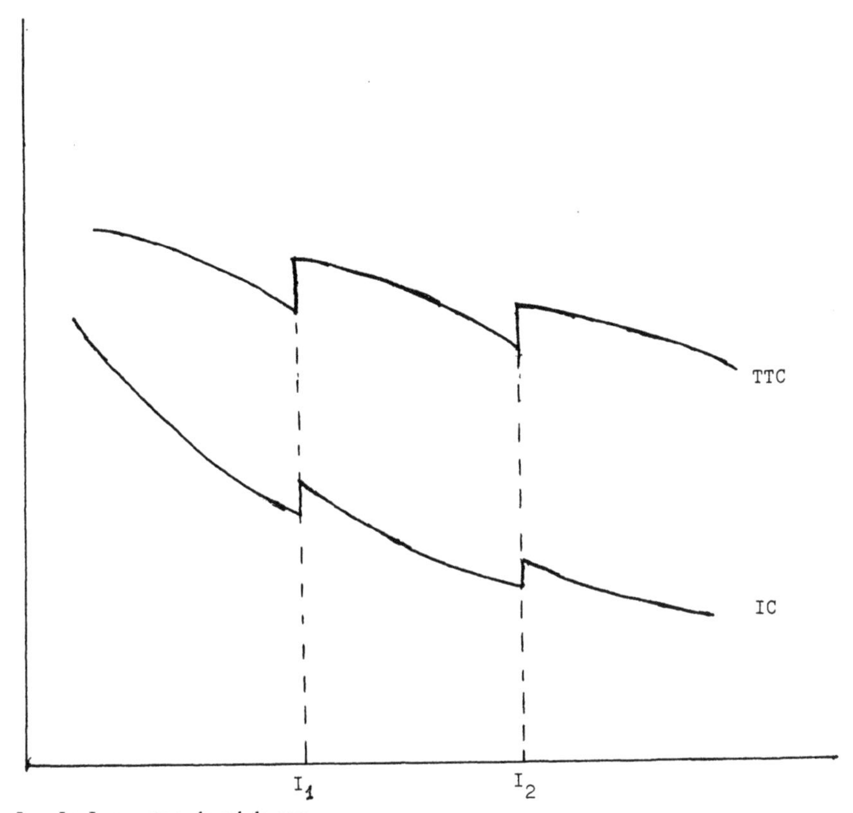

I_1 y I_2: Innovatory breakdowns

Figure 5 Evolution of Transaction costs

assets, name and reputation in the market.[47] This will raise the firm's transaction costs, by making its option of externalised formulas more difficult.

> H12: With all other conditions being equal, the regression towards more open penetration formulas is produced more easily when the firm bases its advantage on technological assets than when doing so on marketing – related ones.

[47] Expressed another way, it is assumed that the firm's asset deterioration produced as a result of dissemination processes is greater in the case of technological assets than in marketing ones.

5. FINAL CONSIDERATIONS

The set of the different forces and trends considered here is, as has been seen, partially indeterminate. We do not mean by that that there is a lack of criteria for analysing the various options, rather that the factors influencing their determination have different signs, which forces us to a specific analysis, in each situation, of the firm and its environment.

To place the analysis in context, it must also be borne in mind that transaction costs are no more than one of the components intervening in the selection process of ways of penetrating international markets. An eclectic consideration of the factors to be remembered, stresses at least three more not considered in the previous exercise.[48]

- In the first place those costs not strictly related to the analysis of the transaction, and which, nevertheless, are important in determining the chosen formula for internationalisation. Such is the case of production costs or transport costs, which could be included under the generic title of location costs. The processes of international delocation and relocation of productive activities, in search of lower costs, indicates the importance of these components when deciding the firm's forms of international projection.

- Secondly, the chosen form of penetration will depend crucially upon the international strategy pursued by the firm. And, thus, it will be very difficult to opt for high control methods of penetration if, for instance, what is being pursued is a strategy of high market dispersion; and, inversely, it will be more difficult for the firm to externalise production or marketing activities in the end market if what it chooses is a strategy highly concentrated on markets and segments. In short, the choice of forms of market penetration is one part – and a basic part – of the firm's international strategy; and has to be in accordance with the aims pursued by such a strategy.[49]

- And, lastly, the forms of penetration depend upon the conditions and climate of competition of the market where the

---

[48] See Hill, Hwang and Kim (1990). A more integrated approach to the strategic content in the different forms of penetration can be found in Kim and Hwang (1992).

[49] See in this respect Alonso and Donoso (1994).

firm operates. Use by rival units of integrated formulas of penetration may force the firm to follow the same mode of behaviour, as an oligopolistic reaction, Knickerbocker (1973).

The option to be finally taken will be the result of the *joint and simultaneous* consideration of an aggregate of situational, strategic and cost variables.

The consideration of this set of factors confirms that the form of market entry is a complex problem, difficult to reduce to a limited set of variables, subject to a determinist option. The firm's experience, moreover, makes a purer study of the phenomenon more difficult since, as a large part of international literature has shown, few firms make a completely conscious, deliberate and rational choice of their options in international markets.

Finally, it must be underlined that the analysis which has been made here is still a very modest one: the options in play have been severely limited and notably restrictive starting assumptions have been applied. The hypotheses that are hinted at thus have no more than a merely heuristic value which they generate from the chosen analytical framework. Even then, their capacity for suggestion reveals the possibilities offered by an analysis such as the one made here.

BIBLIOGRAPHY

Agarwal, S. and S.N. Ramaswami (1992)., "Choice of foreign market entry mode: impact of ownership, location and internalization factors", *Journal of International Business Studies*, first quarter, pp 1–27.

Aharoni, Y. (1966)., *The foreign investment decision process*, Harvard University Press, Mass.

Alonso, J.A. (1993)., "Capacidades exportadoras y estrategia internacional de la empresa", en J. Velarde, J.L. Garcia Delgado y A. Pedreno (eds.)., *Empresas y empresarios espanoles en la encrucijada de los noventa*, Editorial Civitas, Madrid.

Alonso, J.A. and V. Donoso (1994), *Competitividad de la empresa exportadora espanola*, ICEX, Madrid.

Andersen, O. (1993)., "On the internationalization process of firms: a critical analysis", *Journal of International Business Studies*, second quarter, pp 209–231.

Anderson, E. and A. Coughlan (1987)., "International market entry and expansion via independent or integrated channels of distribution", Journal of Marketing, vol. **51**, pp 71–82.

Anderson, E. and H. Gatignon (1986)., "Modes of foreign entry: a transaction

cost analysis and propositions", *Journal of International Business Studies*, vol **17**, pp 1–26.
Ayal, I. and J. Rabal (1987)., "Export management structure and successful high technology innovation", en Ph. J. Rosson and S.D. Reid (eds.). *Managing export entry and expansion*, Praeger, New York.
Bilkey, W.J. and G. Tesar (1977)., "The export behavior of smaller-sized Wisconsin manufacturing firms", *Journal of International Business Studies*, Spring, no. 8, pp 93–98.
Brousseau, E. (1993)., 'Les theories des contrats: une revue", Revue d'Economie Politique, vol 103, jan-fevr. pp 1–82.
Buckley, P.J. (1988)., "The limits of explanation: testing the internalization theory of the multinational enterprise", *Journal of International Business Studies*, vol. XIX, summer, pp 181–193.
Buckley, P.J. (1990)., "Problems and developments in the core theory of international business", *Journal of International Business Studies*, fourth quarter, pp 657–665.
Buckley, P.J. and M. Casson (1979) *The future of multinational enterprise*, Macmillan, London.
Buckley, P.J. and M. Casson (1985) *The economic theory of the multinational enterprise: selected papers*, Macmillan, London.
Cantwell, J. (1988) "Theories of international production", University of Reading, *Discussion Papers in International Investment and Business Studies*, series B, September.
Casson, M. (1979) *Alternatives to the multinational enterprise*, Macmillan, London.
Casson, M. (1982) *The growth of international business*, George Allen and Unwin, London.
Casson, M. (1987) *The firm and the market*, MIT Press, Cambridge Mass.
Caves, R.E. (1982) *Multinational enterprise and economic analysis*, Cambridge University Press, Cambridge.
Cavusgil, S.T. (1980) "On the internationalization process of firms", *European Research*, November, pp 273–81.
Cavusgil, S.T. (1984) "Differences among exporting firms based on their grade of internationalization", *Journal of Business Research*, vol. 12, no 3, pp 1–14.
Coase, R. (1937) "The nature of the firm", *Economica*, vol. 14, no 16, pp 365–405.
Coughlan, A.T. (1985) "Competition and cooperation in marketing channel choice: theory and application", *Marketing Science*, vol. 4, no 2, pp 110–29.
Cyert, R. and J.G. March (1963) *A behavioral theory of the firm*, Prentice-Hall, Englewood Cliffs, N.J.
Davidson, W. (1982) *Global strategic management*, J. Wiley and Sons, New York.
Davidson, W. (1983) "Market similarity and market selection: implications for international marketing strategy", *Journal of Business Research*, vol. 11, pp 439–56.
Davidson W. and D. McFetridge (1985) "Key characteristics in the choice of international technology transfer mode", *Journal of International Business Studies*, vol.16, Summer, pp 5–21.
Denis, J.E. and Depelteau, D. (1985) "Market knowledge, diversification and export expansion", *Journal of International Business Studies*, no. 16, pp 77–89.

Dunning, J.H.(1979) "Explaining changing patterns of international production: in defence of the eclectic theory", *Oxford Bulletin of Economics and Statistics*, vol. 161.

Dunning, J.H. (1988) "The eclectic paradigm of international production: a restatement and some possible extensions", *Journal of International Business Studies*, vol. 19, spring, pp 1–31.

Dunning, J.H. and A. Rugman (1985): "The influence of Hymer's dissertation on the theory of foreign direct investment", *American Economic Review, Papers and Proceedings*, May, pp 228–232.

Erramilli, M.K. (1991) "The experience factor in foreign market entry behavior of service firms", *Journal of International Business Studies*, vol. 22, no 3, pp 479–501.

Forsgren, M. (1989) *Managing the internationalization process* Routledge, London.

Gatignon, H. and E. Anderson (1988) "The multinational corporation's degree of control over foreign subsidiaries: an empirical test of a transaction cost explanation", *Journal of Law, Economics and Organization*, vol 4, no 2, pp 305–35.

Hákansson, H. (1982) *International marketing and purchasing of industrial goods,* John Wiley, Chichester.

Hedlund, G. and A. Kverneland (1985) "Are strategies for foreign market entry changing? The case of Swedish investment in Japan", *International Studies of Management and Organization*, no 15, pp 41–59.

Heide, J.B. and G. John (1988) "The role of dependence balancing in safeguarding transaction-specific assets in conventional channels", *Journal of Marketing*, January, pp 20–25.

Hennart, J.F.A. (1977) *A theory of multinational enterprise*, Ph. dissertation, University of Maryland.

Hennart, J.F.A. (1982) *A theory of the multinational enterprise*, University of Michigan Press, Ann Arbor.

Hennart, J.F.A. (1986) "What is internalization?", *Weltwirtschaflitches Archiv*, Winter, pp. 791–804.

Hennart, J.F.A. (1988) "A transaction costs theory of equity joint ventures", *Strategic Management Journal*, vol. 9, pp 361–74.

Hennart, J.F. (1989) "Can the 'new forms of investment' subtitute for the 'old Forms?'. A transaction costs perspective", *Journal of International Business Studies*, Summer, pp 211–234.

Hill, Ch.W.L. and W. Chan Kim (1988): "Searching for a dynamic theory of the multinational enterprise: a transaction cost model", *Strategic Management Journal*, vol. 9, pp 93–104.

Hill, Ch.W.L., P. Hwang and W.Ch. Kim (1990) "An eclectic theory of the choice of international entry mode", *Strategic Management Journal*, vol. 11, pp 117–128.

Hörnell, E. and J.E. Vahlne (1986) *Multinationals: the swedish cas*e, Croom Helm, London.

Hymer, S. (1976) *The international operations of national firms*, Lexington, Mass.

Itaki, M. (1991) "A critical assessment of the eclectic theory of the multinational enterprise", *Journal of International Business Studies*, vol. 22, no 3, pp 445–60.

Jacquemin, A. (1989) *La nueva organizaciðn industrial*, Vicens Vives, Barcelona.

Jacquemin, A. (1990) "Comportamiento colusivo, I + D and política europea", en X. Vives and J. Gual (eds.): *Concentración empresarial and comeptitividad: Espana en la CEE*, Alianza Economía, Madrid.
Johanson, J. and L.G. Mattsson (1988) "Internationalisation in industrial system: a network approach," en N. Hood and J.E. Vahlne (eds.), *Strategies in Global Competition*, Croom Helm, London.
Johanson, J. and J.E. Vahlne (1977) "The internationalization process of the firm: a model of knowledge development and increasing foreign market commitments", *Journal of International Business Studies*, vol. 18, no 1, pp 23–32.
Johanson, J. and J.E. Vahlne (1990) "The mechanism of internationalisation", *International Marketing Review*, vol. 7, no 4, pp 11–24.
Johanson, J. and F. Wiedersheim-Paul (1975) "The internationalization of the firm: four swedish cases", *Journal of Management Studies*, October, pp 305–322.
Juul, M. and P. Walters (1987) "The internationalization of norwegian firms: a study of the U.K. experience", *Management International Review*, vol. 17, no 1, pp 58–66.
Kim, W.Ch. and P. Hwang (1992) "Global strategy and multinationals' entry mode choice", *Journal of International Business Studies*, first quarter, pp 29–53.
Klein, S. (1989) "A transaction cost explanation of vertical control in international markets", *Journal of the Academy of Marketing Science*, vol. 17, no 3, pp 253–60.
Klein, S., G.L. Frazier and V.J. Roth (1990) "Atransaction cost analysis model of channel integration in international markets", *Journal of Marketing Research*, vol. XXVII, may, pp 196–208.
Knickerbocker, F.T. (1973) *Oligopolistic reaction and multinational enterprise*, Harvard University Graduate School of Business Administration, Boston.
Kogut, B. and H. Singh (1988) "The effect of national culture on the choice of entry mode", *Journal of International Business Studies*, vol 19, Fall, pp 411–32.
Krishna Erramilli, M. and C.P. Rao (1993) "Service firms 'international entry-mode choice: a modified transaction-cost analysis approach", *Journal of Marketing*, vol. 57, July, pp 19–38.
Lee, W.Y. and J.J. Brasch (1978) "The adoption of export as an innovative strategy", *Journal of International Business Studies*, vol. 9, no 1, pp 85–93.
Linqvist, M. (1988) *Internationalization of small technology based firms: three illustrative case studies on swedish firms*, Institute of International Business, Stockholm School of Economics.
Luostarinen, R. (1979) *The internationalization of the firm*, Acta Academic Oeconomicae Halsigiensis, Helsinki.
McKierman, P.(1992) *Strategies of growth: maturity, recovery and internationalization*, Routledge, London.
Melin, L. (1992) "Internationalization as a strategy process", *Strategic Management Journal*, vol. 13, pp 99–118.
Millington, A.I. and B.T. Bayliss (1990) "The process of internationalisation: UK companies in the EC", *Management International Review*, vol. 30, no 2, pp 151–61.
Nordström, K.A. (1990) *The internationalization process of the firm in a new*

perspective, Institute of International Business, Stocholm.
Penrose, E.T. (1959) *The theory of growth of the firm*, Basil Blackwell, London.
Perlmutter, H.V. and D.A. Henan (1987) "La cooperación para competir en el mercado mundial", *Harvard-Deusto Business Review*, no 30, pp 49–58.
Piercy, N. (1981) "Company internationalization: active and reactive exporting", *European Journal of Marketing*, vol. 15, pp 26–40.
Porter, M.E. and M.B. Fuller (1988) "Coaliciones and estrategia global", Información Comercial Espanola, junio, pp 101–120.
Reid, S. (1983) "Firm internationalization. Transaction costs and strategic choice", *International Marketing Review*, no 1, pp 43–61.
Rugman, A. (1980) "Internalization as a general theory of foreign direct investment: a re-appraisal of the literature", *Weltwirtschaflitches Archiv*, v. 116.
Rugman, A. (1981) *Inside the multinationals*, Columbia University Press, New York.
Rugman, A.(1982) *New theories of the multinational enterprise*, Croom Helm, London.
Rugman, A. (1986) "New theories of the multinational enterprise: an assesment of internationalisation theory", *Bulletin of Economic Research*, 2, pp 101–18.
Simmonds, K. and H. Smith (1968) "The first export order: a marketing innovation", *British Journal of Marketing*, Summer, pp 93–100.
Stubbart, C.(1992) "The deceptive allure of developmental model processes", *Strategic Management Society Conference*, London.
Sullivan, D. and A. Bauerschmidt (1990) "Incremental internationalization: a test of Johanson and Vahlne's thesis", *Management International Review*, vol. 30, no 1, pp 19–30.
Teece, D. (1981) "The multinational enterprise: market failure and market power considerations", *Sloan Management Review*, Spring, pp 3–17.
Teece, D. (1985): "Multinational enterprise, internal governance, and economic organization", *American Economic Review*, vol. 75, pp 233–38.
Teece, D. (1986) "Transaction cost economics and the multinational enterprise: An assesment", *Journal of Economic Behavior and Organization*, vol 7, pp 21-45.
Turnbull, P.W. (1987) "A challenge to the stages theory of the internationalization process", en Ph.J. Rosson and S.D. Reid (eds.), *Managing export entry and expansion. Concepts and Practice*, Praeger, New York.
Turnbull, P.W. and J.P. Valla (1986) *Strategies for international industrial marketing*, Croom Helm, London.
Welch, L.S. and R. Luostarinen (1988) "Internationalization: evolution of a concept", *Journal of General Management*, vol. 14, no 2, pp 36–64.
Welch, L.S. and F. Wierdersheim-Paul (1980) "Initial exports: a marketing failure?", *Journal of Management Studies*, vol. 12, no 4, pp 333–43.
Wiedersheim-Paul, F. (1972) *Uncertainty and economic distance: studies in international business*, Uppsala.
Williamson, O. (1975) *Markets and hierarchies. Analysis and antitrust implications*, The Free Press, New York.
Williamson, O. (1985) *The economic institutions of capitalism*, Free Press, New York.
Young, S.(1987) "Business strategy and the internationalization of business: recent approaches", *Managerial and Decsion Economics*, vol. 8, pp 31–40.

PART II
EXPERIENCES FROM EUROPE AND LATIN AMERICA

Technological Innovation and International Competitiveness in Italy

Franco Malerba and Luigi Orsenigo

1. INTRODUCTION

Italy represents one of the success stories of post-war economic growth. Over the past forty-five years, GNP growth has been higher in Italy than in most other industrialized countries. Similarly, productivity and income per capita have risen rapidly and manufacturing exports have increased considerably. In a relatively short period of time Italy has been transformed from an agricultural and semindustrialized country to an advanced industrial economy. In addition, during the 1980s Italy experienced high growth rates in R&D. Yet, Italian international specialization remains mainly in traditional products such as textile and shoes, as well as in mechanics and industrial equipment, whilst the Italian performance in high-technology products is highly unsatisfactory. More generally, the process of internationalization of the Italian industry remains to a large extent limited to exports and to passive multinationalization (especially as far as high technology sectors are concerned).

In this paper, we provide material for a discussion of these contradictory aspects of the Italian performance. First, we examine the main features of innovative activities in Italy and the essential characteristics of the national system of innovation lying at the base of the economic success story of the last forty plus years

Second, we briefly discuss the linkages beween innovative activities, trade performance and processes of internationalization of Italian industry. Indeed, it has been increasingly recognized in the theoretical literature that innovation is a major determinant of the international performance of countries and of economic growth (Dosi, Pavitt and Soete 1987, Cantwell, 1989, Dunning and Cantwell 1991).

We argue that the basic features of the national system of innovation — characterized by the role played by small firms, by a small and weak core of large enterprises, inefficiencies in the academic system and patchy public policies — allowed a rapid process of catching-up but prevented also a further transition towards high-technology industries. This technological backwardness is reflected in an unsatisfactory international performance, which feeds back negatively on the processes of technological accumulation.

The paper is organized as follows:after a short summary of the patterns of post-war economic growth in Italy (Section 2), we examine briefly the conventional indicators of innovative activities (R&D expenditures and patents) and in particular we discuss the main characteristics of the patterns of innovative activities at the sectoral and firm- level (Section 3). Third, we present the essential features of the Italian national system of innovation which may account for the observed patterns of innovative activities (Section 4). Finally, we discuss the links between technological activities, trade performance and processes of multinationalization, focussing on high technology sectors (Section 5).

2. THE PATTERNS OF POST-WAR ECONOMIC GROWTH IN ITALY: AN OVERVIEW.

Italy was a late industrializer. Although industries such as steel, auto, electrical machinery and chemical were already in existence before World War II, Italy did not develop a modern industry until the 1950s. This meant that the growth of the technological and productive capabilities (in terms of labor force, firm organization, managerial skills) and an advanced infrastructure that was typical of other industrialized countries began to emerge only in the last 40 years (Malerba, 1993). In addition, Italy did not have a tradition of industrial R&D that dates back to the end of last century and the first half of this century. Some centers of excellence existed in a few firms (such as Montecatini), but in general Italian firms spent very limited amounts on R&D. Since World War II, Italy has followed a process of catching-up in several high technology industries (Malerba,1988). In this respect, during the 1960s and the 1970s public enterprises active in sectors such as electronics and aerospace have played a major role in maintaining an indigenous capability in R&D intensive industries. In general, however, imports of foreign technology have always exceeded exports of domestic know-how.

The rapid post-World War II economic growth occurred within a dualistic economy in terms of firm size and geographical location. Small firms are quite numerous in traditional and specialized supplier sectors, which constitute a major part of Italian industry. On the other hand the core of Italian industry in scale intensive and high technology sectors is made up of only a few large firms. In addition, most of the large Italian firms and the bulk of advanced industry is located in the Northern regions, while the South of Italy is characterized by a limited degree of industrialization and an absence of progressive high technology industries.

It must be noted that another feature of Italian industry is related to the presence of the public sector in scale intensive and high technology industries such as electronics, steel and food.

Finally, until recently Italian industry has not shown a good degree of internationalization. Italian firms in traditional sectors such as texiles, shoes and furniture have shown a very good international performance in terms of exports. Foreign direct investments by Italian industry however have been limited and the presence of foreign multinational corporations in Italy scarce (Onida-Viesti,1987; Mariotti-Onida, 1988).

3. LEVELS AND STRUCTURE OF INNOVATIVE ACTIVITIES IN ITALY

Against this general background, the level and structure of innovative activities in Italy can be summarized as follows.

3.1 Relatively low levels of innovative activities

In aggregate terms, the technological performance of Italy compares unfavourably with the main industrial countries, despite a slow but steady increasing trend in the 'Eighties. During the 1980s the relative distance between Italy and the other major OECD countries (with the exception of Japan) as far as both total R&D expenditures and R&D intensity are concerned was reduced (Table 1). This growth was partly the outcome of increased R&D efforts of business enterprises. However, public support for business enterprises R&D has also significantly increased. During the 1980s the yearly compounded growth rates of government-financed R&D have been higher than that of most OECD countries. The share of government financed business enterprise R&D over total business enterprise R&D increased from 4.5% (1971) to 24.8% (1986).

At the sectoral level major structural changes in the composition of the R&D undertaken by Italian business enterprises took place. High-technology sectors such as electronics and aerospace significantly increased their relative importance, while other sectors such as transportation (auto, ships, etc) and chemicals reduced their share. This structural change was the consequence of different rates of growth of production and of changes in the R&D intensity of various sectors, such as electronics, drugs and chemicals, and transportation (including in particular aerospace).

In spite of its quantitative growth during the 1980s, the performance of the Italian system remains quite unsatisfactory: in absolute terms and as a percentage of GDP, Italian R&D expenditures are still much lower than the ones of the major OECD countries.

Table 1 Technological activity in the main OCDE countries

	R&D 1990	R&D/GDP 1990
	PPP Million $	%
United States	150.765	2.8
Japan	66.863	2.8
Germany	32.467	2.9
France	23.631	2.3
United Kingdom	19.525*	2.3**
Italy	12.484	1.3

*1989
**1988
Source: OCDE

As is known, R&D expenditures are a highly imperfect indicator of innovative activities, particularly because they do not consider all those processes of learning and accumulation of technological competences which do not take place within the formal structure of R&D laboratories. As a consequence, for instance, R&D data systematically underestimate the technological activities of small companies. Patent data partially overcome these drawbacks, although they suffer from a variety of other shortcomings (Pavitt 1988).

Analysis of patent data provide however similar results: the share of patents applied for by Italian institutions at the European Patent Office has also been increasing, but it remains much lower as compared to the main European countries, reaching 3.4% in the period 1985–91 (Table 2).

3.2 Technological specialization in mature technologies and in "traditional" industries

The low levels of innovative activities are reflected in a marked technological specialization in mature technologies and in "traditional" industries. Moreover, the slight improvement in the aggregate technological performance has taken place through the strenghtening of this pattern of specialization over time.

As is known, technological specialization can be measured by the index of revealed technological advantages (RTA) (Soete 1981). This index has been calculated here on the basis of patent applications at the European Patent Office with reference to the periods 1978–84 and 1985–91 for 32 technological classes derived from the 118 classes considered in the International Patent Classification at the 3-digits level (Table 3). These data show that Italian technological specialization is concentrated in technological classes such as textiles, furniture, foood and tobacco, transport and industrial machinery. On the other hand, the Italian relative technological performance is particularly weak in the fields of electronics and information technologies, chemicals and instrumentation.

In general, Italy appears to be characterized by high levels of concentration of the patterns of technological specialization, a phenomenon which is typical of "small countries" like the Netherlands, Sweden and Switzerland. Moreover, the structure of these patterns of specialization remains quite stable over time and,

Table 2 Patent activities shares of eleven industrialized countries at EPO and USPO

	EPO		
	1978–84		1985–91
Japan	14.48		20.27
United States	26.71		26.32
Belgium	0.90		0.79
France	10.74		8.87
Germany	24.59		21.19
Italy	2.06		3.39
Netherlands	4.11		4.15
United Kingdom	6.95		6.28
Spain	0.15		0.29
Sweden	2.11		2.46
Switzerland	5.34		4.04
	USPO		
	1963–77	1978–84	1985–90
Japan	5.67	15.50	20.89
United States	71.00	57.37	52.46
Belgium	0.36	0.37	0.37
France	2.83	3.38	3.26
Germany	7.15	9.28	9.01
Italy	0.94	1.28	1.40
Netherlands	0.90	1.07	1.07
United Kingdom	4.24	3.61	3.17
Spain	0.10	0.04	0.14
Sweden	1.07	0.12	0.96
Switzerland	1.73	1.83	1.52

Source: Cespri elaborations on EPO and USPO data

if anything, the technological classes denoting technological specialization in the first period tend to remain strong (and often improve) over time, and vice-versa. In general, the Y correlation between the patterns of technological specialization in the two periods considered here (measured by the Pearson correlation coefficient) is equal to 0.93. Whilst the patterns of technological specialization tend indeed to remain quite stable over time in most

Table 3 Technological Specialization of Italy (Revealed technological advantages: RTA((a)

Technological classes	1978–84	1985–91
Agriculture	1.32	1.13
Foodstuffs and tobacco	1.47	1.31
Furniture, Clothing, Footwear	2.70	2.97
Health and entertainment	1.18	0.98
Drugs	0.70	0.93
Preparing and Mixing	0.73	0.69
Machine Tools	1.20	1.48
Industrial machinery and equipments	1.53	1.28
Printing	1.86	1.00
Vehicles, motorcycles, other land vehicles	1.70	1.84
Material handling apparatus	1.71	1.83
Inorganic chemicals	0.59	0.72
Organic chemicals	0.93	1.03
Macromolecular compounds	0.64	0.77
Dyes, petroleum and oils	0.50	0.45
Biochemistry	0.27	0.49
Metallurgy	0.62	0.50
Textiles and flexible materials	3.04	2.92
Paper	0.65	0.72
Building	1.76	1.70
Mining	0.05	0.51
Engines and pumps	1.07	1.37
Mechanical engineering	0.97	1.21
Lighting systems and heating apparatuses	1.41	1.38
Ammunition, weapons	1.26	0.77
Optics and photography	0.43	0.33
Computers	0.41	0.27
Measurement and control instruments	0.69	0.65
Nuclear technology	0.05	0.28
Electrical systems and electronic components	0.55	0.72
Telecommunications	0.64	0.54
Others	0.90	0.84

a) RTA = Patent share in a sector / Total patent share
Source: CESPRI elaborations on EPO data

industrial countries, the stickiness of Italy is particularly high and second only to Switzerland, whilst for instance the correlation

Table 4 Patent shares in high technology sectors of eleven industrialized countries at EPO and USPO

	EPO		
	1978–84		1985–91
Japan	20.59		27.97
United States	31.78		31.68
Belgium	0.65		0.54
France	8.63		6.36
Germany	20.72		15.46
Italy	1.28		1.9
Netherlands	4.16		4.24
United Kingdom	5.11		5.23
Spain	0.04		0.09
Sweden	0.92		0.86
Switzerland	3.56		2.51
	USPO		
	1963–77	1978–84	1985–90
Japan	6.73	15.41	23.11
United States	71.73	57.68	51.65
Belgium	0.34	0.21	0.2
France	3.07	4.71	3.32
Germany	8.13	8.57	8.19
Italy	0.73	1	0.93
Netherlands	1	1.47	1.44
United Kingdom	4.58	4.45	4.14
Spain	0.06	0.01	0.08
Sweden	1.01	0.91	0.95
Switzerland	1.24	1.37	1.16

Source: CESPRI elaborations on EPO and USPO data

coefficient is equal to 0.84 in Germany and 0.67 in the U.S.A.[1]

Focusing the attention on a subset of 12 high technology sectors,[2] Italy's share of EPO patents falls to 1.9%, showing as

[1] *See also* Dosi, Pavitt and Soete, 1987, Cantwell 1991 and Amendola et al. 1993 for a thorough discussion of this issue

[2] This classification has been designed jointly by ENEA, CESPRI at the Bocconi University and by the Politechnic of Milan, specifically with the aim of making

Table 5 Technological specialization in High Tech sectors by country (RTA)

	1978–84	1985–1991
Japan	1.42	1.38
United States	1.19	1.2
Belgium	0.73	0.69
France	0.8	0.72
Germany	0.84	0.73
Italy	0.62	0.56
Netherlands	1.01	1.02
United Kingdom	0.73	0.83
Spain	0.23	0.29
Switzerland	0.67	0.62

Source: CESPRI elaborations on EPO data

strongly and increasingly despecialized (Tables 4 and 5). Over time, however, the share of Italy in these sectors tends to grow, being the only country except Japan that strengthens its position in absolute terms according to EPO data. At a disaggregated level, Italy has technological advantages only in the case of industrial automation (Table 6).

3.3 "Widening" patterns of innovation.

As is well known, innovative activities can take very different forms across sectors and countries, as far as the sources of technological advancement, the organizational structure of learning processes, etc. are concerned. An analysis at the firm and sectoral level allows us to identify some important properties of the patterns of technological change.

The patterns of innovation have been analyzed using patent data (Malerba and Orsenigo, 1994). The OTAF-SPRU data base has been elaborated at the firm level for four European countries: Germany (Federal Republic), France, the United Kingdom and Italy and for 33 technological classes. On this basis, for each of the 33 technological classes, the following indicators of the patterns of

possible a comparative analysis between patent data, trade data and data on the processes of multinationalization. For details, see ENEA 1993.

Table 6 Technological specialization in twelve high-tech sectors: Italy (RTA)

	1978–84	1985–91
Drugs and medicines	0.82	0.93
Plastic, elastomers, fibers	0.93	0.89
Fine chemicals, "specialties"	0.58	0.36
New materials	0.23	0.46
Industrial automation	1.00	1.25
Office automation	0.38	0.23
Consumer electronics and telecommunications	0.82	0.47
Electromedicals	0.36	0.46
Electronic components	0.26	0.51
Aerospace	0.79	0.28
Measurement and control instruments	0.69	0.58
Optics	0.46	0.61

Source: CESPRI elaborations on EPO data

innovative activities have been calculated:

A. Concentration of innovative activities (concentration ratio of the top 4 innovators) and asymmetries among innovators (Herfindahl index);
B. Size of the innovating firms (Share of patents held by firms having more than 500 employees);
C. Change over time in the hierarchy of innovators (Spearman rank correlation coefficient between the hierarchy of innovators in the period 1969–75 and 1975–86);
D. Relevance of new innovators as compared to established ones (number of firms patenting for the first time in the period 1975–86 over the total number of firms holding patents in period 1969–75; share of total patents in the period 1975–86 held by firms patenting for the first time in the same period)

As is known, the patterns of innovative activities differ drastically across technological classes and countries. At the cost of oversimplification, one can distinguish between two polar models. "Widening" patterns of innovative activities (or the Schumpeterian Mark I model) are characterized by technological ease of entry in an industry and by a major role played by new firms in innovative activities. New entrepreneurs come into an industry with new products or new processes, challenge established firms and in such a way they continuously disrupt the current way of production, organization and distribution and wipe out the quasi rents associated with previous innovations. Thus, the innovative base is continuously enlarging through the entry of new innovators and the erosion of the competitive and technological advantages of the established firms in the industry. Deepening (Schumpeter Mark II) patterns of innovation, on the contrary, are related to the dominance of a few, large firms which are continuously innovative through the accumulation over time of technological and innovative capabilities. Large firms have institutionalized the innovation process with the creation of R&D laboratories. With their accumulated stock of knowledge in specific technological areas, their advanced competence in large scale R&D projects, production and distribution and their important financial resources they create barriers to entry to new entrepreneurs and small firms. Of course, widening and deepening Schumpeterian patterns of innovative activities are two extreme cases, which delineate a large number of intermediate cases.

At the sectoral level, in general, at one extreme one finds the chemical group, which follows a deepening pattern of innovation. At the other extreme, in the mechanical group innovative activities follow the widening model. The electronic group is quite similar to chemicals, although the stability of the hierarchy of innovators is less pronounced.

In general, in Italy innovative activities are rather concentrated in a relatively small number of large firms, which are however much smaller in terms of patents as compared to the major competitors. Moreover, the hierarchy of major innovators tends to remain relatively stable even over long periods of time. On the other hand, one can observe also high rates of technological turbulence, i.e many firms enter the club of innovators and many stop patent in the second period. A large fraction of entry is however "lateral entry": that is to say, most of the entrants are firms who had patented before in other technological classes and diversify into related technological classes, so that net entry is actually quite small. Moreover, both entrants and leavers usually hold individually a comparatively small number of patents.

The sectoral patterns of innovative activities in Italy are not very different from those that are observed in other European countries, suggesting that they are strongly influenced by variables related to the very properties of the technologies considered (i.e. what has been defined as the nature of the relevant technological regime See Winter 1984, Malerba and Orsenigo 1990 and 1994). Indeed, the various indicators of the patterns of innovative activities differ consistently across technological classes in all countries, i.e. the patterns of innovative activities in e.g. chemicals are very similar in all countries.

However, one can observe systematic differences in the patterns of technological change across countries in all sectors..In particular, Italy is characterized in most technological classes by higher degrees of technological initiation, lower degrees of stability in the ranking of innovators and a lower role of large firms as compared to the other European countries considered here. Concentration and the role of large firms, however, are not much lower than in the other European countries. (Table 7) Thus, innovative activities in Italy seem somewhat closer to what we have called "the widening" model rather than to the "deepening model" of innovation (Malerba and Orsenigo 1994).

At the other extreme of the Italian case, in Germany deepening patterns of innovative activities seem to prevail, whilst the UK and France are in an intermediate position.

These results, however, might be interpreted as a symptom of

Table 7 Similarities across countries in the patterns of innovative activities.

	Italy	Germany	France	United Kingdom
Index of concentration (C4)	46.52	48.18	43.34	36.80
Herfindahl Index	0.11	0.13	0.10	0.07
Size*	54.24	81.12	76.51	41.34
Spea**	0.39	0.57	0.57	0.53
Newleaders°	41.84	5.97	9.31	16.95
Natality°°	0.58	0.22	0.34	0.38

* Size = Share of total patents held by firms with more than 500 employees
**Spea = Spearman rank correlation coefficient: Variability of the hierarchy of innovators.
°Newleaders = Share of total patents of the 10 most innovative firms held by firms entering the top 10 group in the period 1978/86
°°Natality = Share of patents held by firms patenting for the first time in the period 1978/86
Source: CESPRI elaborations on EPO data

relative weakness vis-a-vis the other countries. In fact, technological advantages in any one country appear to be closely related to the variables which define the degrees of stability and persistence of innovative activities (e.g. positively with the degree of persistence of innovative activities at the firm level and with the stability of the hierarchy of innovators and negatively with the indicators of technological natality and mortality), rather than to the more "traditional" indicators such as concentration or firm size (Patel and Pavitt 1991, Malerba and Orsenigo 1994, Malerba, Orsenigo and Peretto 1993). In other words, technological advantages appear to be associated with processes of "creative accumulation" of technological competences: firms continuously active in a certain technological domain accumulate knowledge and expertise, and are able to effectively master and successfully perform, in that technology.

A similar analysis conducted on the EPO data base for the 12 high technology sectors provides similar results: the number of firms active in high technology is quite limited (513 in the period 1978–91) and the average number of patents per firm is also very low (2.9 in 1985–91). Concentration is quite high, except in industrial automation and precision instruments and large firms hold 72% of all patents. Entry of new innovators is very high, in general, but again entrants are in most cases medium-large companies diversifying into new technological fields (ENEA 1993).

4. THE ITALIAN NATIONAL SYSTEM OF INNOVATION

The aggregate data analyzed so far show that innovative activities in Italy originate essentially from a small core of large firms and a turbulent fringe of smaller companies. Yet, the number of large innovative firms in Italy seems to be smaller as compared to other countries and in general innovative activities appear to be pursued in a less continuous and systematic way as compared to the other major European countries. This structure of innovative activities is reflected in low levels of formalized research activities and in a marked specialization in "traditional" technologies and in mechanical engineering

Aggregate data, however, cannot provide alone a full understanding of the structure of innovative activities in any one country. Indeed, it has long been recognized that technological change originates from a large set of different actors (large and small firms, universities and research laboratories, government agencies, all sorts of institutions, etc.) who entertain complex and intricate relationships among themselves. Thus, the notion of "National Systems of Innovation" has been proposed in order to capture these interrelations (Nelson 1993; Lundvall 1987).

In the case of Italy, one has to recognize that not one, but two different innovation systems are at work in Italy: an informal atomistic learning network and a formal R&D system. These two systems are composed of different actors and are organized in a different way and are linked through a complex organizational system at the national level. The informal atomistic learning network is composed of a large population of small and medium size firms (in some cases located in industrial districts), which interact intensively at the local level. The formal R&D system is composed of large firms with industrial laboratories, small high technology firms, universities, large public research institutes and the national government. The informal atomistic learning network has worked relatively effectively and successfully, while the formal R&D system has not.

Within and across these two systems, dynamic vicious and virtuous cycles have developed over the past decades. Let us briefly examine these two systems and their interrelations.

4.1. The informal atomistic learning network

A large part of Italian industry is composed of a large group of quite dynamic small and medium size firms operating in traditional industries (such as textile and clothing, shoes, furniture) and in the mechanical and equipment supplier industries. These firms are specialized in the supply of custom products and of fashion goods. Most of them assemble and integrate existing components and parts into systems for special applications or specific customers. These firms are highly profitable and quite successful internationally. They are characterized by advanced capabilities of absorbing, adapting, improving and tailoring new technologies (developed externally) to specific market needs. Innovation originates not from formal R&D, but from informal learning by doing, by using and by interacting. Engineering skills, product know-how and understanding customers' requirements are the major sources of incremental innovations and product customization by this group of firms.

Three groups of firms can be identified in this learning network: firms in the industrial district, equipment producers and traditional firms not located in a district.

4.1.1 The industrial district

In industrial districts, characterized by both cultural and social homogeneity, technical change occurs through horizontal linkages among a large number of small and medium size firms (Becattini, 1989). These districts are active in several industries and are located in various Italian regions. In these districts the division of labor among small and medium size firms is high and the productive flexibility and adaptabilty to changing market demand at the final product level is substantial (Becattini, 1987). Most firms specialize in only one stage of the production process: only a few firms eventually internalize more than one stage of the production process and eventually sell the final product. However, the organization of production varies from case to case, according to the specific nature of the relevant technology.[3] Local institutions and associations (local government, banks and professional schools) play a major role in the working of the organization of the district. Regional and local governments, banks and professional schools provide public support, financial resources and qualified labor force to firms. Export and distribution associations help in overcoming the problems faced by small firms in selling the final product on international markets. In some districts associations among firms have been created for the use of some complex and costly production equipment.

---

[3] For example, in shoe districts the design is developed externally, the sole and the heel are purchased from large firms, the various production stages are carried out by small specialized firms, the sale by another firm (which eventually in some cases also internalize some strategic stages of the production process such as cutting). In textile districts, in addition to small firms specialized in a specific production stage, additional actors such as the fashion designer and the CONVERTER are present. Similarly, in the ceramic tiles district, vertically integrated medium size firms and specialized small firms are present (CESPRI, 1990).

Diffusion of process technology within the district is quite fast. Technical change is rapidly diffused within the district through the widespread transmission of information among a large number of producers which share a common culture, have the same level of capability and, because they are similar, are also able to transmit and assimilate tacit and non codified knowledge. Personal contacts and the mobility of technicians among the firms play a major role in this respect (Bellandi,1988).[4] In the district, product innovations are the result of skills in product design and of the ability to focus market requirements and consumers needs. Process innovations are mainly of the incremental type and stem from learning by doing in single specific production stages.

In most cases firms in the industrial district constitute the major market for upstream equipment producers (usually located near or even within the industrial district) which introduce new innovative equipment as a result of close and continuous interaction with the downstream district firms.

Recently in most districts leading firms or local industrial groups have emerged. In the first case some firms, strategically located at the commercialization stage, coordinate the whole production process of the district. In the second case, through acquisitions and partecipations, some industrial groups have been able to control (at the strategic and financial levels) the production of the district, without however interfering with the daily productive operations of the small firms of the group.

4.1.2 Equipment firms

Italian industry is characterized by the presence of a large number of small and medium size equipment producers, which are internationally competitive and highly innovative. This population of firms includes machine-tool producers and robotics producers, as well as other types of equipment producers. These firms are present in various regions in the North of Italy.

The dynamics of entry and exit in this group of firms is quite

[4] Interestingly enough, the diffusion of new capital equipment has been more rapid than the diffusion of electronic information systems within the firms of the district. Firms were able to adopt new machinery because they had the technical capability to insert and adapt the new machinery in their produtive organization. On the other hand most new information systems required a drastic modification in the firm organization and therefore met resistance and delays.

high: new firms have been set up by technicians and engineers who have left other established equipment firms, or by some large users such as FIAT.

Equipment producers generate a continuous stream of incremental innovations in equipment, by tailoring products to users' needs, focusing equipment to specific market segments, and improving and modifying existing equipment. Several times innovations consist of system integration aimed at specific applications or in the solution of specific technical problems of the users.

These firms are characterized by a lively entrepreneurship, a long-standing tradition of technical skills in mechanical equipment production, an effective understanding of users' needs, relevant absorptive and adaptive capabilities with regard to new electronics technologies, and advanced equipment design skills.

Several of these firms do not have a formal R&D laboratory: their knowledge is mostly non-codified, tacit and idiosyncratic, because it is embodied in technicians and engineers. Some firms (mainly flexible automation and robotics producers) maintain close links with engineering laboratories at the university (Camagni,1984). Most firms use consultants for the solution of specific problems.

Learning by interacting through user-producer relationship plays a relevant role in the innovation process. Vertical links with sophisticated users are extremely important in providing an innovative stimulus, a continuous feedback on the use of the machinery and a relevant market. Two main types of users may be identified: large firms (such as FIAT, Olivetti and Zanussi) and firms in industrial districts These links have generated vertical virtuous cycles in Italian industry.

4.1.3 Firms in traditional sectors

A final group of firms is composed of the large population of small and medium size firms operating in traditional industries, but not located within an industrial district. Innovative firms are not very numerous in this very heterogeneous group of firms. New product introduction is driven by marketing and production capabilities linked to fashion design, product tailoring and market segmentation. These firms greatly profit from the innovativeness of upstream equipment producers: embodied technical change in terms of investments in new machinery represents the major source of change in production processes.

It is interesting to note that some large Italian firms active in traditional sectors have maintained some of the attributes of the industrial district by using a very decentralized productive structure, in which a large number of small local firms are specialized in a specific stage of the production process or in the supply of a specific input. Benetton constitutes the best known example of this. Other large firms in traditional industries have also been able to successfully change the organization of production through the introduction of new electronics technologies.

4.2 The formal R&D system

The other part of the Italian national system of innovation is the R&D system, which is highly affected by technological opportunity and demand conditions, and includes a number of different actors: large oligopolistic firms, small high technology firms, university, public research centers, government. The weaknesses of this systems are related to low opportunity and demand conditions, limited number of large firms and small high technology enterprises, ineffective public policy and industry – university interaction.

4.2.1 Limited technological opportunities

The process of creation of endogenous technological opportunity conditions in Italy is characterized by a fragmentation of efforts and a high variance of scientific output.

The level of research at Italian universities varies greatly. High variance exists between some areas of excellence (such as quantum physics, lasers, synthetic chemistry and optoelectronics) and other areas in which research has not reached the level of the international scientific community. Moreover, the growth of areas of scientific excellence are more the result of the efforts of single scientists working at the frontier, than the work of teams of scientists. This situation is aggravated by the limited funds available for research equipment. Finally, multidisciplinary research is still rare and the transfer of technical knowledge to industry is still limited by the low mobility of academicians to industry.

Similarly, the research efforts of the main Italian research centres (the National Research Council (CNR), the National Board for Nuclear and Alternative Energy Sources (ENEA), under the control of the Ministry of Industry, the National Institute of Nuclear Physics, under the control of the Ministry of Education (INFN), the Higher Institute of Health (ISS), under the control of the Ministry of Health) and the experimental stations of CNR) are fragmented. Limited basic research is also performed by a few large firms that have central corporate laboratories such as Ansaldo, FIAT, STET, ENEL, ENI and Montedison.

The generation of scientists, engineers and researchers is still limited. University graduates in the science fields decreased from 11,912 in 1977 to 10,391 in 1987; similarly, graduates in engineering have decreased from 11,313 in 1977 to 9845 in 1987.

4.2.2. Weak demand conditions

In Italy, demand conditions have hindered innovation in the R&D system in well defined ways.

Large firms have rarely provided innovative stimulus to domestic producers simply because they themselves have not shown a high degree of innovativeness. Until recently large firms have preferred to buy state of the art components or equipment abroad, when they were not available domestically, rather than stimulating a potentially innovative domestic supply.

Also public tools on the demand side have not been consciously used as policy instruments for stimulating innovation in Italy. Public procurement has rarely been used as a stimulus for innovation (Pontarollo,1989). The public administration normally purchases existing products from existing producers, as a consequence of norms regarding public contracts, difficulties and delays in financial payments by the public sector, cumbersome bureaucratic procedures, and political or social goals.

Similarly, military demand (with few relevant exceptions) has been generally non technologically progressive. It has also been smaller and more open to imports than military demand in other European countries.

Finally, until very recently for most high technology sectors (as well as for several scale intensive ones) demand has been mostly domestic. Only during the 1980s has demand for the latter two groups gradually moved to the European or global levels, and has consequently put increasing competitive pressure on Italian firms.

4.2.3 A small oligopolistic core

One of the peculiarities of the Italian system of innovation compared to the other main advanced countries is the reduced number and the limited size of large oligopolistic R&D spenders. The core of industrial R&D in Italy is concentrated in a few large groups: FIAT, Ferruzzi-Montedison, ENI, STET (IRI), Olivetti, Pirelli.

In terms of R&D intensity at the firm level, Italian firms are not very different from other countries: in those R&D projects in which they are present, Italian firms are not at a major disadvantage with respect to their major international competitors. The sources of innovation and the organization of the innovative process in these large companies are quite similar to the ones present in other large companies around the world. Innovation is driven mainly by internal R&D, engineering, design and ideas coming from internal functional areas other than R&D. External R&D contracts are given to firms within the same industrial groups. R&D cooperation with public research institutions and with the university, is quite common. Vertical and horizontal cooperative agreements between the oligopolistic core and other Italian and foreign firms are widespread.[5] This small group of large firms has indeed been one of the major sources of change during the 1980s. Following a period of crisis during the second half of the 1970s, and an extensive rationalization of production in the early 1980s, the return to profitability of these Italian firms allowed them to invest more in R&D. This increase has been concentrated in specific technological areas, and was linked to productive specialization.[6] Moreover, growth in R&D was associ-

---

[5] FIAT has quite articulated links with components and part suppliers ; Olivetti has developed a network of alliances and acquisitions and participations, with hardware and software companies; Italtel and SGS (STET) have a range of cooperative agreements with foreign firms.

[6] In the information processing industry Olivetti has followed a successful strategy in several key hardware and software areas; in microelectronics SGS has closed a considerable gap in semiconductor technologies, and has merged with Thomson (France); in telecommunications Italtel and Telettra have developed advanced products; in robotics, firms such as DEA, Jobs, Comau have recently introduced a large number of innovative products; in the aerospace industry firms such as Aeritalia, Agusta and Fiat Aviazione have developed specific capabilities in well defined technologies; in the chemical and pharmaceutical industries Montedison consolidated its position in selected technological areas.

ated with a reorganization of the innovative process, both with the opening up of new networks of cooperative agreements and with the change of existing interfirm agreements.[7] This new technological dynamism of large firms during the 1980s represents, however, nothing else than the continuation of a process of technological accumulation begun by some of these firms during the 1950s and early 1960s. The period of rapid industrial reconstruction and fast growth of the 1950s and 1960s (based on low labor costs and imported standard technologies and centred on mechanics, traditional sectors, and scale intensive sectors such as basic chemicals, auto and steel) was also characterized by a number of indigenous technological developments.[8] These niches of advanced research and of new product developments, however, were not followed by major commitments by large Italian firms to transform original research and development into products manufactured on a large scale and marketed at the international level. The lack of resources able to support complementary activities such as applied research, design, engineering and marketing was later followed by the decision of most firms to discontinue major research efforts and product development in these technological niches. The end of the phase of Italian economic development based on low labor costs,

---

[7] The FIAT case is an interesting example of this second change. During the 1980s FIAT drastically changed its policy towards subcontracting, selecting a limited number of producers and pushing decentralization of component design and innovation. In just a few years time, FIAT reduced the number of its component suppliers from 1200 in 1980 to 850 in late-1980s, in order to increase capacity utilization and decrease production costs, and to move component design to the remaining firms. In order to do so FIAT introduced development contracts linking FIAT with specific component suppliers. Through this mechanism, FIAT supports part of the development cost of a new component. In the event of successful development, FIAT becomes the owner of the technical documentation of the component and may establish a long term supply contract (3 to 5 years) with the same supplier. These types of development contracts have increased from 28 in 1980 to 48 in 1984, and the share of FIAT purchases covered by long term supply contracts following development contracts have increased from 3.7% in 1981 to 7% in 1984. Despite this increase, however, the share is still quite limited as a consequence of the reduced innovativeness of FIAT's auto component producers, which in previous periods were compelled to supply FIAT with products which would meet FIAT requirements exactly.

[8] These developments include the production of advanced computers by Olivetti, and of drugs by Lepetit; activity in nuclear energy by CNEN and in laser technology by CISE and Politecnico of Milan; research in the chemical area at Donegani (Montedison); in the electronics area at CISE; in nuclear energy at Istituto Nazionale di Fisica Nucleare (CNR).

the tension in the labor market and in increasing international competition pushed Italian firms to follow strategies centred on the pursuit of static efficiency (i.e. decentralization and rationalization of what was existing) instead of dynamic efficiency (i.e. innovation).[9] During the 1970s, the focus of the largest Italian firms moved largely away from innovation and R&D at the technological frontier. These firms lacked the financial resources and the economic incentives for a full scale commitment to R&D. The lack of any government R&D support for advanced technological efforts contributed to aggravate this situation. A very similar pattern seems to characterize the early 1990s

Two final remarks on the role of the oligopolistic core in the Italian R&D system can be advanced.First, the increase in R&D of the 1980s is too recent to be effective in terms of international competitiveness in high technology. The lack of advanced technological capabilities of large Italian firms until the early 1980s meant also that these firms could not be successful soon after their increased R&D effort of the 1980s. It takes time and a stable commitment to technological progress to develop advanced technological capabilities.[10] Second, from an evolutionary point of view, the high concentration of limited R&D expenditures within just a few firms implies that the diversity of approaches at the industry level (playing such a major role in fostering technical advance) is greatly reduced. As a consequence, in an uncertain

---

[9] Olivetti decided to remain a producer of mechanical typewriters and sold its electronics operation to General Electric in 1963; CNEN discontinued its activities in the second half of the 1960s; Lepetit was purchased by Dow Chemical; Montedison discontinued the research on advanced new materials of Donegani.

[10] A typical example of this dynamics is represented by SGS, the Italian producer of microelectronics. This firm (after a period of technological dependency from Fairchild during the 1960s) while being highly unprofitable in semiconductor operations, maintained a limited research capability in some advanced semiconductor areas during the 1970s, while being highly unprofitable in semiconductor operations. During the 1980s SGS invested a considerable amount of resources and launched a major effort to regain international competitiveness. It took time however before highly improved design, engineering, productive and marketing skills could be added to SGS research capabilities, so that the firm could regain international competitiveness (Malerba, 1987). Recently, the major merge with the French Thomson and the acquisition of the English INMOS has made SGS-Thomson a major player in the semiconductor industry.

environment, the possibility of having one successful project is reduced.

4.2.4 Few high technology small firms

Another weakness of the Italian R&D system is the limited number of new high technology firms operating in electronics, software biotechnology and services. Some of these firms are closely linked to the oligopolistic core of large Italian companies, such as the small electronics firms in the Canavese region surrounding Olivetti, or the software and service companies in the Milan area. Others are linked to the few scientific parks that exist in Italy. The organization of the innovative process in these firms is centered around design and research activities that are not necessarily formalized into a formal R&D laboratory. Within this restricted group, several firms innovate by integrating components, e.g. hardware and software into systems. This system integration is mainly directed to specific final applications, or to specific customers.

In Italy, demand and dynamic interdependencies are the critical factors driving the establishment of new firms. In a sector such as software, new firms identify a type of unsatisfied demand, utilize existing technology and adapt it to new applications or to potential users by offering a specialized, customized, or segmented product. These firms then grow by entering into product related market segments. It must be noted that these new firms most of the time do not reach large size. On the other hand, cases in which new firms offer new products based on a technological innovation are even rare. This last type of entry however is increasing with time, as a consequence of the growth in the number of electronics engineers and the spin-off of engineers and technicians from large corporations.

In sectors such as robotics, previous accumulated technological capabilities in mechanics and machine tools positively affected the development of the industry and the entry of new firms. On the other hand in electronics, the limited experience and technological capabilities of the Italian electromechanical industry during the 1950s had negative consequences on the successful entry of Italian firms in the early semiconductor firms (Malerba, 1987). Similarly, the late and difficult start of Italian new firms in biotechnology during the 1980s is due to the previous limited R&D capabilities in advanced pharmaceutical research by Italian chemical and drug companies and to the fragmented and limited R&D of the Italian food and processing industry (Orsenigo, 1989).

4.3 The dynamics of the informal learning network and the R&D system: virtuous and vicious cycles through vertical linkages.

One of the relevant aspects of the Italian case has been the presence of virtuous and vicious cycles within and across the two systems of innovation.

4.3.1 Virtuous cycles

Virtuous innovative cycles through vertical linkages take place when downstream technologically progressive and highly competitive users request new advanced capital equipment to upstream producers, which then are able to satisfy users' demand with innovative equipment. With the new equipment, users further improve their technological capabilities and competitiveness, and in turn generate a new demand for improved capital equipment to equipment producers, and so on. A virtuous dynamic vertical cycle is set in motion.

One of the most relevant virtuous vertical cycles has been the one between producers of manufacturing equipment and firms in the industrial district. Virtuous cycles originate because the sophisticated and competitive firms of the district demand better or improved equipment to equipment producers, information which are then able to satisfy their requirements.

This type of virtuous cycle has been very successful because intensive learning by doing, by using and by interacting has taken place between producers and users, through formal and informal communication, on the spot interaction and manpower mobility. Upstream and downstream firms are able to share common tacit and uncodified technological and productive information, and exchange proprietary information.

This type of virtuous cycle has greatly affected the rate of diffusion of new technologies. Given the advanced capabilities of flexible automation producers and the proximity of several producers and users in the North of Italy, the diffusion of flexible automation has been relatively fast in Italy compared to other European countries. On the other hand, EDP, not related to a competitive strength of Italian producers, linked to a different function within firms and acting on a different set of firms capabilities, had a slower rate of diffusion in Italy compared to other European countries.

Virtuous cycles have also taken place when upstream producers with advanced technological capabilities were facing a single large and technologically progressive downstream user. This is the case of the relationship between the robotics and laser industries and FIAT. FIAT had a clear perception of its needs, an advanced knowledge about the production process, and a willingness to invest a large amount of resources in new production processes; robotics producers on the other hand had at their disposal accumulated capabilities in machinery production and an advanced international competitiveness.[11]

4.3.2 Vicious cycles

Vicious cycles have been present when the lack of high competitiveness or advanced technological capabilities in one actor would hinder the development of innovations by a second actor, which is vertically linked to the first one. This in turn would reinforce the uncompetitive situation of the first actor, and so on.

In the Italian formal R&D system, the low level scientific level of most research performed by the university and the public sector and the limited technological capabilities of most large firms reinforced a vicious cycle, and generated a situation in which Italian research and development has remained non technologically progressive.

Vertical vicious cycles took place in specific sectors such as plastics. The lack of interest in plastic materials for auto by both chemical and autos producers seriously damaged the development of plastics for autos on an industrial scale (Amendola, 1989).

Vicious cycles have also negatively affected the introduction of new technologies or the fast entry into new industries in Italy. The lack of a population of advanced small and medium size electronics firms highly impaired the development of small power lasers in the late 1970s (Kluzer, 1989). The limited capabilities

---

[11] Similarly, in the case of lasers, FIAT began promptly a focused and interdisciplinary R&D program on the utilization of lasers in car production, which in turn benefited the production of high power lasers for industrial applications (Kluzer,1989).

and international competitiveness of Italian final electronics goods producers negatively affected the development of advanced indigenous semiconductors during the 1960s and 1970s (Malerba, 1987). The limited experience and technological capabilities of the Italian electromechanical industry during the 1950s had negative consequences on the R&D efforts of Italian firms in the early semiconductor industry (Malerba, 1987). The late and difficult start of Italian R&D in biotechnology during the 1980s is due to the previous limited R&D capability in advanced pharmaceutical research by Italian chemical and drugs companies and to the fragmented and limited R&D of the Italian food processing industry (Orsenigo, 1989).

4.4 Policies supporting innovative activities

A further element accounting for the contradictory technological performance of Italy is given by public policies. Again, policies in favour of the informal atomistic network have been relatively successful, but promotion of innovative activities within the core R&D sector have had – at best – a very limited impact.

4.4.1 Policies in favour of the informal atomistic learning network.

Two types of policies have affected the informal atomistic learning network: policies aimed at fostering the adoption of capital equipment (launched by the central government) and policies aimed at developing a local technological infrastructure (launched both by the central government and by regional and local authorities).

The former type of policies – in particular the Law 1329/1965 (the Sabatini Law) which calls for deferred payment of the entire expenditure up to five years, in the case of machine tool purchases and the Law 696/1983, concerning tax deductions on the purchase or leasing of advanced equipment such as automation equipment – has been based on fiscal instruments and has been successful in reaching a large number of potential adopters. also thanks to the simplicity of the required bureaucratic procedures.[12]

[12] The scope of the intervention of the Sabatini Law can be demonstrated with a few figures: in 1987 Mediocredito Centrale distributed about 444 billion lire (approximately 352 million dollars) in subsidies against more than 30,000

Less satisfactory results have instead been achieved by other types of intervention, usually based on the granting of financial incentives and aiming at more selective goals (e.g. regional reequilibrium as in the Presidential Decree 902/1976). The functioning of these provisions has been extremely difficult because of the highly complicated nature of the programs.

Policies for information and technology diffusion have been characterized by a blending of national policies and of regional and local initiatives, arising in a decentralized and bottom up way. These initiatives include broad programs aimed at constituting centers and structures for research, experimentation, personnel training, production upgrading and technical consultancy,[13] and general centers of support for diffusion (especially in Lombardy, in Emilia and in Liguria), aiming to provide information and training,and to organize pilot projects and demonstrative activities to stimulate industrial awareness in the use of new technology.

Mixed results have been obtained by support policies focused on the creation of centers for technology transfer, specialized by industrial sector and targeted at specific local industrial situations. These centers are concentrated in Emilia, Marches and Lombardy and conduct experimentation, engineering, design and consultancy. In general, these are mixed agencies: promoted and managed jointly by regions, regional financing companies, chambers of commerce and, in some cases, research institutes, and by private firms and industrial associations. Initiatives of cooperation for technology diffusion have taken place also among firms. At the local level these initiatives have been quite successful, as the experience of a few regions like Emilia and Lombardy demonstrates.[14]

---

operations involving capital outlays of over 4000 billion lire (approximately 3.2 billion dollars). In 1986 the subsidies were 203 billion lire (approximately 136 million dollars) for 9000 applications involving 6000 billion lire (approximately 4 billions dollars) in investments. Law 696 includes also a grant equal to 25% of the expenditures (net of VAT) for firms located in Northern and Central Italy and 32% for those located in Southern Italy. More on this in Malerba, 1993.

[13] Such as the Tecnotex Program at Biella in the textile industry, the Trieste Research Area (which also includes the international genetic engineering center promoted by UNIDO) and Tecnopolis in Bari (the only true science park existing in Italy).

[14] In Lombardy, for example, there is a specific set of provisions to stimulate intercompany exchanges of technological expertise for the creation of new products, the application of new technologies and the intercompany use of

4.4.2 Public policy for innovation

Public policy in support of technological innovation does not have a long tradition in Italy. During the 1950s and 1960s there was no policy. While other advanced countries began to support the electronics industry, in fact, Italian public policy focused its support on sectors with standard technologies and large-scale economies, such as steel and basic chemicals with the aim of increasing the productive capacity of the country in these sectors. In most cases this policy created inefficient or duplicative large plants. The Italian government did not support Olivetti's research and production of computers. Nor did it intervene in the purchase of Olivetti's computer operations by General Electric in 1964. Similarly, it did not adopt any policy of support for the new semiconductor industry during these years (Malerba,1987). Even the first attempts of policies of support of high technology industries (Law 1089 in 1968 and law 675 in 1977) were characterized by limited resources, and by a lack of precise reference models.

The timing of public policy of support of high technology sectors has been determined to a large extent by the emergence of industrial and scientific lobbies in advanced sectors. This characterized the decisions to support the electronics industry during the late 1970s and early 1980s and the biotechnology industry during the second half of the 1980s (Adams and Orsenigo,1988).

Contemporary public policy towards the support of innovation in Italy is implemented at three different levels. At the basic research end of the innovation process are located the Finalized Programs of the National Research Council (CNR). These programs were originally intended to guide basic research towards economic applications and to stimulate the transfer of basic results from the universities and research organizations to industry. Further downstream in the innovation process there are the National Research Plans of the Ministry of Scientific and Technological Research (MRST). These plans are designed to stimulate cooperation in R&D in high-risk projects. Finally, at the applied and development stage of the innovative process, industrial R&D support is performed through the Applied Research Fund and the

---

advanced technical services (quality and reliability testing). The role of public intervention is to promote the search for partners and the agreement between the various actors. The development of specific, short-range forms of cooperation has led, in some cases, to the formation of true intercompany technical service centers.

Fund for Technological Innovation (Law 46/1982). The first aims to support applied industrial R&D, while the second focuses on development and prototype production.

Several problems and flaws are present in Italian public policy of support for technological innovation. First, public policy still remains centered on direct financial support of firms' R&D and innovative activities. This instrument is the easiest to manage for the public sector, but reliance on it has greatly reduced the spectrum of policy tools available and the possible goals attainable by the government (Momigliano, 1986). Second, the spectrum of sectors at the technological frontier chosen for support is very broad. While the Applied Research Fund does not indicate any sectoral or technological priority, the sectors chosen in the Innovation Fund include a wide range of products and processes, not necessarily at the technological frontier. The selection of specific technological areas would allow a more focused government intervention and a clearer technological target to firms. Third, there is a lack of coordination between the fund which supports applied research (Applied Research Fund) and a fund which supports downstream activities (Innovation Fund). Finally, the decision making process and the bureacratic procedures still take an unreasonable amount of time.

It must also be noted that fiscal incentives have not been used in Italy as an incentive to R&D activity. There is in fact an almost total lack of legislation in this sense, particularly regarding R&D expenditures. Finally in Italy there is no explicit policy in favor of the birth of small Schumpeterian firms active in high technology industries. In particular, there is a total absence of initiatives aimed at stimulating the creation of this type of firm, especially regarding the procurement of necessary financial resources.

A final weakness of the Italian R&D system regards the interfaces among the various actors of the R&D system and the successful technological cooperation between university, research organizations and industry. One reason is the limited number of centers of excellence in Italian universities, the limited mobility in and out of the university system, and the bureacratic and institutional structure of universities. Public policy has tried to overcome some of these difficulties, but has succeeded only in part.[15]

[15] Some forms of cooperation have shown satisfactory results — as in the case of cooperation between CNR and industry within the framework of the Finalized

4.4.3 The effects of internationalization, cooperative agreements and European technology policy on the Italian R&D system

The globalization of international technological competition and the increasing complexity and cost of the innovation process in several sectors has pushed Italian firms to increase their degree of internationalization. In the early 1980s therefore Italian firms began to follow an articulated policy of internationalization and cooperation in R&D. These policies and networks differed extensively from firm to firm and from sector to sector. They were also favoured by the launching of several European programs of international cooperation in R&D such as ESPRIT, BRITE, Biotechnology and EUREKA.

With the benefit of the doubt deriving from the sources used for the calculations (newspapers and economic magazines), it is possible to claim that the number of international cooperative agreements of Italian firms has been sharply increasing during the 1980s; and R&D has been one of the main motivators of international cooperative agreements by Italian firms (Malerba, 1988).

These newly established networks of international cooperative agreements in R&D broadened the knowledge base of Italian firms and provided them with complementary technological competences. Because they represented a quite recent and new phenomenon for Italian firms however, these networks of international cooperative agreements could not immediately exert their full effects on R&D performance: Italian firms had to learn how to cooperate and how to extract the maximum benefit from a relationship with partners based on a continuous interaction and exchange of information.

Also the participation of Italian firms in European-wide technology policy has helped to overcome some of the weaknesses of the Italian R&D system, by allowing Italian firms or research centers to cooperate with centers of excellence in research.

In their participation in European programs, Italian firms have

---

Projects, the industrial promotion projects of ENEA, which concern component testing and the creation of joint ventures with equity participation or cooperative with universities, CNR, local government, firms,the programs of the INFN, designed to commercially exploit scientific results in collaboration with companies that operate in advanced technologies. Similarly, the Higher Institute of Health (ISS) has increased interaction with industry not only in the usual phases of testing and new drugs authorization, but also within the Finalized Projects of CNR and the National Research Plans of MRST.

undoubtedly benefited from the exchange of information with the other partners in these projects and have broadened their knowledge base. Italian participation in ESPRIT (12% of total ESPRIT funds) and in other programs such as EUREKA, reflects the strengths and weaknesses of Italian industry. Large firms such as Olivetti, STET and FIAT are present in areas such as computer integrated manufacturing, office systems and lasers. Italian high technology small firms on the other hand have a limited presence.

5. TECHNOLOGICAL INNOVATION, TRADE PERFORMANCE AND MULTINATIONALIZATION

The notion that technology plays a fundamental role in the determination of the trade performance of countries was already at the basis of the "technological gap theory" of international trade (Posner 1961) and has received more recently further corroboration in various empirical studies (Amendola et al. 1993, Cantwell and Dunning 1991, Dosi, Pavitt and Soete 1987). Similarly, the role of technological advantaged is central in the theories of the patterns of internationalization, particularly as it concerns the processes of multinationalization (Cantwell 1989). According to this view, the technological assets of any one country do not only influence the development of the flows of foreign direct investments, but constitute also a powerful factor of attraction of multinational enterprises (MNEs) (Cantwell and Dunning 1991). Thus, it has to be recognized that a further link exists through the influence that the processes of multinationalization exert on the accumulation of domestic technological capabilities. The deployment of R&D laboratories by MNEs in foreign countries strengthens in fact the technological capabilities of the receiving countries. And at the same time, the evaluation of the technological potential of any one country can be grossly biased, in some cases, if its foreign activities are not considered in the analysis (Patel and Pavitt 1991).

In this section, we examine briefly the relationship between tecnology, trade and multinationalization in the case of Italy, focusing in particular on the subset of high-technology industries and products. The data and the results are drawn from research carried out in 1993 under the auspices of ENEA by researchers of CESPRI at Bocconi University, of ENEA, and of the Polytechnic of Milan (ENEA 1993).

5.1 The Italian position in high technology sectors

To begin with, it is very well known that Italian trade specialization reflects quite faithfully its technological position and its patterns of technological activities (See Amendola et al. 1993 and Guerrieri and Milana 1990). Just as an example, it might be worth remembering that over the last decade, Italian export penetration in the OECD markets has been substantially growing: the Italian share in OECD markets has increased from 4.1% in 1983 to 5.3% in 1990. Italy now ranks as the sixth world supplier of OECD markets (it was eighth in 1983), with a share very close to that of the UK. This growth, however,has been obtained essentially through the strengthening of the traditional areas of specialization of the Italian industry. The competitive position of Italy remains particularly strong in the traditional industries (as defined according to Pavitt's taxonomy- see Table 8), despite a negative trend. The market share of Italy grows instead in an another conventionally strong area, i.e. in the mechanical engineering industries and in other specialized sectors. The share of Italy remains finally quite low in the scale-intensive and in the high-technology-based sectors. In other words – and at the risk of oversimplification – the comparative advantages of Italy are to be generally found in industries characterized by "mature" technologies (whatever a mature technology is), which do not necessitate a strong commitment to formalized R&D activities, but where the tecnological activities of a few large companies and – above all – of the

Table 8 Market shares in imports of manufacturers of seven main industrial countries (four sectors as per Pavitt taxonomy)

	Manufacturing	Traditional sectors	Scale intensive sectors	Specialized suppliers	Science sectors
CEE Countries					
1982	40.9	40.3	42.3	43.7	33.9
1989	38.7	36.1	41.9	41.8	30.3
1990	41	38.3	45.2	43.9	30.8
ITALIA					
1982	6.2	12.3	4.3	6	2.6
1989	5.8	10.5	4.2	6.1	2.6
1990	6.2	11	4.7	6.5	2.7

Source: ICE elaborations on DRI data

informal learning network compensate for the growing competition of the NICs.

Conversely, the Italian competitive position in the high-technology sectors is rather weak (Table 9). In the years 1989–90, the export share was only 3% and the negative trade balance amounted to $10.5 million. The trade deficit was largely concentrated in the electronic sectors and in chemicals and pharmaceuticals, whilst only aerospace showed a surplus. However, in the Eighties the Italian export share of high-technology products remained quite stable, in contrast with other EEC countries (except the UK). In particular, sectors which are characterized by strongly negative trade deficits show some improvements (plastics and fibers, electronic components, specialty chemicals, office machines excluding EDP) and only pharmaceuticals, consumer electronics, telecommunications and office machines – EDP show a further decline.

On the other hand, the indices of relative competitive position (IRCP) show a declining trend over the last decade. The deficit of

Table 9 Export shares and index of relative competitive position (IRCP) of Italy

Sectors	Shares			IPCR		
	1980–82	1984–86	1988–90	1980–82	1984–86	1988–90
Drugs and medicines	5.3	5.1	4.6	0.3	– 0.9	– 3.4
Plastic, elastomers, fibers	4.4	4.6	5.5	– 3	– 3.1	– 4
Fine chemicals, "specialties"	2.9	3	3.1	– 2.8	– 2.8	– 4.1
Office automation (EDP)	5.4	4	3.4	– 0.1	– 1.8	– 2.6
Office automation (others)	2.7	2.8	3.6	– 2.5	– 1.3	– 0.3
Consumer electronics	1.4	0.8	1.2	– 3.9	– 3.3	– 6.8
Telecommunications	2.3	1.9	2	0.3	1.1	– 1.3
Electromedicals	2.6	2.5	2.8	– 2.2	– 2	– 2.9
Electronic components	2.5	2.4	2.9	– 3.1	– 2.6	– 3.5
Aerospace	1.4	1.6	1.8	0.2	0.6	0.6
Measurement and control instruments	2.8	2.6	2.8	– 2.1	– 1.9	– 3.4
Optical instruments and materials	1.4	1.5	2	– 2.8	– 1.8	– 2.8

Source: Data base COMEST-ENEA

the whole group of high technology sectors grew from 1.6% to 2.5% of the high-technology trade of OECD countries. Only aerospace shows a mildly positive and growing balance, whilst all other sectors are characterized by growing negative balances (except office machines excluded EDP and optical instruments and materials). It is worth noting that even in the sectors showing growing export shares their competitive position worsens: that is to say, the the relative growth of exports in high technology sectors has been supported by a process of increasing international integration of productions and thus from a growing import penetration.

In general, Italy is characterized by despecialization in high technologies, as shown by the index of specialization, calculated as the world export share of a country in a specific sector over the world export share of the same country in a particular macro-aggregate (in this case both the total manufacturing export and the export of high technology sectors), (Table 10). Moreover, during the Eighties the sectors characterized by a relative specialization show a declining tendency,and vice-versa. In other words, the Italian model of specialization in high technologies shows a tendency towards the convergence to the patterns of specialization of the other OECD countries, although it remains structurally very weak. In particular, Italy appears reatively weaker in the whole

Table 10 Trade specialization of Italy in high tech sectors (a)

	1980–82	1984–86	1988–90
Drugs and medicines	0.73	0.78	0.62
Plastic, elastomers, fibers	1.04	1.06	0.84
Fine chemicals, "specialties"	0.45	0.53	0.49
Office automation (EDP)	0.95	0.63	0.57
Office automation (others)	0.4	0.42	0.56
Consumer electronics	0.21	0.13	0.25
Telecommunications	0.5	0.55	0.38
Electromedicals	0.43	0.41	0.42
Electronic components	0.49	0.44	0.49
Aerospace	0.48	0.58	0.52
Measurement and control instruments	0.44	0.47	0.47
Optical instruments and materials	0.24	0.26	0.29

(a) Export share in a sector/export share in manufacturing
Source: Data base COMEST-ENEA

electronic group (especially where consumer electronics, and telecommunications are concerned), whilst the areas of relative specialization are to be found in pharmaceuticals, plastics and fibers and office machines.

Finally, the analysis of the geographical composition of the bilateral normalized balances indicates that the Italian model of specialization in the high technology sectors is typical of the countries characterized by intermediate levels of development. Italy entertains positive balances only with Spain and non OECD countries (but notably excluding the Asian NICs). During the Eighties, the negative balance vis-a-vis the world grew as a consequence of the reduction of the positive balances and the growth of the negative balances with Japan and the Asian NICs. Yet, the negative balances with the USA and the EEC countries tended to diminish, indicating a slow process of catching-up vis-a-vis the highly developed countries, but a loss of competitiveness against the growing countries with intermediate levels of development.

5.2 The processes of multinationalization.

The structural weakness of Italy in high-technology is broadly confirmed also by the analysis of the processes of multinationalization (Mariotti, 1989; ENEA 1993).

Despite a marked quantitative development of Italian foreign direct investments (FDI) in the Eighties, a substantial gap between active and passive internationalization still exists in high technology sectors. Indeed, by the end of 1991, for the first time in Italian history, the number of productive employees of Italian companies in foreign countries (511 000 employees) was slightly bigger than the number of employees of foreign companies operating in Italy (508 500).[16]

Yet, as far as high technology sectors are concerned, at the beginning of 1992 the stock of inward FDIs was still twice as big as outward FDIs in terms of number of employees and participating firms, and three times bigger in terms of sales. Specifically, only in aerospace does Italy show a positive value of the normalized internationalization balances (NIB). In four sec-

[16] Active internationalization stemmed from the investments in 1150 industrial companies with the participation of 263 Italian investor groups, for total sales of around Lit. 108 000 billion. These figures compare with 1450 firms with the participation of 820 foreign investors, for total sales of Lit. 152 000 billion in 1990.

Table 11 Patenting activity, foreign trade and multinazionalization of Italy in high tech industries

Sectors	Technological specialization 85–91 (a)	Normalized balances (b)	Normalized international balances (c)	Outward internationalization (d)	Inward internationalization (e)	Export shares of MNEs
Pharmaceuticals	-0.04	-0.34	-67.37	19.30	51.00	14.12
Plastic, Elastomers, Fibers	-0.06	-0.28	9.85	30.40	20.05	25.78
Fine chemials, "specialities"	-0.47	-0.32	-86.46	14.60	67.80	30.32
New materials	-0.37	n.d.	-54.39	n.d.	n.d.	20.11
Industrial automation	0.11	-0.01	-9.56	1.20	1.50	57.29
Office automation	-0.63	-0.17	-39.55	32.80	43.70	66.74
Consumer electronics and telecommunications	-0.36	-0.47	-70.60	14.30	53.10	19.00
Electromedicals	-0.37	-0.32	-93.72	5.30	69.90	37.05
Electronic components	-0.33	-0.31	13.47	103.70	52.20	51.54
Aerospace	-0.56	-0.09	95.60	32.90	0.70	11.04
Measurement and control instruments	-0.27	-0.28	2.62	29.30	22.80	38.78
Optical instruments and materials	-0.24	-0.39	-49.91	11.20	25.90	22.41

a) RTA* = (RTA – 1) / (RTA + 1). For a definition of RTA. see Tab 3
b) (Exports – Imports) / (Exports + Imports)
c) = Outward FDI employees (sales) – Inward FDI employees (sales) / Outward FDI employees (sales) + Inward FDI employees
d) = Employees in foreign companies with italian participation / Employees of Italian companies in Italy
e) = Employees of Italian companies with foreign participation / Employees of Italian industry

Source: Politecnico of Milan – Economics Department

tors, (new materials, consumer electronics, electromedical instruments and apparatus, optical instruments and materials) the negative value derives essentially from very low Italian FDIs; in the other four sectors (office machines, telecommunications, pharmaceuticals and fine chemicals), active internationalization reaches non-marginal levels, but still lags far behind the foreign penetration of FDIs in Italy.

In general, around 30% of domestic employment in high technology sectors operates in foreign-controlled companies, as against 10.7% of total Italian industry. If also non-majority participations are considered, the degree of internationalization in high technology sectors rises to 35.9% and reaches 46% if aerospace and industrial automation are excluded, where FDIs are not an important means of expansion in foreign markets. Conversely, the degree of active internationalization is 25.8% and 29.7% excluding aerospace and industrial automation.

The Italian internationalization gap in high technology derives essentially from the limited number of large Italian firms capable to operate at the frontier of technology. Indeed, only a handful of companies had at the beginning of 1992 at least 1000 employees in foreign markets in high technology sectors (Olivetti, Montedison, Elsag-Bailey and Enichem) Most of the other large Italian companies have only recently started a systematic strategy of internationalization, in particular as far as State-owned companies and specifically the IRI group are concerned. In addition to these few large groups, a handful of medium-sized companies pursue systematic internationalization strategies, often in specific product niches.

5.3 The relationships between innovation, trade and multinationalization

The above analysis confirms the existence of a vicious circle between limited processes of advanced technological capabilities, trade performance and the process of internationalization in high technology sectors.

Table 11 provides a synthetic overview of the competitive profile of Italian industry in the 12 high technology sectors considered here. All sectors (except industrial automation) show values of technological specialization (in terms of patents) lower than the Italian average; all sectors show negative normalized trade balances; only as far as multinationalization is concerned is the picture not so uniformly negative. Further suggestive corroboration of these results is provided by a more disaggregated analysis considering 53 high technology sectors (see ENEA 1993 for details about the construction of this data-base). Inspection of the data, (not reported here) shows that only in the case of numerically controlled machines has Italy both a positive technological specialization and a trade surplus; most other sectors are characterized by technological despecialization and trade deficits. Similarly, if normalized trade balances are regressed against the normalized indices of technological specialization (independent variable), the latter variable turns out to be statistically significant but with very small explanatory power of the Italian performance in high technology sectors (Adjusted R2 = 0.12) That is to say, in high technology sectors Italy not only is characterized by technological despecialization, but finds it also very difficult to translate its limited advanced innovative capabilities into trade performance (Amendola and Pianta 1993).

The relationship between technological specialization and multinationalization is even weaker: no significant relationship emerges between the two indicators. Although, a better test should distinguish between the effects of technology on active and passive multinationalization (Cantwell and Dunning 1991), this result constitues further indirect evidence of the limited impact that low technological capabilities can exert on the processes of internationalization in high technology sectors.

6. CONCLUSIONS

This paper has shown that Italy is an intermediate technolologically developed country, characterized by insufficient commitment to formalized R&D efforts, a marked specialization in "mature", low R&D intensive technologies, and to a large degree occasional involvement in innovative activities. Technological progress is generated by a small club of large companies and a large number of smaller firms, which are however unable to operate systematically in high technology sectors.

Thus, two systems of innovation with a quite different organization coexist within the same country. In one — the informal atomistic learning network — small firms compete and interact at

---

[17] To be sure, a more articulated analysis which considered other indicators would provide much more differentiated results. See for instance ENEA 1993.

the local level. In the other — the formal R&D system — large firms, new high technology firms, large public institutions, universities and the national government operate in an intricate and complex web of relationships.

The lesson that can be learned from the Italian case is that a country may enter the club of advanced industrial economies, and even prosper and grow, without a developed formal R&D system. In this way the Italian experience of growth in the absence of an advanced R&D system resembles that of Denmark.

However,such a system cannot provide the scale, the commitment, the organizational capabilities and the continuity of efforts that are necessary to sustain a stable industrial growth and a satisfactory performance in foreign markets in the long run. Indeed, the weakness in high technology may constitute a major hindrance to the maintenance and further development of international competitiveness and domestic growth. This leads one to wonder how high Italian economic growth rates may be in the 1990s if the country is able to reorganize its research institutions and render its formal R&D system more effective.

BIBLIOGRAPHY

Adams P. and Orsenigo L. (1988) "Tecnologie emergenti e politica industriale in Italia", Rivista trimestrale di scienze dell'amministrazione, 2.

Amendola G. (1989), La diffusione dei materiali polimerici nell'industria automobilistica, in Onida F. and Malaman R.

Amendola G., Dosi G. and Papagni E. (1993), The Dynamics of International competitiveness, Weltwirtschaftliches Archiv".

Amendola G. and Pianta M. (1993), The technological specialization of advanced countries, Kluwer, Dordrecht.

Becattini G. (1987), "Mercato e forze locali: il distretto industriale", Bologna, Il Mulino.

Becattini G. (1989) Modelli locali di sviluppo, Bologna, Il Mulino.

Bellandi M. (1989), Capacita innovativa diffusa e sistemi locali di imprese, in Becattini (1989).

Camagni R. (1984) Il robot italiano, Milan, Il Sole-24 Ore.

Cantwell, J. (1989), Technological Innovation and Multinational Corporations, Oxford, Basil Blackwell.

Cantwell J. and Dunning J.K. (1991), MNEs, Technology and Competitiveness of European Industries, Aussenwirschaft, vol.1, n. 46.

CESPRI (1990) L'integrazione internazionale del sistema di industria e servizi dell'Italia: mutamenti strutturali e strategie verso il 1993", IV Rapporto CESPRI-Bocconi, Camera di Commercio, Milan.

Dosi, G., Pavitt K, and Soete L. 1987, The economics of technical change and international trade, Wheatsheaf, Brighton.

ENEA, 1993, Competitivitα dell'Italia nelle alte tecnologie, Energia e innovazione, n. 5–6, May–June.
Guerrieri P. and Milana C. (1990), L'Italia e il commercio mondiale, Bologna, Il Mulino.
Lundvall, B.A. (1987) National Systems of Innovation: Towards a Theory of Innovation and Interactive Learning, Pinter Publishers, London.
Kluzer S. (1989) Il settore dei laser commerciali", in Onida F. and Malaman R.
Malerba F. (1987), Dalla dipendenza alla capacitα tecnologica autonoma, Milan, F. Angeli.
Malerba F. (1988) "La dinamica di lungo periodo della R&S dell'industria italiana", Rivista di politica economica, April.
Malerba F. (1993), "Italy", in Nelson R.R. (ed.) National Systems of Innovation, Oxford, Oxford University Press.
Malerba F. and L. Orsenigo (1990), "Technological regimes and patterns of innovation: a theoretical and empirical investigation of the Italian case", in A.Heertje and M. Perlman (eds.), Evolving technology and market structure, Ann Arbor, Michigan University Press, pp. 283–306.
Malerba F. and L.Orsenigo (1994), "Schumpeterian Patterns of Innovation", Cambridge Journal of Economics, forthcoming.
Malerba F., L.Orsenigo and Peretto P., (1993). "On persistence of innovative activities", Bocconi University, mimeo.
Mariotti S. (1989) Innovazione, strutture industriali e strategie d'impresa: l'Europa nel confronto con le altre grandi aree industriali, in Ruberti A. (ed.) Europa a confronto, Laterza , Bari.
Mariotti S. and Onida F. (1986), "L'Italia multinazionale", Milan, Il Sole — 24 Ore.
Momigliano, F. (1986), Le leggi della politica industriale, Bologna, Il Mulino.
Nelson R. (1993) "National Innovation Systems" Oxford, University Press Oxford.
Nelson R. and S. Winter (1982), An evolutionary theory of economic change, Cambridge, Mass., The Bellknap Press of Harvard University Press.
Onida F. and Malaman R. (1989), Industria italiana ed alte tecnologie, F. Angeli, Milan.
Onida F. and Viesti G. (eds), (1987), Italian Multinationals, London, Croom Helm.
Orsenigo, L. (1989) The emergence of biotechnology, London, Pinter Publishers.
Patel P. and Pavitt K. (1991) Large firms in the production of world technology: an important case of Non-Globalisation", Journal of International Business Studies, First Quarter, pp 1–21.
Pavitt K. (1988) "Uses and abuses of patent statistics", in Van Raan A. (eds.) Handbook of Quantitative Studies of Science and Technology, Amsterdam, Elsevier.
Pontarollo E. (1989) "Domanda pubblica e politica industriale: FS, SIP, ENEL", Milan, Marsilio.
Posner M. (1961) International Trade and Technical Change, Oxford Economic Papers, vol. 13 pp. 323–341.
Ruberti A. (ed.) (1989), Europa a confronto, Laterza , Bari.
Soete L. (1981) A general test of technological gap trade theory, Weltwirtschaftliches Archiv, Band 117, pp 639–657.
Winter S. (1984), Schumpeterian competition in alternative technological regimes", Journal of Economic Behaviour and Organization.

Innovation in Portuguese Manufacturing Industry

Vitor Corado Simoes

1. INTRODUCTION

The perspective of the innovation phenomenon has dramatically changed over the last decade. It became widely accepted that innovation is not just the outcome of research and development (R&D) activities as the linear or "ladder of science" (Gomory, 1989) model suggested. Innovation is increasingly seen as a cumulative learning process that largely exceeds the boundaries of formal R&D, and where organisational aspects play a paramount role. This is acknowledged by the "chain-link" model of the innovation process, presented by Kline and Rosenberg (1986).

In the same vein, the firm is now seen as a set of competencies, accumulated along technological trajectories. A firm's technological base is, therefore, the result of a process of accumulation of specific knowledge and has a strong tacit component. Innovative opportunities open to a firm are conditioned by its track record and core business (Pavitt, 1989). Furthermore, the process of technological change is largely based on localised learning, stemming from the relationships between the firm and its environment (Cantwell, 1989; Cohendet, Herand & Zuscovitch, 1992): cooperating with customers, suppliers, competitors and with local scientific and technological infrastructure.

Innovation is neither just a matter of superior scientific knowledge, nor of breakthrough inventions. Technological change is, to a large extent, the outcome of a process of interaction and learning between the firm and its environment and inside the firm itself. As Pavitt remarked (1989:83) innovation permeates the whole firm and requires "continuous and intensive collaboration and interaction amongst functionally and professionally specialised groups". But, at the same time, it largely depends on absorptive capacity, that is the capacity to identify, select, assimilate and transform knowledge from outside (Cohen & Levinthal, 1990). Innovation may, thus, be characterised as an inter-active process of generation, acquisition, transfer and use of knowledge, aiming at developing and/or adopting new products and/or processes. As Sahal (1981) has shown, the technology diffusion process encompasses a significant innovative component, since it requires the adaptation and use of knowledge in new environments. Seen from this perspective, innovation concerns all sorts of firms: not only leaders, but also followers and even "laggards"; not just the so-called "high-tech" industries, but "traditional" industries as well, as the rapid rate of technological change in textiles and clothing industries, despite the low level of R&D expenditures, shows.[1] Such a perspective also implies that challenges are not just technical, but also organisational and cultural (in the sense of both the socio-cultural environment and firm's culture).

This view of the innovation process is particularly accurate to deal with the issues of technological change in "middle-of-the-road" countries like Portugal. In fact, Portuguese firms are neither global players, nor world technology leaders: they will hardly develop "new-for-the-world" products. But they have, nevertheless, innovative activities, namely through the adoption, with variable time lags, of products and/or processes developed by other organisations. It is worth recalling that this wider perspective of the innovation process has been, to a large extent, taken up in the recent Community Innovation Survey, launched by the E.C. Commission on the basis of the OECD Oslo Manual. This survey aims at assessing the situation of innovative activities in the Community and is not so much concerned with technological breakthroughs or "new-for-the-World" products, but rather with products and processes which are new for the firms in the enquiry.

Having this background in mind, we may now focus on the

[1] I am grateful to John Cantwell for stressing this point.

main features of innovative activities by Portuguese manufacturing firms. The purpose of this article is to provide a brief picture of those features and to identify the main issues raised by the process of strengthening the innovative capabilities of such firms.

The paper includes three parts. In the first, a general characterisation of Portugal's industrial structure and scientific and technological (S&T) capacity will be presented. The second deals with the present technological base and innovative activities of Portuguese firms, interpreting the information provided by existing technology input and output indicators and by a few studies on technology innovation and diffusion in Portugal.[2] The third part will concern the main factors which explain the low innovative performance of Portuguese firms. The analysis developed clearly suggests that the main problems lay in "soft" aspects, in strategic thinking, management and human resources issues, and not in the "hard", in the access to machinery and equipment.

2. INDUSTRIAL STRUCTURE AND S&T CAPACITY: AN OVERVIEW

As was explained in detail elsewhere (Simoes, 1991 and 1993) the Portuguese economy experienced a swift internationalisation process, following EC entry in 1986. Such a process resulted in an increased Europeanisation of the economy, translated into a boom in inward investment and in a growing share of EC countries as trading partners. Foreign firms played a key role, actively profiting from the opportunities opened by regional integration, while Portuguese enterprises adopted a more reactive stance. The weight of foreign-owned firms in Portugal's international trade experi-

[2] The main works considered in drawing up that perspective were the following: CISEP/GEPIE, *InovaĆao Industria Portuguesa – Observatorio M.I.E.*, Lisboa, GEPIE, 1992; Joao Martins Pereira, *Estudo sobre Tecnologia, Qualidade e Design nas PMEs Portuguesas*, Porto, Forum das PMEs, 1991, 2nd. ed.; Joao M. G. CaraÇa et allii; *Study of the Impact of Community RTD Programmes on the Portuguese S&T Potential*, Lisboa, SECT, 1992, 1991; OECD, *Reviews of National Science and Technology Policy – Portugal*, Paris, OECD, 1993; Vitor Corado Simoes, *Oportunidades de Desenvolvimento Tecnolégico das Empresas Portuguesas Através de Contractos de LicenÇa*, Lisboa, AIP, 1992; JNICT, Inquérito ao Potencial Científico e Tecnolégico Nacional em 1990, Lisboa, JNICT, 1993.

enced a significant increase, either through direct exports by affiliates or subcontracting relationships established with Portuguese manufacturs.

There was a considerable expansion in industrial investment, largely with the support of E:C: funds, especially of PEDIP (Specific Programme for the Development of Portuguese Industry). Foreign manufacturing investments concentrated in the automotive sector, where a handful of big projects took place: General Motors set up a plant producing electronic devices and ignition systems; Ford launched the manufacturing of car-radios; the Finnish firm Valmet started to produce tractors; and the Brazilians of Cofap manufactured automotive components. The main investment, by far, has been undertaken by a joint-venture between Ford and Volkswagen with the purpose of manufacturing a new multi-purpose vehicle; it is the largest foreign investment ever made in Portugal, involving a total investment in fixed assets of almost 450 billion escudos. This drive towards the automotive industry amounted to an upgrading of the average technological content of foreign manufacturing investments, although the breath and depth of the linkages to be established with domestic suppliers still remains to be seen. It should be noted, on the other hand, that these investments were heavily subsidised, with incentives approaching 30% of the amounts invested.

Portuguese firms also profited from PEDIP to invest, especially in the acquisition of new equipment vintages. However, this was not paralleled by a significant change in strategic capability. Production strategies, based on technological upgrading of hardware, prevailed over market and learning oriented approaches. Due account has to be taken of the emergence of a few new technology-based firms.

Portugal's specialisation pattern has remained basically unchanged in the last decade. International competitiveness rested on traditional and resource-based sectors (textiles and clothing, footwear, wood, pulp and paper). Although positive signs of new strategic behaviour were identified (product differentiation approaches, increase in the value added content of several goods and own internationalisation moves by a few firms, setting up commercial affiliates abroad), it should not be concealed that the challenges faced by sub-contracting and price-competing firms are very hard, their profit margins being squeezed by sub-contractors and by increasingly fierce competition from the new industrialising countries.

The wave of foreign investments at the turn of the decade is not yet apparent in trade statistics. They will, for sure, lead to the decline of traditional industries in the overall export stucture. Their effects in terms of technological change in the domestic manufacturing fabric will, however, dramatically depend on the kind and intensity of linkages to be established with domestic firms.

The scientific and technological system exhibited a growth trend, but figures are still far behind EC averages. S&T expenditures reached 0,61% of GDP for 1990 (and are expected to amount to 0,7% for 1992), from 0,4% in 1984; the share of researchers within the active population is also fairly low, approaching 0,12%.

The last few years witnessed a growing concern with science and technology matters, and with the need to invest in this field. Two EC-funded programmes were launched aiming to strengthen Portugal's S&T potential: the CIENCIA and the STRIDE – Portugal programmes. However, the links between these programmes (especially the first) and the PEDIP (industrial development) are not so strong as they should be, to articulate a real innovation policy. As Professor Rothwell put it, "to some extent, the system was based on the idea that the more science and technology you pushed in at one end, the more new products and innovations came out in the other hand"; however this is a very biased and incorrect perspective, since "innovation is not synonymous with R&D". (OECD, 1993: 143, 156).

Signs of change became apparent in the last decade. Worth mention are the growth of polytechnical education (aimed at overcoming one of the heaviest handicaps to Portugal's industrial development – the shortage of skilled technicians and middle managers), the establishment of a large number of R&D centres, institutes, laboratories and technology-support organisations, mainly in the form of private non profit institutions, and the "internationalisation" (better, Europeanisation) of the Portuguese S&T system (CaraÇa et alii, 1992; OECD, 1993). However, the overall system remains weak and lacks adequate "bridges" with industry. Its main shortcomings remain very much those identified in the 1982 review of national S&T policy developed under the aegis of OECD:

- paucity of human and financial resources devoted to R&D activities;
- excessive dispersion and fragmentation of research units (although some excellence groups emerged, reaching the required critical mass);
- weakness of the higher education system;
- insufficient links between R&D organisations and industrial units; and
- very low effort in the business enterprise sector and in experimental development activities.

Having sketched this general view of the main features of Portugal's industrial fabric and S&T system, we may now examine a more detailed picture of innovation patterns at the firm level.

3. INNOVATIVE ACTIVITIES BY PORTUGUESE FIRMS

3.1. A framework for analysis

The measurement of innovation suffers from serious difficulties due to the very characteristics of the innovative process, to its qualitative nature (largely behavioural and social and organisationally-embedded), to the various forms that an innovation may take (from technological breakthroughs to minor improvements) and to the different appropriation mechanisms used by firms. The issue is further compounded by four additional factors. First, as was stressed above, the linear or "ladder" model of innovation — assuming that the more R&D you pump in, the more new products will come out — is not correct. The "chain-link" perspective shows that innovations are an interactive process where (i) R&D expenditures are just one of the components, and not necessarily the critical factor, and (ii) a given amount of inputs is not automatically translated into a corresponding volume of outputs. Second, investments in innovation take many forms (OECD, 1992) and there is a trend towards an increased recourse of firms to external technology sources, including licensing-in, acquisitions and technology-based cooperative agreements (Friar & Horwitch, 1986). Third, as Pavitt has shown, industries have different patterns of technological accumulation, with significant differences in the importance ascribed to "in-house" R&D. Finally, the relevance of S&T indicators is contingent on the industrial structure and development level of the countries concerned: for Portuguese firms, technology change and the accumulation process, as well as innovation performances, are much more dependent on strategic thinking, management attitudes, marketing capabilities and upgrading of skills than on R&D effort as such (Godinho & CaraÇa, 1990; Simoes, 1991; OECD, 1993).

Usually the assessment of the various aspects of the innovation process is undertaken through two main kinds of measures – input and output indicators (Molero & Buesa, 1993). The first refer to the resources fed into the S&T system or into the firm (R&D expenditures, technology acquisition). The second concerns the outcomes of the innovation process (breakthrough innovations, trade in technology-intensive products, patents granted, licensing-out). However, most authors look at both types of indicators independently, overlooking the links existing between them and the very process of "transformation" of inputs into outputs. We need, therefore, a framework to encompass this process, bearing in mind that it largely takes place within the firm.

Granstrand and Sjollander (1990) presented a framework for studying technology strategies, founded on the concept of the technology base of the company, which acts as a "translator" of technology procurement strategies into exploitation ones. This idea may be applied in a different context, to build a "bridge" between input and output indicators. In other words, the technology base may be envisaged as a "reaction space" which enables the "conversion" of inputs (technology sourcing or investment) into outputs (innovation performance). Innovative activities of firms may, therefore, be assessed through this framwork, using technology indicators instead of the "technology strategies" suggested by those authors. Our analysis of the innovative behaviour of Portuguese firms will, then, be based on three building blocks – technological investment, technology base and innovation performance.

Technological investment encompasses the various mechanisms used by firms to enhance its technological base. It includes different forms of technology development and/or acquisition: "in-house" R&D activities, the purchase of technology embodied in machinery and equipment, licensing-in, and technology-based cooperative agreements. The technology base corresponds to the asset of technological competence that the company possesses (Granstrand and Sjollander, 1990:39). The possibilities of absorbing and "transforming" technology inputs into outputs depend on three main factors: strategic intent,[3] that is, the strategic motives underlying the decision of technology sourcing; learning capabilities (or "absorptive capacity" to use the wording of Cohen and Levinthal, 1990); and commitment to internalising technology (Hamel,1991).

3.2. Technological Investment

Unfortunately there is no estimation of the weight of the various forms of technology investment in the whole process of technology upgrading by Portuguese firms. There is, however, some information on the importance ascribed to the various "factors of innovation", on the basis of a survey undertaken by CISEP/GEPIE (1992). The purchase of equipment was by far the leading factor, with a score of 1136 points. Other factors ranked high were equipment improvements (627), employment of skilled people (474) and project design capabilities (321). In contrast, R&D activities (192), purchase of patents and licensing-in (95) and cooperation with research centres (83) exhibited very low scores. This clearly shows that, by and large, the acquisition of new machinery and equipment is regarded by Portuguese firms as the paramount vehicle for technology upgrading. Such a pattern is partly due to the very pattern of Portugal's manufacturing fabric (where supplier-dominated industries have a remarkable importance), but also reflects an attitude of entrepreneurs towards innovation.

Having in mind these aspects, let us turn now to a brief overview of the recent trends exhibited by those mechanisms of technology acquisition for which information is available.[4]

Acquisition of embodied technology – Perceived by Portuguese entrepreneurs as the main device for technology upgrading, the acquisition of machinery and equipment may be assessed through foreign trade statistics. In fact, due to the weakness of the domestic industrial fabric in this area, periods of buoyant investments are immediately translated into increased imports of capital goods, as

[3] The term "strategic intent" is borrowed from Hamel & Prahalad (1989).

[4] Since we are mostly concerned with the process of technological investment by domestic firms, and not so much with a macro-perspective, FDI inflow will not be considered as a mechanism for technology acquisition (as it should be if a macro approach were taken).

happened in the post-accession period, when capital goods reached more than 30% of total imports and exhibited annual growth rates in volume exceeding 20%. From 1989 onwards there was a slowdown, expressed in an average growth rate of around 9% for the period 1989–92.

It should be recognised, however, that Portuguese firms have made scarce use of reverse engineering by comparison with their Japanese or Korean counterparts. If in a few more mature areas of metal-working and electrical machinery, some Portuguese firms have been able to generate endogenous technological capacity, there is a lack of internationally competitive firms in the industrial machinery industry. User-producer linkages are generally weak, and high demanding customers go abroad to fulfil their needs.

Statistical data indicate that there was, in recent years, a significant modernisation of Portuguese firms in terms of machinery and equipment. However, many firms are now discovering, to their own cost, that equipment modernisation per se is not enough to achieve competitiveness.

R&D Activities – The low commitment of Portuguese enterprises towards R&D activities may be clearly shown through a few indicators:

- small number of firms reporting R&D expenditures (in 1990 there were 194 only, 163 of them in manufacturing);
- very low share of business enterprises in the performance and financing of R&D expenditures: their percentage in financing gross domestic R&D expenditure was 27% in Portugal (1990), compared to levels of 62% for Germany, 51% for the Netherlands, 44% for Italy, 60% for Ireland and 47% for Spain;
- small size of R&D units: the average R&D unit in business enterprises, according to 1990 statistics, employed (in full-time equivalent) 2,3 scientists and engineers and 8 technicians and auxiliaries and had an R&D expenditure of 70 million escudos. This suggests that most units will be behind the critical mass needed to achieve significant results.

Besides this weak R&D commitment, another important feature deserves a reference. It concerns the low spending on related S&T activities, a set of activities (including inter alia quality control and scientific information search, analysis and storage) instrumental in backing up and linking R&D to the production system.

R&D activities in manufacturing were, in 1990, heavily concentrated in electrical machinery, electronics and transportation equipment. These industries accounted for almost one half of R&D expenditures, followed by chemicals with a share of 70%. However, the concentration of R&D at the firm level is not much above the figures recorded in other, more industrialised, small countries: the 8 largest manufacturing R&D performers account for slightly more than 60% of expenditures. Half of the members of the top-8 are foreign-owned affiliates. Bearing in mind these features and the very low amount of business enterprise R&D, this means that there are no "research champions" that may have a say in the international arena.

How to interpret this low R&D effort of Portuguese firms?

An initial explanation stems from the fact that Portugal's industrial fabric has a strong share of traditional sectors, where technology upgrading is largely equipment-embodied or where product innovations are related to aesthetic design. This feature does not tell the whole story, however. What happens is that, in general, Portuguese firms are still a stage below that where formal R&D effort is relevant. Their weakness is not due to the low formal R&D activity. It has deeper roots: shortage of skilled people, management capacity and behaviour, price-based competition strategies and lack of an appropriate network of business and technical services.

Contractual technology transfer including licensing-in — Available statistics show that the early nineties were characterised by a significant increase in payments stemming from contractual technology transfer (licensing-in of know-how and industrial property rights, software licensing, engineering services and technical assistance), after a slow growth in the eighties. Technology payments rose at an yearly average of 64% for 1990–92. A closer analysis shows that this trend was mainly due to engineering services (associated with the building up of infraestructures and a few large manufacturing projects), and not to licensing contracts.

Licensing seems to have lost ground as a consequence of European integration. The ratio of licensing payments to GDP declined to 1,8%0, for 1990–92, from around 2,9%0 for 1982–85, despite the existence of a few signs of recovery in 1992 data. It should be noticed that more than two thirds of licensing payments were undertaken by foreign-owned firms. Nevertheless, both statistical and case-study evidence shows that the recourse of domestic firms to licensing as a vehicle for technology upgrading and new product launching has lessened. This pattern may be explained by two factors, both linked with Portugal's EC entry. First, some former licensees were taken over by their licensors in industries such as food processing, beverages, chemicals, pharmaceuticals and machinery; in some cases, reduced risk perception, market growth prospects and the easing of trade flows (enabling the Portuguese market to be supplied from abroad) led the former licensors to take an equity share, often a majority one, in their licensees; in others (fewer), it was the licensee who, fearing increased competition, endeavoured to forge a stronger link with his former licensor. Second, in sectors where licensing agreements had been entered into mostly as a means to circumvent tariff barriers, as happened with cosmetics, market integration led to the discontinuation of licensing and contracts were changed into agency arrangements. All in all, the freedom of licensees appears to have been curtailed by EC accession.

The analysis of the licensing experience of Portuguese firms indicates that the main motives behind licensing are market-driven and not technology-driven. Licensing has been used mainly as a means to get new products marketed in the domestic market, and not so much as a vehicle for internalising technological knowledge. It appears that licensing is envisaged as a means to substitute the low "in-house" capacity to develop new products more than as a support to the strengthening of "in-house" technological effort. This is not to say, however, that licensing-in has not been a positive factor in technological upgrading. Of course, it was; but, in our opinion, its potential has not been fully exploited, due to a lack of strategic perspective and commitment (Simoes, 1992).

Other non-equity technology cooperative arrangements — The involvement of Portuguese firms in the recent wave of technology-based cooperative arrangements, both inter-firm and with research and technology organisations has been limited.

One of the main determinants of this non-cooperative behaviour is, most probably "the low capacity of Portuguese firms to correctly identify their technological needs" (Lopes, 1993). Going a little further, it may be said that this is a consequence of an insufficient level of "in-house" technological needs and of management weaknesses. A recent work on the sourcing of external services by Portuguese firms (Ferrao, 1992) shows that the main discriminants of firm behaviour are not size or industry, but rather organisational structure, the level of education of entrepreneurs and their socio-professional paths, export propensity and the strength of the relationships previously set up with other firms.

Unlike other small European countries, the network of technology inter-firm relationships in Portugal is very sparse. Customer supplier links are weak and, in general, insufficient to generate cooperative technological developments. The feebleness of the capital goods and intermediate goods sectors are additional hindrances to such developments. Similarly, University-Industry linkages remain limited, and are not considered by the majority of managers as relevant (CISEP/GEPIE, 1992). In recent years, and largely with the support of PEDIP and other EC programmes, a large number of science and technology organisations, mostly in the form of private non-profit institutions, were created and/or developed(technology institutes, technology centres, Innovation Agency, etc.). However, the demand for these services remains limited and the matching of industry needs and technology services leaves much to be desired.

Portuguese firms played a minor role in international technology-based cooperation agreements. A press survey undertaken by our team for the period 1988–91 identified only 10 agreements, 8 of them concerning licensing and technical assistence. This means that technology cooperation was very scarce, inward oriented and had a minor technology-development content. As we noted elsewhere (Simoes, 1991), this may be interpreted as indicating that Portuguese companies are still technologically too weak to be regarded as interesting partners for a two-way technology exchange.

With regard to EC cooperative research programmes the overall picture is not very different. As a rule, involvement by firms is low, BRITE/EURAM being the only noticeable exception. Portuguese participants seldom have leadership positions, thereby hindering their capacity to profit from such projects. Despite these shortcomings, the evaluation of EC programmes is positive, insofar as they opened new opportunities for technology learning and transfer and supported the development of research teams (in private non-profit making organisations), capable of further networking with domestic firms.

A final reference should be made to the relationships with

foreign affiliates established in Portugal. One study, commissioned by the Ministry of Industry and Energy, on the technological profile of a sample of 23 foreign majority-owned firms indicated that they had an "off-shore" positioning, generating very few linkages with domestic enterprises. This is, in our opinion, an overstated conclusion. Undoubtedly a large number of foreign investments (mostly manufacturing platforms and some integrated manufacture) are "enclave-type" subsidiaries. In other instances, the purchase of Portuguese firms by foreign concerns led to a significant decline in their innovative activities. It should be noted, however, that in general the presence of foreign affiliates had a positive effect on the technological and organisational level of Portuguese firms, mostly due to three factors. First, through the demonstration effect: Portuguese entrepreneurs copied technological and organisational innovations introduced by foreign affiliates. Second, through professional mobility, processes and behaviours were extended to domestic firms. Third, sourcing by foreign affiliates (including sub-contracting) contributed towards a significant upgrading in the technological level of domestic firms and generated positive organisational bonds.

Synthesis — Portuguese firms' level of technological investment may be considered as low, whatever indicator one chooses, except the acquisition of embodied technology. In fact, the concept of investment in innovation, giving rise to a learning process and design-production-marketing to the accumulation of knowledge stemming from interaction, is largely absent from Portuguese enterprises. This is also associated with a strategic positioning of price competition (trying to squeeze direct prodution costs and staking everything on low labour costs) instead of product differentiation. Furthermore, in spite of the existence of a few clusters (Monitor Company, 1993), firms are, in general, very insulated, with scarce technology linkages which might generate virtuous circles of innovation.

3.3. Innovation performance

The two technology output indicators most commonly used to portray innovative performance are patents granted in the United States and the share of turnover or exports due to new products.[5]

[5] Other indicators used at a macro-level are technology balance of payments and trade in technology intensive products (see, for instance, Molero & Buesa, 1993).

For our purposes, data on patents granted in the United States are not appropriate. As a matter of fact, the average number of US patents granted to Portuguese firms per annum is so low (less than 10) as to become meaningless for analytical purposes. Portuguese industry has not yet attained the technology development and internationalisation levels which render US patents a relevant indicator of innovative performance.

We should, thus, turn towards information on the relevance of new and/or improved products for the firms concerned.

According to the innovation survey undertaken by CISEP/GEPIE (1992), almost 70% of the 1026 respondent units had introduced improvements in their existing products and 36% stated they had launched one or several new products during the period 1987–1989. With regard to process innovations, the corresponding shares were very similar: 74 and 36%, respectively. These figures should be interpreted with some caution, and cannot be taken on their face value. As innovation and technology development became – at least in the word – key issues, one may well understand that firms would like to "ice the cake", claiming to have done something in the field. There is also an inherent difficulty in defining the "newness" of a product: do successive minor improvements accumulate to change a product's nature, i.e., to make it a new product? Furthermore, the emergence of new products depends on the characteristics of the industry: in "fashion industries", such as clothing, footwear or cosmetics, the speed of "development" of a "new" product is much higher than in capital goods industries. These problems cannot be adequately tackled through a broad postal survey like the CISEP/GEPIE one.

Nevertheless, the survey shows that most Portuguese firms have some kind of innovative activities, at least through the acquisition of new equipment vintages or through the introduction of minor improvements in existing products or processes. It is worrying, on other hand, that only one third of the firms surveyed claimed to have launched new products. Though "laggards" may be found everywhere, such a reliance on existing products may be a sign of difficulty in adapting to changing market requirements.

The survey enables us to go a little further in this matter, since it included a question on the share of "innovations" in turnover.[6]

---

[6] It was formulated in the following way: what is the share of turnover (or output) due to innovations introduced in 1987/1988/1989?

The first finding (very important, in our opinion) is that only one third of the firms surveyed replied to this question. This may be interpreted as indicating that firms are not very familiar with the accountancy of innovation outputs and/or that the weight of "innovations" on sales was so low that they refrained from responding. Focusing on the 347 firms for which information is available, the majority indicated shares between 5 and 25% of sales; units whose innovations accounted for more than 50% of output represented 18% of total (presumably a significant part of them are new firms).

Judgements on the magnitude of these figures are very hard, since internationally comparable references are lacking. Assuming that firms are evenly distributed in each cell, the average figure is 30%, meaning that 30% of turnover in 1989 concerned innovations introduced in the preceding three years.[7] Such a figure looks relatively high when compared with percentages of 32% for Sweden (Deiaco, 1992) and 20% for Norway (Smith & Vidvei, 1992). Comparisons cannot be pushed too far, since there are significant discrepancies in the criteria used. In Portugal, data refer to the "percentage of sales due to innovation", no restriction being made as to the kind of "innovation" considered (thus meaning that product improvements and all types of process innovations might have been included). In contrast, the Swedish and Norwegian surveys were much more precise, focusing on product innovations only. Sound conclusions cannot be derived from these comparisons. We are convinced, however, that figures for Portugal are somewhat inflated due to the broadness of the concept used. Therefore, if the survey had followed the concept adopted in the recent EC Harmonised Innovation Survey ("products significantly changed from a technological viewpoint or newly introduced") and if a higher response rate were ensured, the share would have dropped sharply, especially for domestic owned firms.

The limited innovative performance of Portuguese firms may be confirmed by two additional remarks on other output indicators. First, Portugal's balance of trade in technology intensive products is largely negative and a significant share of exports is accounted for by foreign affiliates. Second, Portugal's technology exports are very low (they are estimated to reach some 10% of imports) and

[7] A similar exercise on data provided in Pereira (1991:35) for 50 SMEs, restricted to product innovation, leads to a share of 20%.

mainly correspond to engineering services and technical assistance to less developed countries' organisations.

Having reviewed both input and output indicators, we now face the need to link them, in order to understand better the process, which at the company level, facilitates the selection of inputs and their "transformation" into outputs. In other words, we should assess the "technology base", i.e. the set of technological capabilities and weaknesses of Portuguese firms.

3.4. Linking inputs and outputs: the technology base

The identification of a firm's technology base is obviously a difficult task that can only be carried out for small samples. As far as we know, the only available work broadly aimed at performing such a task was carried out by Joao Martins Pereira (Pereira, 1991) and refers to a sample of 50 SMEs. Technological capabilities of these firms were analysed on the basis of the following 8 criteria: productivity (value added per worker), integration (value added divided by turnover), age of equipment, worker skills and qualification, use of "new technologies" in the manufacturing process, R&D projects, recourse to external technical services and level of investment. Unfortunately there are no elements concerning the characteristics of management (and of managers) and the organisational structure. The author identified two contrasting groups:

- (i) Firms with above average "technological level", employing relatively skilled personnel, adopting "new technologies" (especially electronics) in manufacturing processes, benefiting from technical assistance from independent organisations and having recourse to diversified sources of information, and
- (ii) Firms characterised by low productivity, low skilled labour force, insufficient training effort, having limited external relationships (or, in other words, with very restricted task environments) and applying simple, traditional labour-intensive technologies.

It is interesting to remark that the first group is spread throughout the whole manufacturing fabric, encompassing not just "modern" industries[8] but also traditional sectors (garments, cork...). This means that the divide is not basically between "traditional" and "modern" industries – but rather between technologically prepared and weak firms.

But at the same time we should not conceal the fact that the second group of firms (those with low technological levels) are mostly concentrated in traditional sectors – those that are "dominated in Portuguese industrial structure and account for a significant share in our exports" (Pereira, 1991: 41). Furthermore, competitiveness in enlarged markets requires much more than technological capacity strictu sensu – it basically requires strategic thinking and the formulation of correct strategies, matching marketing, technological and organisational aspects.

The relevance of strategic thinking and of commitment in undertaking technology investments has also been stressed in our research on the opportunities for technological development through licensing-in (Simoes, 1993). It was found that licensing-in usually involves the communication of manufacturing and marketing know-how, but very seldom the transfer of know-why, of basic design capabilities. The use of licensing-in as a vehicle for upgrading a firm's capability to absorb and internalise technological knowledge and to design and develop new products seems to be contingent on six main, interrelated factors: (i) the strategic approach towards technology acquisition (a "technology investment" perspective should be present from the phase of technology search and selection onwards); (ii) preparation for the contract; (iii) learning capacity and commitment (the more successful cases were those of firms which already had a relevant technology capacity or which endeavoured to build up that capacity to absorb the technology); (iv) balanced linkages with the licensor, developing cooperation without seriously curtailing autonomy; (v) industry characteristics, the generation of design capabilities being much more difficult in science-based industries; and (vi) synergies between licensed products or processes and the licensee's activity and experience.

The "conversion" of technology inputs into innovative outputs

---

[8] "Modern" industries were defined as those that gained importance in the last 10–15 years, exporting products with tight specifications or working in the field of "new" technologies: precision mechanics, automotive components and electronics and telecommunications products (Pereira, 1991:15).

thus requires a managerial attitude which understands the importance of learning and the potential benefits derived from the application of such learning into marketable products; in other words, it demands a "technology investment" perspective. But learning is only possible when a minimum knowledge basis already exists; hence the importance of human resources within the firm, to identify needs and to absorb knowledge. Finally, marketing capabilities are important for generating returns from innovative products and, through a feed-back process, for suggesting new ideas for product improvement and design.

The above analysis may be summarized in a few words: in general terms, the technological (and strategic) capability of Portuguese firms is weak; they envisage technology upgrading mostly as a matter of equipment modernisation and not so much as a learning process of accumulation of tacit knowledge. Therefore, their innovative performance remains limited. Putting together the three blocks described above (technology inputs, performance indicators and technology base) we may take a final step in our task: the identification of the main issues in promoting the technological development of Portuguese firms.

4. INNOVATIVE CAPACITY: THE MAIN ISSUES

In our view innovative capacity is closely associated with "soft" and internal aspects, and namely with management skills and commitment to devise correct strategies to foster learning (and to adapt judiciously to environmental changes) as well as to structure the organisation and motivate people. Of course, environmental influences and external relationships are important. But to identify and exploit opportunities, internal capacity and vision are needed.

The critical problems regarding the innovative capacity of Portuguese manufacturing enterprises may be clustured around half-a-dozen closely inter-related axes: weakness in strategic thinking; insufficient concern with the "soft", intangible aspects which are at the heart of innovation (organisation, tacit knowledge, information, quality); insufficient focus on marketing; paucity of "in house" technical skills; scarce backward and forward balanced and demanding linkages; and scarce use of the national network of technical support services.

The weaknesses in strategic thinking are, most probably, the main shortcoming and the source of many of the other problems identified. Such weaknesses are translated into an absence of a forward-looking approach, a lack of vision, an incapacity to anticipate changes in industry conditions and, of course, into a mediocre innovative performance. The lack of strategic capability is due to a host of factors where one may stress the insufficiencies of entrepeneurs in terms of technical and management knowledge (risk taking and entrepreneurial behaviour is not necessarily associated with strategic vision), the resistances to change, the family – owned nature of many businesses (where the transmission of management posts within the family prevails over the separation between ownership and management), and the lack of industrial groups that might act as "rationality centers" in structuring the behaviour of SMEs.

Linked with the weaknesses in strategic thinking is the insufficient concern of Portuguese entrepeneurs with the management of "soft" technology issues, information, quality and marketing. A survey commissioned by the Commission of the European Communities on the strategic reactions of European firms to Single Market challenges (Buigues, Ilzkovitz & Lebrun, 1990) shows a sharp contrast between Portuguese and Spanish firms. While Portuguese entrepreneurs rank production strategies first, giving less importance to the impact of the Single Market on distribution, product design and R&D – the Spanish placed much more emphasis on the latter three approaches. This survey provides a clear message: Portuguese firms usually follow production strategies, showing little concern with product design and marketing.

Portuguese firms have been much more concerned with the "hard" than with the "soft" and for most of them innovation still means new equipment. They are starting to learn, at their cost, that in the new competitive framework production strategies are no longer suited and that the competitive environment is more and more based on intangible factors, facilitating product differentiation.

The focus on production instead of marketing deprives Portuguese firms of one of the main innovation leverages – the knowledge of market needs and of customers' desires and requirements. Many Portuguese firms export, but don't sell their products abroad, in the sense that they lack their own sales networks. This "cutting off" from final customers makes the reading of "market signals" more difficult and, therefore, hampers innovation. Associated with this problem is the weakness of user-producer interaction in Portugal. The existence of sophisticated and demanding buyers is one of the key factors in fostering innovation, well recognised in Porter's diamond (Porter,1990) or in Lundvall's "national systems of innovation" (Lundvall, 1988). However, the setting up of cooperative user-producer networks to develop new products and/or to upgrade existing ones is not a common feature of Portugal's manufacturing fabric.

Another barrier to innovation is the shortage of technically skilled personnel. This is partly the result of the drive of many firms on cost-cutting and on price-based competition, relying on low-skill, low-wage workers. But it is also due to structural factors and to the bottlenecks of the education system: the suppression of vocational education in 1975 had very negative consequences, generating a shortage of middle managers and some types of skilled workers (Simoes, 1991). There is also a shortage of scientists and engineers, especially in the areas where industrial experience is a significant facet of the skills required. The CISEP/GEPIE (1992) survey shows that firms consider the low skills of the workforce as the main barrier to innovation, largely exceeding other factors, such as financial constraints or the lack of public support.

The weakness of in-house technical skills and R&D effort is not compensated by a significant recourse to technological support services. Despite the strong growth in private non profit interface organisations, whose share in total R&D jumped from 1,6% to 12,4% between 1986 nd 1990, the links between University and Industry remain very slender. The only exceptions came from: (i) a few firms (including foreign-owned ones) with an internal technological base that enables them to formulate specific demands and to define targets in their dialogue with the University (research teams; and (ii) the emergence of new technology based firms, many of them founded by former researchers, that kept strong links with the Higher Education system. The use of technology centers (Centros Tecnologicos), launched with the purpose of spreading technology and providing technical assistance to firms, has also remained limited, and mostly addressed towards quality control or sporadic advice.

The picture is slightly gloomy. It is true that Portuguese firms, in general, are now better equipped and have fairly recent models of machinery. However, the transition from mere production strategies to more innovative behavior – involving the upgrading of human resources, more efficient and strategic management approaches and increased awareness of "dynamic competitiveness factors" – is still in its early stages. The response to innovation weaknesses requires, first of all, a change in attitudes and actions aimed at developing strategic thinking, and upgrading the quality of general management in Portuguese firms.

REFERENCES

Buigues, P., Ilzkovitz, F. and Lebrun, J. F. (1990), *The Impact of the Internal Market by Industrial Sector: The Challenge for Member States*, Commission of the European Communities, Brussels.

Cantwell, J. (1989), *Technological Innovation and Multinational Corporations*, Oxford, Basil Blackwell.

CaraÇa, J. M. E. et allii (1992), *Study of the Impact of Community R&D Programmes on the Portuguese S&T Potential*, SECT, Lisbon.

CISEP/GEPIE (1992), *InovaÇao Indústria Portugesa – Observatório M.I.E.*, GEPMIE, Lisbon.

Cohen, Wesley M. and Levinthal, Daniel A., Absorptive Capacity: A new Perspective on Learning and Innovation (1990), *Administrative Science Quarterly*, Vol. 35, pp 128–152.

Cohendet, Patrick, Heraud, Jean-Alain and Zuscovitch, Ehud (1992), Apprentissage Technologique, Réseaux Economiques et Appropriabilité des Innovations, in D. Foray and C. Freeman, eds., *Technologie et Richesse des Nations*, Economica, Paris.

Deiaco, Enrico (1992), Points de Vue Nouveaux sur l'Activité et les Performances Technologiques: Enquête Suédoise sur l'Innovation, STI Revue, no 11, Dec. 1992.

Ferrao, Joao (1992), ServiÇos e InovaÇao, Celta Editora, Oeiras.

Foray, Dominique and Mowery, D. C. (1990), L'Intégration de la R&D Industrielle: Nouvelles Perspectives d'Analise, Revue Économique, Vol. 41, no 3.

Friar, John and Horwitc, Mel (1989), The Emergence of Technology Strategy: A New Dimension of Strategic Management in M. Horwitch, ed., *Technology in the Modern Corporation*, Pergamon, N. York.

GEPIE (1993), *Workshop InovaÇao na Indústria Portuguesa* – NORTEC 93, GEPIE, Lisboa.

Godinho, Manuel M. and CaraçA, Joao M. G. (1990), InteracÇao Tecnologia – Desenvolvimento em Portugal, *Estudos de Economia*, Vol XI no 1 Oct, Dec. pp 67–103.

Gomory, Ralph E. (1989), From the "Ladder of Science" to the Product Development Cycle, *Harvard Business Review*, Nov.–Dec., pp 99–105.

Granstrand, Ove and Sjollander, Soren (1990), Managing Innovation in Multi-Technology Corporations, *Research Policy*, Vol 19, 1990.

Hamel, Gary (1991), Competition for Competence and Inter-partner learning

within international strategic alliences, *Strategic Management Journal*, Vol 12, pp 83–103.
Hamel, Gary and Prahalad, C. K. (1989), Strategic Intent, *Harvard Business Review*, Vol 67, no 3, May–June, pp 63–67.
Jnict (1993), *Inquérito ao Potencial Científico e Tecnológico Nacional em 1990*, JNICT, Lisbon.
Kline, S. J. and Rosenberg, N. T. (1986), An Overview of Innovation, in National Academy of Engineering, *The Positive Sum Strategy: Harnessing Technology Growth*, The National Academy Press, Washington D.C.
Lopes, Ernani et allii (1983), *Relatório sobre Política Industrial em Portugal nos Anos 90*, Report to the EC Commission, Lisbon.
Lundvall, B. A. (1988), Innovation as an Inter-Active Process: From User Producer Interaction to the National System of Innovation, in G. Dosi, C. Freeman, R. Nelson, G. Silverberg and L. Soete, eds, *Technical Change and Economic Theory*, F. Pinter, London.
Molero, José and BUESA, Mikel (1993), Recursos Tecnológicos in J. L. Garcia Delgado ed. *Lecciones de Economia Española, Civitas, Madrid.*
MONITOR COMPANY (1993), *A Competitividade de Portugal: Desenvolver a AutoconfianÇa,* Exame/Cedintec, Lisbon.
OECD (1992), *La Téchnologie et L'Économie – Les Relations Déterminantes*, OECD, Paris.
OECD (1993), *Reviews of National Science and Technology Policy – Portugal*, OECD, Paris.
Pavitt, Keith (1989), Strategic Management in the Innovation Firm, in Roger Mansfield, ed., *Frontiers of Management – Research and Practice*, Routledge, London.
Pereira, Joao M. (1991), *Estudo Sobre Tecnologia, Qualidade e Design nas PMEs Portuguesas*, Porto, Forum das PMEs, 2nd Ed.
Porter, Michel (1990), *The Competitive Advantage of Nations*, Mac Millan, London.
Sahal, Devendra (1981), *Patterns of Technological Innovation*, Addison Wesley, New York.
Simoes, Vitor Corado (1991), *Globalisation and the Small Less Advanced Countries – The Case of Portugal*, FAST, Brussels.
Simoes, Vitor Corado (1992), *Oportunidades de Desenvolvimento Tecnológico das Empresas Portuguesas Através de Contratos de LicenÇa*, AIP, Lisbon.
Simoes, Vitor Corado (1993), Going Global or Going European? The Case of Portugal, in Marc Humbert, ed., *The Impact of Globalisation on Europe's Firms and Industries*, Pinter Publishers, London.
Smith Keith and Vidvei, Tor (1992), Les Activités d'Innovation et les Outputs de l'Innovation dans l'Industrie Norvégienne, *STI Revue*, no 11, Dec. 1992.

Factors in the Siting and Commercial Behaviour of Multinational Companies in Spain

José Molero, Mikel Buesa and Montserrat Casado

1. INTRODUCTION

The extent of the process of internationalisation and the important role that multinational companies have played in it have awakened a growing analytical interest regarding the behaviour of this type of agent. This has given rise to the creation of several hypotheses — largely complementing each other — which, though not constituting a complete theory, enable empirical analysis to focus on those internal and external elements which impinge on their decisions on foreign investment, and, stemming from this, on the makeup of the activities of their subsidiaries in the countries where they are located.

It is not our aim in this work to have an abstract discussion on the theory of internationalisation,[1] but rather to present the results we have obtained from our research — inspired by it — on the type of strategies followed by subsidiaries of German and Dutch multinationals located in Spain. Though our work covers production, commercial, technological and the use of human capital aspects of these strategies, in this chapter we refer to the factors determining the locating of these firms in Spain. Furthermore, given the importance which along with these factors, is acquired

[1] See for this the text by J. A. Alonso included in this volume.

by their relationship with domestic and outside markets, we also analyse their commercial behaviour.

The chapter has been divided into three parts. The first part refers to the evolution of direct foreign investment in Spain and, particularly, that from Germany and Holland. The purpose of this is to show the importance of capital from these two countries among the total investment flow into the Spanish economy.

In the second part, we present the empirical evidence that has been gathered regarding the factors giving rise to investments from the aforementioned multinationals, looking at it from a double standpoint. On the one hand, that of the specific advantages in the technological and commercial fields, which provide them with a valuable capacity in the international context and, more specifically, in the Spanish market. On the other hand, that of elements regarding this market which constitute factors attracting this type of investment.

Thus, the analysis is to be found within the standpoints adopted by the most recent literature on internationalisation processes, and a set of factors is adopted similar to that used in other works on the subject (Brooke and Buckley, 1988; Corado Simoes, 1992), which enables the case of Spain to be compared to that of other countries.

And in the final part, a study is made of the commercial strategy employed by the subsidiaries which we are going to analyse. There are two points which our argument hinges around: the first refers to how intensively there is an orientation towards the domestic market and the competitive position they occupy therein; and the second centres on the characteristics of their activity in international markets, evaluating the relative importance and the geographical location of their foreign trade relations, as well as how these take shape in the interchanges developed within the multinational group.

As we have pointed out, the empirical analysis on which this work is based uses as a reference firms controlled by Dutch and German capital who are located in Spain. The fact that the subsidiaries studied come from two countries- justified insofar as these two capital inflows are important within the whole area of foreign investment in Spain, — enables us to highlight the similarities and differences in the behaviour of multinational firms of different origins.

The methodology used to obtain the information required in the work has two foundations, on the one hand, the collection of existing data from Spanish, Dutch and German sources on the companies we are interested in, and, on the other, the carrying out of a survey among them on the different subjects that we were researching.

The first of these procedures has enabled us to discover the existing flows and stock of German and Dutch investments in Spain, and also to establish the payroll of the 734 subsidiaries of multinationals from the former and the one hundred from the latter which are based in Spain.[2] Furthermore, through the use of published sources we have obtained individualised data of variables such as the sector of activity, sales, employment, exports, leading position in the local market, and technological activities, with regard to these companies.

Furthermore, the survey has provided plentiful information – especially of a qualitative nature, on factors leading to investment and the shape of the strategies adopted by subsidiaries that we have researched. The survey was sent to all firms with Dutch capital but, on the other hand, only to industrial firms with German capital,[3] which obliged us to bear this situation in mind when comparing the results of both groups. The number of valid questionnaires obtained was 23 for the former and 113 for the latter, which represents a percentage of answers of 23 and 38.5, respectively. Firms in the sample have a 23.1 per 100 share, in the Dutch case, in employment and 36.5 per 100 of total sales of the whole group of Dutch multinational subsidiaries established in Spain. These percentages rise to 65.2 and 68.1 for employment and sales of the manufacturing subsidiaries of German origin. All of this enables us to consider that the data obtained from the cases analysed are sufficiently significant.

---

[2] The information on foreign firms in the hands of Spanish government organisations is not available to researchers, since it is considered classified material. This has forced us to build up the census of the population studied from different trade directories – such as the ones published by *Fomento de la Producción* or *Alimarket* – and from the lists of companies based in Spain, as prepared by the Chamber of Commerce of each investing country. This procedure ensures a very wide coverage of the whole sector of firms being studied, since the above-mentioned directories only exclude those very small firms whose economic significance is, in any case, slight.

[3] It must be borne in mind that German investment in Spain is largely concentrated in manufacturing sectors, even though in recent years a clear progression is noticeable in the greater amount of investment going into services.

1. FOREIGN INVESTMENT IN SPAIN: THE ROLE OF GERMAN AND DUTCH CAPITAL

Foreign investment ever since in 1959, with the Plan de Estabilizacion, a steady opening up to foreign markets began, has been considered as one of the decisive elements of Spanish economic development.[4] Throughout the sixties and up to 1973, there was a noticeable increase in the inflow of foreign capital, with a growth of about 12% a year in real terms.[5] The 70's crisis, plus the existing climate of political uncertainty till, finally, the country clearly opted for setting up a democratic system, had a negative influence on this capital inflow.[6] From this latter year onwards, and until the mid-eighties, the growth path picked up at a rather higher speed than the previously mentioned one- an annual 14 per 100 – till, as a result of Spain joining the European Community, direct foreign investment rose to an unprecedentedly high figure of an annual 38 per 100.[7] The argument that the entry of a new member in an enlarged economic space means an extra attraction for a foreign investor (Dunning and Cantwell 1987), is thus clearly supported by the Spanish experience.

This notable evolution of foreign investment, particularly in recent years, has meant an important change in the influence exercised by multinational companies on the Spanish economy. As an expression of this change we have the marked increase in these companies' share of the country's industrial production,[8] and which coincided with a broad restructuring of their international activities (Yannopoulos, 1992; Cantwell, 1992.)

Thus, it is in the context we have just described that we must

---

[4] The presence of foreign capital in the Spanish economy is not a recent phenomenon. Its importance in the early stages of the industrialisation process in Spain, as well as its continuing major role over time has been amply highlighted in several works (Muñoz, Roldan y Serrano, 1978; Buesa y Molero, 1988; Iranzo, 1991; Martinez Serrano y Myro, 1992)

[5] Valued at constant 1980 prices, direct foreign investment rose from 27 500 million pesetas in 1964 to 76 600 in 1973.

[6] The total volume of direct foreign investment in 1976, valued at 1980 prices, was 29 500 million pesetas, that is, a figure almost matching that for 1964.

[7] In 1990, also valued at 1980 prices, direct investment reached its historic peak of 481 100 million pesetas.

[8] The most reliable estimates show that, in 1981 firms controlled by foreign capital achieved 11% of Spanish industrial production. This share rose to 36.5 per 100 in 1990. See in this respect, Martinez Serrano y Myro (1992).

place the evolution of direct Dutch and German investment. As far as Holland is concerned, the data in Table 1[9] enable the

Table 1 German and Dutch foreign direct investment in Spain. 1975–1990. (Billions of 1980 constant pesetas)

Years	A. Total FDI in spain	B. FDI European Union	C. Dutch FDI	D. German FDI
1975	64.16	12.05	2.28	3.42
1976	27.14	14.91	3.18	4.43
1977	42.59	19.49	1.29	6.23
1978	78.02	29.53	2.36	11.84
1979	95.17	33.78	8.72	8.01
1980	85.42	35.68	6.75	10.01
1981	69.31	35.60	2.41	6.56
1982	143.62	49.22	12.78	14.82
1983	110.38	57.15	7.35	14.47
1984	172.94	61.44	11.75	17.19
1985	166.23	67.29	11.87	16.75
1986	225.48	114.35	17.14	57.26
1987	388.71	190.87	65.45	14.04
1988	429.47	241.02	94.94	31.01
1989	601.67	312.30	91.86	39.31
1990	830.52	570.30	175.48	54.45
1975/79	307.08	109.76	17.83	33.93
1980/84	581.67	239.09	41.04	63.05
1985/90	2642.08	1496.13	456.74	212.82
1975/90	3530.83	1844.98	515.61	309.81

Source: Own elaboration with data from the Ministry of Economy.

growing importance which this country has acquired as a source of investment in Spain to be seen. In fact, while in the second half of the seventies it had a share of about 6 per 100 of the total foreign capital invested in the Spanish economy, — or 16% if all the

[9] It is worth pointing out that the fact that the data in this table do not coincide with those mentioned in previous notes is due to the latter referring to net investments recorded in the Balance of Payments, whilst the former correspond to gross investment operations authorised or verified by the Spanish authorities which may take place over a period of several years.

European Union countries are taken as reference, — a decade later, that percentage had tripled, to more than 17 per 100 in the second half of the eighties — or 30 per 100 with regard to the whole community area. Expressed another way, Holland has become the main European investor in Spain.

Now, it should be mentioned that the Low Countries in recent years have taken on an important role as intermediaries in international investment processes, so the figures in Table 1 overvalue the *real* incidence of capital in Spain originating from that country. In order to discover the real figures of this situation use has been made of the information offered by the *Nederlandsche Bank* regarding the net flow of investment in Spain, in which intermediary operations carried out by ad hoc companies established in Holland are excluded. The corresponding data[10] clearly show that, throughout the eighties, direct Dutch investment was 5.5 per 100 of the whole of foreign investment in the Spanish economy. This means that — not counting the effect of intermediaries — Holland has not changed its role in providing capital for Spain; a role which, moreover, as a result of its size, can be considered as important.

As far as German investment is concerned, according to the data shown in Table 1, it can be shown that its share of the whole of foreign capital invested in Spanish firms is more than 8 per 100 in the period under consideration. This percentage has dropped between the periods prior and subsequent to Spain's entry into the European Community; but this does not prevent it being said that these investments have been very stable during that period — and even since the sixties[11] — and this indicates very well-established relationships between the latter's multinationals and their Spanish subsidiaries, as seen in the strategic nature given by the former to their presence in the Spanish market.

[10] These data in their evolution over time show close parallels with those provided by Spanish sources. Thus, the linear correlation ratio between the corresponding series (0.9121) is significant with a reliability level of 99.95 per 100. Nonetheless, the values of these series show a marked difference in themselves.

[11] During the period 1962–1988 German investment in comparison with total foreign investment in the Spanish economy was 12.15 per 100 (valued in real terms). The high volume of direct foreign investment flowing into the Spanish economy during 1989 and 1990 meant a lesser significance for German capital as a whole, despite the latter showing no decline.

Furthermore, it can be pointed out that, at the end of the eighties, the value of German capital stock invested in Spanish firms was 14.3 per 100 of the figure for accrued foreign net investment in Spain since the sixties; and that, in the case of Holland, this percentage rose to 4.9 per 100.[12] In short, it can be seen that the two countries selected for this study have an outstanding role as investors in the Spanish economy.

2. FACTORS IN SITING MULTINATIONAL COMPANIES IN SPAIN

The motives leading to direct investment abroad make up an important qualitative element of analysis which leads to a greater insight into the strategies of multinationals. Specialist literature has frequently dealt with this topic,[13] and has drawn up two groups of determining factors in this investment. They are, on the one hand, the existence of specific assets in these firms which provide them with a competitive advantage in the international field; and, on the other, aspects of the internal makeup of the countries where the subsidiaries are to be set up, operating as magnet factors for the corresponding investment.

The empirical analysis of the factors to be found in the first of these preceding types is not an easy task, due to there being insufficient information of the type required. Nevertheless, it is possible to make a tentative approach to this topic by checking for coincidence between the sectors attracting direct investment and the branches of production in which the countries providing the investment have acquired advantages in the commercial and technological fields.

Within the Spanish economy the sectoral distribution of Dutch and German direct investment — according to information

[12] According to the *Statistiches Jahrbuch*, German capital stock in Spain rose in 1989 to 10 502 million DMs, equivalent to 734.9 thousand million pesetas. Also, the Nederlandsche Bank (*Afdeling Betalingsbalansen*) valued Dutch capital stock in Spain for the same year at 4497 million gilders — which is the equivalent of 253.7 thousand million pesetas. Accrued direct net foreign investment in Spain, from 1964 to 1989, valued at 1980 prices, was 5,139.3 million pesetas.

[13] A synthesis of literature dealing with this point can be consulted in, among others, Buckley (1991a). Also in Hood and Young (1990) emphasis is given to the role played by the different factors giving rise to direct foreign investment, from a theoretical viewpoint.

provided from available sources[14] – is as shown in Table 2. Although the breakdown of the data is made in a different way in each case and, particularly for the Dutch one, a serious discrepancy can be seen between them[15] a common pattern can be seen between them regarding the relative importance, within industry or services, of the different sectors looked at.

Dutch capital, although geared more towards the service sectors, has an important presence in industry, especially in chemicals, electric and electronic machinery and material and food. Furthermore, German investment is more centred in the industrial sectors, mainly in the chemical industries and in the construction of mechanical, electrical and electronic material and the car industry, although in recent years there has been gradual growth in investment in some service sectors. This trend in the sectoral destination of German investment in Spain coincides with that of German foreign investments as a whole. (Dunning and Cantwell, 1987).

Moreover, the profile of the technological and commercial advantages of the two investing countries considered is as shown in Table 3. In preparing it we have taken into account available studies of the technological advantages of Germany and Holland, both on the international[16] plane and with regard to the Spanish domestic market[17] and in turn their commercial advantages have been analysed, by taking into consideration their specialisation in exports with regard to OECD countries as a whole, as well as the

[14] The first part of the table records Spanish data on authorised or verified investment flows since 1984. This time limitation is due to the fact that the Ministerio de Economía has only published this type of information with a country-by-country breakdown regularly since that year. In the second part of the table figures for capital stock invested in Spain are provided, according to official German and Dutch estimates.

[15] As has been stated previously, the role assumed by Holland as an intermediary in international investment processes has a marked effect on data from Spanish sources. Carrascosa (1991) from an analysis of verified Dutch investments in 1988 has calculated 80 per 100 of them are from firms in other countries. His findings make it possible to confirm that, as a result, official Spanish figures overvalue real Dutch investment, especially in the financial sector.

[16] The analysis of the technological advantages was carried out with information on patents registered in the United States, bearing in mind the findings of works by Soete and Wyatt (1983) and Patel and Pavitt (1991a).

[17] The analysis has been carried out from information on patents awarded by the Spanish Patent Office, using the findings of Buesa (1992).

Table 2 Sectoral breakdown of German and Dutch FDI in Spain.

I. Authorised investment flows (1)

	Holland		Germany	
Sectors	Total	%	Total	%
0. Agriculture	4.35	0.86	3.05	1.30
1. Power and Water	9.74	1.92	0.17	0.07
2. Mining and Chemistry.	36.10	7.13	21.29	9.08
3. Metal. transformation and Machinery.	18.41	3.64	111.46	47.52
4. Other manufacturings	82.40	16.28	27.85	11.87
Total industries	146.66	28.97	160.78	68.55
5. Building	5.01	0.99	1.57	0.67
6. Wholesale and Retail Trade, Tourism.	66.28	13.09	36.00	15.35
7. Transport and Communication.	5.27	1.04	1.92	0.82
8. Finance, Insurance and Real Estate.	275.70	54.47	28.88	12.34
9. Other Services.	2.92	0.58	2.38	1.01
Total Services.	350.17	69.18	69.18	29.49
Total	506.19	100.00	234.56	100.00

II. FDI Stock (2)

Holland			Germany		
Sectors	Millions of Florins	%	Sectors	Millions of Marks	%
Agricuture and fishing	7	0.2	Chemical industry	2114	20.1
Industries	2075	46.1			
• Mining. Oil and Chemistry.	841	18.7	Non-electrical Machinery	636	6.1
• Metallurgy and Electrical Ind.	630	14.0	Electrical and Electronic		
• Food and Beverages	530	11.8	Machiery and Material	1254	10.9
• Others Industries	74	1.6			
Services	2415	53.7	Trade	136	1.3
• Trade	296	6.6			
• Transport and Communication	20	0.4	Finances	406	3.9
• Finance and Insurance	418	9.3	Portfolio societies	1190	11.3
• Other Services	1681	37.4	Other sectors	4766	45.4
Total	4497	100.0	Total	10502	100.0

Sources: Own elaboration with data from the Ministry of Economy (Section I), Nederlandsche Bank and Statistiches Bundesamt (Section II).

(1) Billions of 1980 constant pesetas (1984–1990)

(2) 1989 Position in national currency

Table 3 Technological and commercial advantages of Holland and Germany

	Holland				Germany			
Sectors	(1)	(2)	(3)	(4)	(1)	(2)	(3)	(4)
1. Mining	−	−	+	−	−	−	−	−
2. Gas and Oil refining	+	+	+	−	+	−	−	−
3. Electric power	−	−	−	−	−	−	−	−
4. Basic metallurgy	−	−	−	−	−	−	+	−
5. Non-metallic products manufacturing	−	−	−	−	−	−	−	−
6. Chemical industry								
a. Chemicals (except consumption goods)	−	−	+	+	+	+	+	+
b. User chemistry	+	+	+	−	−	+	+	−
7. Metal products	−	−	−	+	−	−	+	+
8. Mechanical machinery and equipment	−	+	−	−	−	+	+	+
9. Office and computer machinery	+	+	+	−	−	−	−	−
10. Mechanical and electrical machinery and equipment	+	+	−	+	−	−	+	+
11. Vehicle industry	−	−	−	−	−	+	+	+
12. Shipbuilding	+	+		−	−	+		−
13. Other transport material	−	−	−*	−	+	+	−*	−
14. Food, drink and tobacco industry	+	+	+	+	−	−	−	−
15. Textiles	−	−	+	−	+	+	+	−
16. Leather industry	−	−	−	−	+	−	−	−
17. Footwear and clothing industry	−	−	−	−	−	−	−	−
18. Timber and wooden furniture industries	−	−	−	−	−	−	+	−
19. Paper, printing and publishing	−	−	−	−	+	−	−	−
20. Processing of rubber and plastics	−	−	+	−	−	+	+	−
21. Other manufacturing industries	−	−	−	+	−	−	−	+

Source: Own elaboration from OCDE (1992); Buesa (1992); Patel & Pavitt (1991); Soete & Wyatt (1983) and Dunning & Pearce (1985).
(1). technological advantages in spain. estimated with data from the spanish patent office (1967–1986).
(2). international technological advantages. estimated with data from the usa patent office (1963–1988).
(3). commercial specialisation with regard to the oecd countries (1986–1991).
(4). commercial specialisation of country's mncs with regard to the world largest mncs.
*including shipbuilding.
| + | relative advantage
| − | relative disadvantage

commercial specialisation of their main multinationals.[18] All of this serves as an approach to discovering the specific factors of investing country firms which favour their move abroad.

Thus, in the above table it can be seen that Holland bases its technological and commercial strengths on the industries of *oil, end user chemistry, office, electric and electronic machinery*, and *food*. And, in the case of Germany, the advantages are diversified to a greater extent, being located in the sectors of *chemicals, mechanical and electrical machinery and equipment, the car industry, other transport material, textiles, rubber and plastics.*

These profiles, discounting inevitable differences in breakdown, show a fairly general parallel with those for sectoral distribution of Dutch and German investment in Spain. This means that these countries' specific advantages in industries and companies[19] are among the factors spurring investment in Spain, thus verifying — even if on a still rudimentary plane — one of the elements which has been stressed in the theoretical and empirical literature on the internationalisation of production.[20]

The existence of that type of company advantage is not enough to offer a complete explanation of the reasons for its international expansion. As has been mentioned above, the advantages of siting offered by the investment-receiving countries must also be taken into account. In the various works which, both from the theoretical and empirical standpoint, have dealt with this subject (Brooke and Buckley, 1988, Hood and Young, 1990; Buckley 1990), different types of factors impinging on siting decisions of multinational subsidiaries have been indicated. Among them, synthet-

[18] It must be observed that the breakdowns used in the studies which have served as a basis for the preparation of Table 3, differ from each other. Consequently, we have opted for a qualitative presentation of the findings which must be taken as a simple approximation.

[19] It must be underlined that our findings coincide very closely with those obtained for German and Dutch firms by Patel and Pavitt (1991) in their analysis of sectoral distribution of the world's main 660 multinationals.

[20] The recognition of the existence of specific competitive advantages for the firm — the nature of which may be productive, technological, financial, commercial or political — as one of the important factors in explaining international investment, stems from the works of Hymer (1960) and Vernon (1966), as systemized by authors such as Caves (1974) or Lall and Streeten (1977), and incorporated into a broader view — which takes into account the internationalisation of transactions and the theory of the advantages of siting- by authors such as Buckley and Casson (1976), Dunning (1977 and 1988) and Cantwell (1990).

ically, the following can be mentioned:

i) Those relating to the shape of the local market (size, growth potential).
ii) Those referring to availability and cost of factors of production labour, inputs).
iii) The possibilities offered by the host country in vertical integration processes.
iv) Sociopolitical factors (political stability, cultural proximity).

In our case, through the survey carried out among the subsidiaries of Dutch and German multinationals, exploration has been made of the role played by some of these factors in foreign investment processes. This is completed with an analysis of the different ways in which these companies enter the Spanish economy. In Tables 4a and 4b the information recorded in this respect is shown.

As far as the first of these subjects is concerned, the results for the whole of the subsidiaries interviewed show that the most attractive element for investors is the size and characteristics of the domestic market,[21] with aspects relating to the costs of factors of production and those of an institutional nature taking second place. This profile is similar to the one obtained from other recent studies which consider countries with a relatively broad market size[22] (Papanastassiou and Pearce, 1993; Taggart, 1993), but different from what is seen in portugal, where the most important siting factors are labour costs and access to raw materials. (Corado Simoes, 1992).

Nevertheless, the most noticeable trait shown in our results is the strong contrast existing between Dutch and German subsidiaries. Thus, among the former, cost and institutional factors and access to foreign markets are the central elements, while the local market conditions are given low importance. On the contrary, the

[21] Bear in mind that Spain, by size, is fifth among European Union countries. Its GDP, valued at 573.7 thousand million dollars in 1992, represents 8.4 per 100 of the whole of these countries; and its population — 38.9 million inhabitants — 11.9 per 100.

[22] Nevertheless, in these studies the growing importance is shown of accessibility to foreign markets as an important factor in siting. In our case we have noticed this trend in the interviews we have had with directors of some of the subsidiaries analysed.

profile of factors attracting German investors is the opposite, so that, for them, the makeup of the Spanish market is seen to be essential and far above any other cost or institutional consideration.

It is interesting to notice in this respect that German firms show a similar pattern to the one reflected in Robinson and Barber's study on the subsidiaries of American multinationals operating in Spain at the end of the sixties. Furthermore, this pattern is compatible with the results of breakdown studies which have dealt with the question, where emphasis is laid on the crucial role of the size of the domestic market and, in a more secondary fashion, of certain elements of macroeconomic stability, and one can see the slight influence exercised by costs of the labour factor on investment flows (Bajo, 1991; Martinez Serrano and Myro, 1992). Obviously, this compatibility does not exist in the case of Dutch subsidiaries.

All this indicates that, in short, for the same country receiving inward investment, siting factors can play a different role according to the characteristics, experience and culture of the investing companies. With the information we have we cannot go more deeply into this subject; but it can be noted that the presence of German multinationals in Spain has a long tradition- which is not the case with the Dutch- and that between the two of them there are differences regarding the shape of their commercial strategies, as will be shown later.

The existence of different patterns in the siting factors influencing the investment decisions of German and Dutch multinationals is not reflected in the forms that their entry in Spain adopts. These, as is seen in Table 4, are not significantly different from between both groups of firms and, in turn, are similar to those seen in the case of American subsidiaries at the end of the sixties.[23] That supports the idea that, in the choice between starting up a new company or taking over another existing one, there do not seem to be any general rules of conduct, so that each case corresponds to the particular nature of the aims sought by the investors and the particular conditions of the host country (Brooke and Buckley, 1988).

---

[23] The χ^2 test applied on our data and those provided by Robinson and Barber (1971) give as a result a value not significantly different to zero.

Table 4a Factors determining the investment decisions.

	Dutch subsidiaries		German subsidiaries		Total	
Investment factors	Number of Firms *	%	Number of firms *	%	Number of firms *	%
* Labor force costs	20	87.0	34	30.1	54	39.7
* Tax incentives	21	91.3	12	10.6	33	24.3
* Favourable social environment	21	91.3	9	7.9	30	22.1
* Size and features of the Spanish market	3	13.0	97	85.8	100	73.5
* Favourable legal Conditions	20	87.0	3	2.7	23	16.9
* Access to foreign markets	22	95.7	25	22.1	47	34.6
* Others	–	–	14	12.4	14	10.3
Total firms	23	100.0	113	100.0	136	100.0

Source: Own elaboration
*Number of firms which considers positively each factor.

4b Entry forms in the Spanish market.

	Dutch subsidiaries		German subsidiaries		Total	
Forms of entry	Number of Firms	%	Number of firms *	%	Number of firms (1)	%
* Takeovers	8	34.8	53	46.9	61	44.9
* Greenfields	14	60.9	54	47.8	68	50.0
* Not available	1	4.3	2	1.8	3	2.2
Total firms	23	100.0	113	100.0	136	100.0
Chi-cuadrado test: 1.8682		Not significant at 95 %				

Source: Own elaboration
*We have not included four firms acquired through the stock market.

3. COMMERCIAL STRATEGIES OF SUBSIDIARIES LOCATED IN SPAIN

Complete understanding of the internationalisation process requires going beyond internal and external factors for multinational companies which influence their decisions, and making a more profound examination of the strategies employed in countries where their subsidiaries are located. Thus, in this section, we refer to the commercial aspects of those strategies, since, on the basis of them, the role played by these factors can be better understood. Consequently, we attempt to study the commercial behaviour of the subsidiaries, both in the Spanish domestic market and in foreign ones.

Our starting point is the consideration of the commercial orientation of Dutch and German subsidiaries towards both markets. In this respect, the first item of data to be taken into consideration is that, taking as a reference point all these subsidiaries, more than 96 per 100 of Dutch sales are made in Spain, while that percentage falls to 80 per 100 in the case of the Germans. Correlatively, exports represent only 4 per 100 of sales in the former case and 20 per 100 in the latter.[24] There is, therefore, a noticeable difference between both groups of firms, which is also reflected in the results of our survey summarised in Table 5.

Table 5 Sales in the domestic market.

Sales percentages	Dutch subsidiaries		German subsidiaries	
	Number of firms	%	Number of firms	%
100 %	11	47.8	16	14.2
75–99 %	9	39.1	52	46.0
50–74%	2	8.7	24	21.2
1–49%	–	–	21	18.6
Not available	1	4.3	–	–
Total	23	100.0	113	100.0
Chi-cuadrado test: 17.3563		Confidence level = 99.9%		

Source: Own elaboration

It is true that this differentiation does not prevent the majority of the subsidiaries analysed here gearing their commercial activity towards the local market — more intensively in the Dutch case —

[24] *See*, later on, Table 7.

and exports are subordinate. This statement is similar to what has been obtained in other studies where it has been concluded that the commercial strategies of European multinationals, through direct investment abroad, is particularly focused on supplying local markets.[25] And the same occurs in the case of American subsidiaries located in Spain.[26]

In this context, it is of great interest to discover what position is held by the firms analysed within the Spanish market. Their replies to our survey — which are recorded in Table 6 — show that

Table 6 Leading position of foreign subsidiaries

	Dutch Subsidiaries		German subsidiaries	
Position	Number of firms	%	Number of firms	%
First firm of the sector	2	8.7	34	30.1
Among the five firsts	14	60.9	56	49.6
Among the ten firsts	4	17.4	9	8.0
Other positions	2	8.7	12	10.6
Not available	1	4.3	2	1.8
Total	23	100.0	113	100.0

Source: Own elaboration.

around 90% of them claim to be among the top ten in their sector of activity, with the leader position being very frequent, particularly among the Germans. Though this result, due to the characteristics of the sample, may show an upward bias compared to the situation of the whole of the firms making up the group analysed, it leaves no room for doubt that a large number of the multinational subsidiaries enjoy an outstanding competitive position in the domestic market.[27]

---

[25] *See*, among others, the analysis of Franko, (1976).

[26] See Robinson and Barber (1971, page 36). The global exporting propensity of these firms is 10 per 100 of sales. It must be remembered that this work refers to the situation as recorded at the end of the sixties, so it is possible that, at the present time, there has been some modification in the commercial strategy of American subsidiaries

[27] This result is consistent with the estimates of Martinez Serrano and Myro (1992) on the market share of firms with foreign capital share in Spanish

The gearing of these subsidiaries towards the local market – due to the size of the latter and the advantageous position they hold in it – does not rule out relationships with foreign markets, as has been pointed out previously. Consequently, it is now worth analysing how the latter is made up, by making a reference to exporting activities and intergroup trade.

The literature on multinationals has devoted important attention to this question on the basis of a consideration of the existence of imperfections in the markets which give rise to forms of international competition different from those described in the models based on the classical assumptions of the theory of comparative advantages. The most important aspects which have been highlighted in this respect are the following[28]

i) Firstly, there is a difference in conduct among companies controlled by national capital and those with foreign shares, with the latter showing a greater degree of opening up to the outside.
ii) Stemming from the above, multinational groups control an important part of world interchange. And it is characteristic in these to find important commercial relationships involving only the parent company and its subsidiaries; that is, an intergroup trade representing a substantial part of their international trading activity.
iii) As a consequence, these firms' operations must give rise to important effects in the external balance of the countries where they operate. The nature of such effects is not predetermined, it depends on the aims, characteristics and type of activity of the different groups.

In this respect, the distinction established by Kojima (1975 and 1978) is interesting for the distinction made between companies whose subsidiaries are export-oriented, trade oriented – trying to take advantage of the comparative advantages of the country where they are located, and those following the opposite path – anti-trade oriented, whose aims centre on exploiting the

---

industry. This figure in 1990 reached 36.5 per 100 of manufacturing production, but reached more than 50 per 100 in industries such as *electrical and office machinery, electronics, transport material, chemicals, metal products and cork and plastic products.*

[28] For a synthesis of the literature on this subject the work by Alonso and Donoso (1989), ps 149 to 155 can be consulted.

advantages of the parent company within the market where its subsidiaries are situated. Between both extremes one can find intermediate cases and even transitions from one to another over time, depending on the changes in the advantages and institutional conditions of the countries providing and receiving international investment, as well as the corresponding firms.

In the specific case of the Spanish economy, the different studies made on this matter[29] allow emphasis to be made, within a tight synthesis, that even though before the beginning of the sixties the companies with foreign capital showed a clear preference for the domestic market with a lesser tendency to export than companies with national capital, from the mid-sixties onwards, this behaviour showed a radical change. In all studies subsequent to this period not only a higher percentage of foreign sales by multinational subsidiaries but also a greater showing on their part in Spanish exports was observed, so that most of the latter is explained by their activity. Furthermore, there is general agreement that the import propensity of companies with foreign capital is clearly higher than those with national capital. It is likewise observed that the balance of all this leads to worse overseas trade balances, since they are more negative, for the former companies rather than the latter.

So, this is the context in which one must place the analysis of the foreign commercial activities of the subsidiaries of Dutch and German multinationals located in Spain. The basic data for exports[30] are shown in Table 7. With these data it can be shown that the likelihood of exporting is almost the same in both groups – 39 and 36 per 100, respectively- but a consideration of the breakdown stresses that that probability shows a noticeable difference in the different sectors. In general, among German industrial firms there is a higher proportion of exporters than among those with Dutch capital.

Moreover, most of the Dutch subsidiaries operating in overseas markets show very slight exporting propensities, in clear contrast to what happens with German subsidiaries. This is reflected in the

---

[29] See once again the synthesis of Alonso and Donoso (1989), pages 155 to 162.

[30] The primary source for these data is the Censo de Exportadores prepared by the Instituto de Comercio Exterior from Customs information. Therein is recorded all the firms with more than ten million pesetas worth of exports annually, so Table 7 can be regarded with a very small margin of error as a true reflection of exports by the whole of the subsidiaries studied in our investigation.

Table 7 Export activity of Dutch and German subsidiaries

I. Dutch subsidiaries

Sectors	[1] N* of firms	[2] Exporting firms	[2]/[1] %	Firm's distribution according to their propensity to export (Sales percentage): n.a	Up to 10%	from 10 to 20%	More th 20%	[3] Exportation in 1987 (Mill. Pts)	[3] As % of Sales
Industry	64	31	48.4	3	21	2	5	17,719	3.88
– Chemistry	22	9	40.9	1	6	1	1	6,599	5.32
– Metalmechanical, Electrical and transport material	22	13	59.1	–	10	1	2	7,800	3.70
–Other industries	20	9	45.0	2	5	–	2	3,320	2.72
Services	27	3	11.1	–	2	–	1	183	0.12
Other sectors	9	5	55.6	2	2	–	1	1,001	8.07
Total	100	39	39.0	5	25	2	7	18,903	3.04

II. German subsidiaries

Sectors	[1] N* of firms	[2] Exporting firms	[2]/[1] %	Firm's distribution according to their propensity to export (Sales percentage): n.a	Up to 10%	from 10 to 20%	More th 20%	[3] Exportation In 1987 (Mill. Pts)	[3] As % of sales
Industry	327	199	60.9	5	82	36	76	444,966	24.53
– Chemistry	80	51	63.8	29	29	8	11	34,910	8.34
– Metalmechanical, Electrical and transport material	153	99	64.7	2	33	21	43	391,944	33.53
–Other industries	94	49	52.1	–	20	7	22	18,112	7.99
Services	202	31	15.3	1	18	5	7	3,940	1.17
Other sectors	8	5	62.5	2	–	1	2	1,064	21.85
Not available	197	27	13.7	26	–	–	1	5,286	6.17
Total	734	262	35.7	34	100	42	86	455,256	20.32

Source: Own elaboration

global average of sales going to the overseas market which, among the former, hardly exceeds 3 per 100, while, among the latter, it reaches more than 20 per 100. This difference is seen, to a greater or lesser extent, in all the sectors considered.

Nevertheless, though the German subsidiaries are more geared to the international market, this does not mean that their exporting propensity is outstanding in the framework of the Spanish economy. In fact, only a third of them reached a level of overseas sales comparable to the average of Spanish exporting firms,[31] which is explained by their lateness in joining exporting processes, compared to other foreign subsidiaries[32] (Casado, 1992).

To sum up, in the light of the above-mentioned evidence, it can be stated that subsidiaries of Dutch multinationals operating in Spain show an *anti-trade oriented* behaviour, according to Kojima's previously-mentioned classification. This may appear contradictory with the emphasis shown on accessibility to overseas markets and their low valuation of the domestic market, when the factors determining their location are highlighted. But this contradiction is solved, at least in part, if it is borne in mind that a very important part of these firms' activity consists of marketing imported products.[33] Meanwhile, the behaviour of German subsidiaries, more open to overseas markets, though below the average level of companies which are controlled in Spain by foreign capital, may be estimated to be in an intermediate category between the former and Kojima's *trade oriented* classification. Logically, behind these global patterns lurks a wide variety of cases falling between the two extremes, as is shown by the data in Table 7.

Another aspect of exporting where a marked contrast is reflected

---

[31] Though the calculation of the average exporting propensity of Spanish firms with overseas sales is not an easy task, it may be considered that a figure around 25 per 100 constitutes a good approximation if the findings of studies dealing with this subject are taken into account. *See* Maravall and Rodriguez De Pablo (1982) and Alonso and Donoso (1985 and 1989).

[32] For example, by the end of the sixties, 36 per 100 of American multinational subsidiaries located in Spain exported an amount above 20 per 100 of their sales. In this respect see Robinson and Barber (1971), page 50.

[33] From the findings of our survey we calculate that in this group of subsidiaries imports account for half their sales (Buesa and Molero, 1993). in the case of the germans we have not been able to obtain the necessary information to make a similar calculation.

between German and Dutch subsidiaries is that referring to its geographical distribution, as can be seen in Table 8. In fact, the

Table 8 Exports' geographical distribution (in % of exporting firms)

Geographical destination	Dutch subsidiaries	German subsidiaries
Mother house country	10.1	27.8
European union*	24.9	44.7
Other developed countries	1.9	2.3
Developing countries	63.1	25.2
Total	100.0	100.0

Source: Own elaboration
*Except mother house country

latter concentrate their foreign sales in lesser developed countries, having little relationship with those of the European Union and only a very slight one with Holland. On the contrary, German subsidiaries show the opposite profile, so that export operations are centred on the parent company country and the others from the European Union.[34]

The last of the elements related to overseas trade which we are interested in dealing with here, is the one referring to intragroup trade. With regard to this subject, the literature on multinational companies has stressed that exchanges between parents and subsidiaries constitutes one of the essential variables in their commercial strategy, and that its importance has grown as the internationalisation process has progressed.[35] From the empirical standpoint, studies made of the subject have highlighted the following aspects:[36]

i) Firstly, the incidence of intragroup trade on each country's foreign trade is greater in the case of industrialised rather than underdeveloped ones.

[34] Something quite similar was the case at the end of the sixties with American subsidiaries, though in this case exports to the United States were relatively small and those to Europe quite high. See Robinson and Barber (1971).

[35] See for this works by Buckley (1991b), Casson (1986) Caves (1982) and Hood and Young (1990).

[36] See the synthesis made by Van Den Bulcke (1987) in which the aspects listed below are developed.

ii) Secondly, there are significant differences in the use of this type of trade according to the area where the multinationals have their home.

iii) And, finally, intragroup trade depends on the multinational maturity of the parent companies, the level of control of the subsidiaries and the degree of technological complexity of the sector where those firms are operating. Also, economic integration processes favour the growth of this type of trade (Dunning, 1990).

In the case of the subsidiaries of Dutch and German multinationals situated in Spain, the information is available as is shown in Table 9. There it is clearly seen that intragroup trade has grown markedly throughout the second half of the eighties, and this concurs with the results of other recent studies on this topic (Savary, 1992; Van Der Bulcke and Lombard, 1992). this,

Table 9 Intrafirm trade of Dutch and German subsidiaries

I. Exports to other firms of the group (% of the firms)

% Of total exports	Dutch subsidiaries		German subsidiaries	
	1985	1990	1985	1988
0 %	73.9	47.8	14.2	13.3
1–49%	13.0	34.8	27.4	36.3
50–100%	13.0	17.3	23.8	32.7
Not available			34.5	17.7
Total	100.0	100.0	100.0	100.0
Average intragroup trade (in % of exports)	14.1	21.2	24.6	33.2

II. Imports from other firms of the group (% of the firms)

% Of total exports	Dutch subsidiaries		German subsidiaries	
	1985	1990	1985	1988
0 %	39.1	26.1	11.5	10.6
1–49%	30.4	34.8	33.6	32.7
50–100%	30.4	39.1	29.2	34.5
Not available			25.7	22.2
Total	100.0	100.0	100.0	100.0
Average intragroup trade (in % of imports)	34.6	42.7	30.1	33.7

Source: Own elaboration

basically, is explained by the fact that several of these firms were initiated in this type of trade in the above-mentioned period; and, also, because subsidiaries who were already trading with their group further developed their relationship with it. Both reasons may stem from the opening up of the market as a consequence of Spain's entry into the European Community, which would give support to Dunning's (1990) theory on the intensification of intragroup trade in economic integration processes.

Furthermore, it must not be overlooked that among the two groups of subsidiaries we are analysing there are noticeable behaviour differences. Thus, while the Germans head towards standardisation between intragroup rates of exports and imports, the Dutch still have a marked imbalance between both, so that this type of trade is much more important with respect to their imports than to their exports. This reflects the importance for the latter held by the marketing of imported products – as we have indicated above – as well as the different intensity and geographical orientation of the exporting activity of both groups of subsidiaries.

To sum up, though there is not a general pattern delimiting the intensity of intragroup trade, empirical evidence confirms that the strategies of subsidiaries based in Spain is oriented towards a growing commercial integration with the multinational group to which they belong. This integration is, nevertheless, unequal, being more intensive in exports for the Germans than for the Dutch, and more important in imports for the latter than the former.

In conclusion, the findings of our analysis – which are situated in the time horizon of Spain's negotiating and entering the European Community, when the Single Market project was clearly formulated – have shown up the existence of substantially different commercial strategies between the subsidiaries of Dutch and German multinationals based in the country. These results point in the same direction as the works in which the thesis is maintained that the building of the European Single Market will not produce standardisation of company strategies among European firms (Buckley, Pass and Prescott, 1990; Prescott, 1991); and, in turn, contradict the theory that that same Single Market would lead to a reduction in the degrees of multinationality, especially with regard to horizontal integration processes (Itaki and Waterson, 1990/1991).

4. CONCLUSIONS

From the experience of the subsidiaries of German and Dutch multinationals developing their activities in Spain, in this work we have analysed the factors determining the direct investment decisions of these companies and the makeup of their commercial strategies. The results obtained in general fit the theoretical explanations which stress the role played by the specific advantages of investing firms and the advantages of siting for the host countries, in the internationalisation process.

But beyond this generalisation, our study clearly shows that that framework of factors gives rise to different situations between companies. Thus, between Dutch and German multinationals a clear contrast is seen with regard to their valuation of siting factors such as the size and characteristics of the market receiving the investment, the cost conditions prevailing in that market or the institutions to be found there. Our empirical evidence makes it clear that, in this contrast, the influence comes from the investing country, so it could be thought there exist elements of a national character reflected in the cultures and management styles, producing different approaches to internationalisation strategies. However, it may be that that influence is conditioned by the type of competitive advantage developed in each investing country, which becomes specific in the nature of the economic sectors in which the activity of internationalising countries takes place. Given that these sectors differ among themselves in terms of their market structure, the form of their demand and the characteristics of their technology, the national differentiation we have discovered probably hides, at least in part, an intersectoral difference. In any case, due to analytical limitations imposed by the size of the sample we have used, our research has been unable to progress in that field.

Furthermore, we have observed that the differences in the determining factors in investment are not reflected in the ways in which foreign multinationals enter the Spanish market. This occurs, whatever the nationality of the investing firm, particularly through the creation of new firms, though there is also a significant number of takeovers of local firms.

Our analysis has also centred on the makeup of the commercial strategies of the subsidiaries of Dutch and German multinationals located in Spain. In this field we have also found important differences between the two; differences affecting the intensity of their orientation towards the local market — though the latter is always the most important and many of the subsidiaries analysed act to a certain extent as leaders, — the relative volume and geographical distribution of their exports, the size of their intragroup trade and, within this, the imbalance between import and export operations.

To sum up, our research has provided evidence that shows the existence of a noticeable heterogeneity in the strategies of multinational companies. This should be borne in mind by national governments when framing policies to attract international investment, since not all subsidiaries are interwoven in the same way in the local economy and, as a result, their effects on it, whether beneficial or harmful, are not always produced in the same way, nor do they lead to an identical result.

REFERENCES

Alonso, J. and Donoso, V. (1985): *La Empresa Española frente a Iberoamérica y la CEE*. Ed. Cultura Hispónica. Madrid.

Alonso, J. and Donoso, V. (1989): *Características y Estrategias de la Empresa Exportadora Española*. Instituto de Comercio Exterior. Madrid.

Bajo, O. (1991): "Determinantes macroeconómicos y sectoriales de la inversión extranjera directa en España" in *Información Comercial Española*, núms. 696–697. August-September.

Brooke, M. and Buckley, P. (1988) *Handbook of International Trade*. Macmillan Publishers. London.

Buckley, P. (1990) *International Investment*. Gower House. London.

Buckley, P. (1991) "Foreign market servicing strategies and competitiveness: a theoretical framework" in Buckley, P. and Collaborators: *International Business Strategy*. Management Centre. Bradford.

Buckley, P. (1991a) "The foreign investment decision: the motives" in Buckley, P. and Collaborators: *International Business Strategy*. Management Centre. Bradford.

Buckley, P. (1991b) "The role of exporting in the market servicing policies of multinational manufacturing enterprises: theoretical and empirical perspectives" in Buckley, P. and Collaborators.: *International Business Strategy*. Management Centre. Bradford.

Buckley, P. and Casson, M. (1976) *The Future of Multinational Enterprise*. Ed. MacMillan. London.

Buckley, P, Pass, C. and Prescott, K. (1990) "The impact of the Single European Market Act on the foreign market servicing strategies of British manufacturing firms" in *Paper B.A.M./1992-3*. Management Centre. Bradford.

Buesa, M. (1992): "Patentes e innovación tecnológica en la industria española (1967–1986)" in Garcia Delgado, j.: *economía española, cultura y sociedad. homenaje a juan velarde fuertes*. eudema. madrid.

Buesa, M. and Molero, J. (1988) *Estructura Industrial de España.* Fondo de Cultura Económica. Madrid.

Buesa, M. and Molero, J. (1993) *Estrategias de las Empresas de Capital Extranjero en España. El caso de las filiales de multinacionales holandesas.* Mimeo. Instituto de Análisis Industrial y Financiero. Complutense University. Madrid.

Cantwell, J. (1990) "The growing internationalization of industry: a comparison of the changing structure of company activity in the major industrialized countries" in Webster, A. and Dunning, J. (Eds.): *Structural Change in the World Economy.* Routledge. London.

Cantwell, J. (1992) *Multinational Investment in Modern Europe. Strategic Interaction in the Integrated Community.* Edward Elgar. Aldershot.

Carrascosa, A. (1991) "Notas sobre el origen geográfico de la inversión extranjera directa en España" in *Revista de Economía, núm. 9.*

Casado, M. (1992): *Las Estrategias de las Empresas Multinacionales en España dentro del Nuevo Espacio Económico Europeo: el caso de las filiales alemanas.* Ph.D.dissertation. Faculty of Economics. Complutense University. Madrid.

Casson, M. (1986) *Multinational and World Trade.* George Allen & Unwin. London.

Caves, R. (1974) "The causes of direct investment: Foreign firms share in Canadian and U.K. manufacturing industries". *Review of Economics and Statistics,* núm. 56.

Caves, R. (1982) *Multinational Enterprise and Economic Analysis.* Cambridge University Press.

Corado Simoes, V. (1992) "European integration and the pattern of FDI inflow in Portugal" in Cantwell, J.: *Multinational Investment in Modern Europe. Strategic Interaction in the Integrated Community.* Edward Elgar. Aldershot.

Dunning, J. (1977) "Trade, location of economic activity and the MNE: a search for an eclectic approach" in Ohlin, B.; Hesselborn, P. and Wijkman, P. (Eds.): *The International Allocation of Economic Activiy.* Macmillan. London.

Dunning, J. (1988) *Explaining International Production.* Unwin Hyman. London.

Dunning, J. (1990) "Changes in the level and structure of international production: the last one hundred years" in Buckley, P. (Ed.): *International Investment.* Gower House. London.

Dunning, J. and Cantwell, J. (1987) *Directory of Statistics of International Investment and Production.* Macmillan. London.

Dunning, J. and Pearce, R. (1985) *The World's Largest Industrial Enterprises 1962–1983.* Gower Publishing. Hants.

Franko, L. (1976) *The European Multinationals.* Harper & Row. London.

Hood, N. and Young, S. (1990) *The Economics of Multinational Enterprise.* Longman. London.

Hymer, S. (1960) "The international operations of national firms: a study of direct foreign investment". Ph.D. dissertation, Masachusetts Institute of Technology. MIT, Masachusetts.

Iranzo, S. (1991) "Inversión extranjera directa: una estimación de la aportación real y financiera de las empresas extranjeras en España" in *Información Comercial Española,* num. 696–697. August–September.

Itaki, M. and Waterson, M. (1990) "European multinationals and 1992". *Discussion Papers in International Investment and Business Studies.* Series B. Vol. III. Reading University.

Kojima, K. (1975) "International Trade and Foreign Investment: Substitutes or Complements". *Hitosubashi Journal of Economics*, vol. 16.

Kojima, K. (1978) *Direct Foreign Investment: A Japanese Model of Multinational Business Operations*. Croom Helm. London.

Lall, S. and Streeten, P. (1977) *Foreign Investment, Transnationals and Developing Countries*. Ed. MacMillan. London.

Maravall, F. and Rodriguez De Pablo, J. (1982) *Exportación y Tamaño de las Empresas Industriales Españolas*. Instituto de la Pequeña y Mediana Empresa Industrial. Madrid.

Martinez Serrano, J. and Myro, R. (1992) "La penetración del capital extranjero en la industria española" *in Moneda y Crédito*, núm. 194.

Muñoz, J., Roldan, S. and Serrano, A. (1978) *La Internacionalización del Capital en España*. Edicusa. Madrid.

OECD (1992) *Foreign Trade by Commodities*. Volumes 1, 2 and 5. Paris.

Papanastassiou, M. and Pearce, R. (1993) "Global innovation strategies of MNE's and European integration: the role of regional R&D facilities" in Corado Simoes, V. (Ed).: *International Business and Europe after 1992*. EIBA 19th Annual Conference. Lisbon.

Patel, P. and Pavitt, K. (1991) "The innovative performance of the world's largest firms: some new evidence" in *Economics of Innovation and New Technology*.

Patel, P. and Pavitt, K. (1991a) "Large firms in the production of the world's technology: an important case of non-globalisation" in *Journal of International Business Studies*, vol. 22. num. 1.

Prescott, K. (1991) *Restructuring of European Business after 1992*. European Economic Integration Papers. Management Centre. Bradford.

Robinson, H. and Barber, B. (1971) *Las Inversiones Norteamericanas en el Desarrollo de España*. Stanford Research Institute y Cámara de Comercio Americana en España. Madrid.

Savary, J. (1992) "Cross-investments between France and Italy and the new European strategies of industrial groups" in Cantwell, J.: *Multinational Investment in Modern Europe. Strategic Interaction in the Integrated Community*. Edward Elgar. Aldershot.

Soete, L. and Wyatt, (1983) "The use of foreign patenting as an internationally comparable science and technology output indicator" in *Scientometrics*, vol. 5. num. 1.

Taggart, J. (1993) *Strategic Conflict in the MNE: Parent and Subsidiary*. EIBA 19th. Annual Conference. Lisbon.

Vanp Den Bulcke, D. (1987) "El comercio intra-empresa en las empresas multinacionales" in *Información Comercial Española*, núm. 643. March.

Van Der Bulcke, D. and Lombaerde, P. (1992) "The Belgian metalworking industries and the large European internal market: the role of multinational investment" in Cantwell, J.: *Multinational Investment in Modern Europe. Strategic Interaction in the Integrated Community*. Edward Elgar. Aldershot.

Vernon, R. (1966): "International investment and international trade in the product cycle" In *Quarterly Journal of Economics*, núm. 80. May.

Yannopoulos, G. (1992) "Multinational corporations and the Single European Market" in Cantwell, J.: *Multinational Investment in Modern Europe. Strategic Interaction in the Integrated Community*. Edward Elgar. Aldershot.

Technological Strategies of MNCs in Intermediate Countries: The Case of Spain

José Molero, Mikel Buesa and Montserrat Casado[1]

I. INTRODUCTION

The phenomenon of increasing technological activity internationalization is one of the most frequently discussed within the current literature of Multinational Corporations (MNCS). In fact, it is part of a more general trend of a new and growing role of subsidiary companies within the MNCS to which they belong (Dunning, 1994; Granstrand et al, 1993; Papanastassiou & Pearce, 1993; Cantwell, 1993). In spite of the intensity of the debate the complexity of the process makes it very difficult to understand its meaning globally. Our doubts are centred on two main aspects. first, how new is the internationalization of r&d and how extended is it nowadays and, second, what are the causes explaining this process, whatever its extent is?

There is a relatively admitted approach which emphasizes the novelty of the phenomenon. Thus, until the 1970's MNCS had a very concentrated organization of R&D within parent firms headquarters. However, in the last twenty years we have witnessed a rapid development of R&D internationalization through the

---

[1] A previous version of the paper was presented by José Molero in the 19th Annual Conference of the European International Business Association. Lisbon, December, 1993.

establishing of MNCS' laboratories in an increasing number of countries. Nevertheless, recent research results (Cantwell, 1993a) have shown neither that the process is so new nor the growth of the last decades is so general.

As far as the extension of the process is concerned, after initial views which saw the internationalization of technological activity as a consolidated part of the general process of globalization (Howell, 1990; OECD, 1992), a growing number of empirical studies offer results which allow us to put it in a more balanced context (Patel & Pavitt, 1991a; Patel, 1993; Cantwell, 1993a; Dunning, 1994). Thus, considering the existence of different stages on the way towards globalization, there is strong support for confirming the global exploitation of technology and only partial and less conclusive evidence in favour of the existence of global technological collaboration. The importance of global generation of technology – the last grade – is much less according to the evidence which underlines the crucial role of the national systems of innovation. (Archibugy & Michie, 1993).

The theoretical explanation of the process is still weak. The starting point is the analysis of the forces which press for keeping the production of technology centralized and other ones pushing it into a more decentralized and international framework (Granstrand et al 1993). The first group includes the following: a) the companies' need to protect firm-specific technologies; b) the existence of significant scale economies in R&D and the difficulties of reaching "critical mass" in decentralized laboratories; c) the role played by home market conditions in creating and maintaining firm specific technological advantages and d) the wish to minimize coordination and control costs.

On the other side of the balance there are also reasons for decentralizing the technology-creation mechanism (Cantwell & Hodson, 1991; Pearce & Sight, 1991). Dunning (1994) has summarized them in four types: i) product, material or process adaptations or improvements, which include a very important process of evolving from technical support activities into proper development projects (Granstrand et al, 1993); ii) basic material or product research, usually undertaken for two reasons: the immobility of such a kind of resources and the need for continual testing and interaction with customers; iii) research for rationalizing or cost minimizing productions and iv) to acquire or gain an insight into foreign innovating activities. This last point basically affects to R&D extension to countries belonging to the "Triade" (Patel, 1993, Dunning, 1994).

From another point of view, the literature highlights the existence of task division among parent companies and affiliated companies (Pearce & Sight, 1991; Pearce & Satwinder, 1992; Häkanson, 1991; Von Boehmer 1991; Molero & Buesa, 1993). thus, basic research is almost exclusively done in parent company laboratories; applied research for obtaining new product and processes is shared many times, although there is a clear imbalance in favour of headquarters' installations. finally, the activities related to the improvement or adaptation of products and processes are also shared between central and subsidiary firms, albeit with an increasing presence of the latter.

A previous work (Molero & Buesa, 1993), dealt with the technological component of MNC strategies operating in Spain. Within a framework made up from the new theory of technological change (Dosi et al, 1988; Freeman, 1990) and new developments of technological competition of MNCS (Cantwell, 1988; Chesnais, 1991), we studied the behaviour of German industrial subsidiaries (GS) operating in Spain throughout the period of its integration in the EEC.

The main results can be summarized in two points. First, GS have a significant technological activity in Spain which obliges us to avoid any identification of the Spanish case with others the literature relates to less developed countries (LDCS). This activity in turn has two features which are worthy of comment. On the one hand, it is higher than what can be seen in current Spanish firms; this result contradicts other findings available for more advanced countries (Dunning, 1994). On the other hand, it is lower than technological tasks carried on by other GS in more developed markets (Wortman, 1991). Thus the denomination of "Intermediate case" seems to be very adequate for describing the Spanish position. Nevertheless, the globalization thesis is of little help, at least in its most extreme form.

Additionally, the fact was highlighted that there is a great variety of behaviours. So, after a complex taxonomy effort, a map was drawn including cases from "Passive adaptation" to "Partial Technology Autonomy" types of subsidiaries. However we did not find any example of Spanish subsidiaries entering into high level research activity.[2]

The aim of this paper is to improve our knowledge about the weight MNCS have in the Spanish Innovation System and the strategies they pursue. Besides this, there is the intention of contributing to the open debate about MNCS' role in the international creation and diffusion of technology.

For these purposes we have new evidence coming from newly available statistics and later pieces of research completed in recent months. The first one deals with Dutch subsidiaries (DS) established in Spain. Here we have followed the same methodology used for GS investigation. The comparison of the two cases will allow us to know whether GS were special cases or not.

In spite of the accumulation of recent research, there is still scarce evidence on the influence of MNCS international activity upon the host economies (Cantwell, 1993a; Dunning, 1994). The second work is a contribution to this debate. It refers to technological regimes (Orsenigo, 1989; Malerba & Orsenigo, 1991) followed by MNCS doing technological innovation in Spain in relation to Spanish innovative firms.[3] The similarities and differences which can be found, will highlight their influence on the Spanish Innovation System.

II. GENERAL CONSIDERATIONS ABOUT TECHNOLOGICAL ACTIVITIES OF MNCS IN SPAIN

Before entering the core of the discussion, it is useful to draw a brief contextual panorama concerning MNCS' activity from a historical perspective.

We can consider three stages in recent times. The first goes from the 1950's until 1974/5 and is characterized by having one of the highest rates of growth of the OECD. The second can be defined as a transition period and lasts until the mid-eighties, when Spain entered the EEC. The last one is still alive and represents the end of the opening up process of our economy.

During the first stage the MNCS' technological activity was

[2] In fact, from 20 German parent companies which answered our questionnaires, no one said their Spanish subsidiary did basic or advanced research.

[3] It comes from full research carried out about innovative firms in the Madrid region the main results of which have been published in Buesa & Molero, 1992.

fundamentally the importation of multiple production and organization technologies for exploiting their firm's advantages and two basic local factors;[4] first, the possibilities of a rather large and growing market very closed to foreign trade. Secondly, the availability of a cheap labour force hitherto accumulated in an extremely backward agriculture.

Thus technology transfer was very active both through embodied (capital good importation, direct investment) and disembodied forms (licences, technical assistance). As in others' experiences, this had a positive balance if we look at its incidence on Spanish productive firms and different negative consequences if we consider direct and indirect costs (payments, abusive clauses, etc). About the activity developed in Spain, they carried out very little research, so the repercussion on the Spanish research system was poor.[5]

In the transition stage, the international transformations we witnessed had a peculiar development in Spain as a consequence of its integration into the EEC.

With regard to technological development, there was an increasing awareness of our important international backwardness. It led to the first serious political actions in this field, such as the creation of the Centro Para el Desarrollo Tecnologico e Industrial (CDTI) in 1977.

In this context, MNCS' activity underwent significant changes. After a short period of FDI stagnation — due to the instability of the political transition — foreign investments continued growing at a very rapid rate. Of course it was due, principally, to MNCS' renewed action. To explain it we need to consider a twofold argument. On the one hand, the profound need Spain had to reorganize its economy to compete better in the new international economy. It made many existing firms seek outside collaboration. On the other hand, the interest of many MNCS in reinforcing (or starting) their presence before Spanish entry into the EEC.

From a strategic point of view, one must underline the shift of many MNCS to a more active exporting role. It demanded significant changes in laws regarding their relationships with local firms and new decisions about technological activities developed

---

[4] Among others the following works can be consulted: Muñoz, Roldan & Serrano, 1978; Buesa & Molero, 1988.

[5] This was dealt with in Molero, 1983.

in Spain. In fact, in the mid-1980's MNCS had a crucial weight in most technological indicators such as R&D, external payments or the introduction of innovations (Molero, 1992).

We arrive at the present phase in which the integration of the Spanish economy to the international economy is very progressive. As in most cases, it assumed a liberal orientation of the economic policy which, among other things, implied a strong accent on the role played by foreign investments in restructuring our productive system. Moreover in these years, we witnessed very dynamic changes of the internationalization process; one of the most outstanding being the new international distribution of MNCS technological activities (Casson, 1991, Cantwell, 1993).

It is in this complex and changing scenario that we have to place our analysis of MNCS' technological strategy in Spain.

III. BEHAVIOUR AND TECHNOLOGICAL STRATEGIES OF MNCS IN THE SPANISH ECONOMY

In order to understand correctly the technological activity of MNCS operating in Spain, we need to have an approach to the importance they have in the Spanish Innovation System. We also should know the extent to which they participate in the international division of technical change.

Regarding the first point, we have summarized in Table 1 the basic data coming from official Spanish R&D statistics. There you can see the very central position MNCS have within our R&D system. They carry out more than 40% of total entrepreneurial activity and – more important – they contribute with more than 53% of total firms' resources.[6]

The same source allows us to add two qualitative complements. First, the share of MNCS in Spanish official aids to support R&D is very reduced, contrasted wiht their R&D activity. In fact they receive about 11% of public administration funds. Consequently, the origin of MNCS' R&D financial resources has a distinct composition from that corresponding to Spanish firms. While the last group contributes about 70% of the resources they manage, and receive around 20% from the administration, foreign firms'

[6] In these estimates we have put together firms with a majority of foreign capital and those "controlled" by foreign capital, which means adding a group of firms with foreign investment between 20% and 50% of their share capital.

Table 1 Sharing of firms, classified on their level of foreign penetration and different indicators of R&D

Types of firms conform their grade of participation of foreign capital	Sharing in total R&D expenditures of firms	Sharing in the funds proceeding from the public administration	Sharing in the contribution in R&D of funds of business enterprises
Without foreign capital	45.21	75.71	43.22
Foreign participation <20%	11.83	13.27	3.48
Foreign participation 20% < 50%	4.22	4.21	4.67
Foreign participation > 50%	38.73	6.81	48.62
Total	100.0	100.0	100.0

Source: Elaborated by the authors with dates of the INE (1993)

self-financing goes up to more than 90% and they only receive marginal help from the Spanish administration (INE, 1993). From the output point of view, all available evidence confirms the higher performance of the MNCS subsidiaries in comparison to the Spanish firms (Molero, 1992). Interestingly the stricter is the concept the higher is the position of MNCS in relation to Spanish firms.

Although there are no statistics of R&D internationalization, several studies have tried to produce some basic data (Warrant, 1991; Cantwell, 1991). Unfortunately the number of experiences developed in Spain make it included in groups like "other countries" or "rest of Europe". One of the few exceptions is the study by Warrant (1991) which takes information from the leading industrial groups of most developed countries. About the Spanish position, two facts summarize it. On the one hand, there is no significant Spanish firm's laboratory outside Spain. On the other hand, the number of R&D centres other MNCS have established in Spain is very limited, less than 2% of the total.

The next step is to analyze the strategy followed by MNCS in Spain. Although the samples of firms we are going to use only refer to German and Dutch subsidiaries, we think they can cast light on the general situation because both Germany and Netherlands have been very active countries in FDI in Spain in recent years (Molero & Buesa,1993; Buesa & Molero, 1993).

Table 2 Origin of the technology used by MNCS' subsidiaries in Spain (% of total*)

	Product technology		Process Technology	
	German Firms	Dutch Firms	German Firms	Dutch Firms
Developed by subsidiary in Spain	46.9	30.4	54.0	43.5
Acquired from other Spanish companies	6.2	0.0	3.5	0.0
Imported from parent company	68.1	73.9	60.2	52.2
Imported from other foreign company	10.6	4.3	12.5	4.3
Data not available	2.7	0.0	4.4	0.0

* They are not exclusive percentages, so vertical additions do not equal 100
Source: Molero & Buesa, 1993 and own elaboration

The starting point in our research was to know the origin of the products those companies commercialize. An initial approach gives the impression there is a difference between DS and GS behaviour because while 70% of DS claims to develop partially or totally their products in Spain, only 40% of GS answer in the same way. Nonetheless, an in-depth analysis leads us to the conclusion that, regardless of the number of participants, most are in a minority position and only about 20% share a significant part of the total.[7]

This position of Spanish subsidiaries has its reflection in the origin of their production technologies. In fact, as Table 2 shows, the parent companies are the main suppliers of product technology. As far as process technology is concerned, the position is more balanced between parent companies and subsidiaries. That close technological relationship is not extended to firms outside the group. It is especially true with regard to other Spanish firms and a little more pronounced in the case of DS. Both distributions show a similar general pattern of technological acquisition.

There is a majority of Spanish subsidiaries which do not develop R&D programmes. Nonetheless, as Table 3 shows, the

[7] In DS, 4.3% of the firms declare an exclusive participation and other 17.4% participate with more than 50%. The figures are similar in GS: 6.6% and 17.% respectively.

Table 3 R&D Activity of MNCS' subsidiaries in Spain (% of total*)

	German firms	Dutch firms
A) Companies carrying out R & D programmes	44.2	43.5
B) Distribution of companies carrying out R & D programmes on the basis of turnover allotted to its financing (total = 100)		
Less than 0.5% of sales	12.0	20.0
Between 0.5% and 2% of sales	62.0	60.0
Between 2% and 5% of sales	22.0	20.0
More than 5% of sales	4.0	0.0

* They are not exclusive percentages, so vertical additions do not equal 100
Source: Molero & Buesa, 1993 and own elaboration

number of firms with this sort of task is not negligible: in both cases it is close to 44% of the corresponding samples.

The financial effort of most of them is established between 0.5% and 2% of sales volume. Only in about 20% of the cases do the resources devoted to R&D exceed 2% of the sales. The estimated average level of effort is 1.86% of sales volume for GS and a little lower for DS: 1.5%. In both cases, it is clearly superior to the average behaviour of local firms (Buesa & Molero, 1993; Molero & Buesa, 1993). however we do not see a parallel higher level of resources as far as personnel is concerned; in fact, the relative research teams have a position similar to the spanish companies. combining the two elements we arrive at the conclusion that mncs' subsidiaries usually make more intensive research effort compared with spanish firms.

In cases for which there are available comparative data, we have proved that effort is significantly lower than that of other subsidiaries in most advanced counties (Wortman, 1991). This is one of those results which enables us to reach the conclusion about the intermediate character of the Spanish position in the recent international division of technology creation. About R&D objectives, both studies show a very similar pattern followed by DS and GS;[8] the highest emphasis is put on product development and improvement while other tasks related to process technologies or

[8] This is confirmed through an χ^2 test between the two distributions; it reaches a value of 0.4634 and is not different from zero at 95% of confidence; See Buesa, Molero, 1993.

imported technology adaptation occupy secondary positions.

The last group of questions we have explored deals with some technological results of the firms. We have used two indicators: one about the rate followed for innovation introduction and the other related to technology exports.

The "effective innovation introduction" refers to new products and processes incorporated by the firms. The way to approach the importance of such changes is through the weight those shifts have on the final output of the company.

Table 4 summarizes the results obtained for GS and DS, together with others coming from similar studies carried out for other Spanish groups.

As can be seen, both GS and DS are quite active in introducing products and processes. DS are even more dynamic, which puts

Table 4 Innovations introduction of different groups of firms with residence in Spain (Percentages)

	Product innovation				Process innovation			
Groups of firms	A	B	C	D	A	B	C	D
Dutch firms (23)	91.3	56.4	60.4	60.4	73.9	47.8	60.7	60.7
German Firms (113)	82.3	20.4	30.2	34.8	78.8	17.7	27.6	32.9
Large Spanish firms (439)	44.4	16.9	21.7	37.5	30.1	na	na	na
- Multinationals (136)	61.8	27.6	30.3	41.5	38.3	na	na	na
- Public Enterprises (57)	33.3	12.3	17.3	37.4	24.6	na	na	na
- Spanish private enterprises (246)	37.4	12.2	17.3	34.0	26.8	na	na	na
Innovative firms of Madrid	91.4	50.7	53.4	55.7	63.6	36.4	52.2	56.0
Firms of the Bask Country (484)	36.3	na	na	na	19.0	na	na	na

Source: Own elaboration with data of our own questionnaires (dutch firms); Molero y Buesa (1993) (german firms); Circulo de Empresarios (Large Spanish Firms); Buesa & Molero (1992) (Innovative firms of Madrid) and IKEI (1990) Firms of the Bask Country.
A: Firms that have introduced some product (process) in the last 5 years
B: Firms for which the new products (processes) are involved in more than 50% of the sales.
C: Estimation of the sales of firms (or products produced by new processes) in relation with the sales of the total group of firms (excluded firms of which the data are not available)
D: Estimation of the sales of new products (or products produced by new processes) in relation to the sales of the innovative firms of each group of firms
** Data of each group of firms are not strictly comparable with the rest because they refer to the firms who are considering their products are innovative or that are using innovative processes on a significant way
** The numbers in parenthesis are the number of the firms of each group of firms

them in a very different position among all studied cases.

From a general point of view, two features summarize the behaviour of our two samples. First, they confirm the greater technological activity of MNCS in comparison to large Spanish firms. Secondly, DS and GS behave very similarly to most active Spanish companies.

One must be cautious in drawing conclusions. In fact we think a twofold interpretation can be proposed. On the one hand, those results confirm the crucial role of MNCS in the current technological pattern. On the other hand, one must emphasise that the consequences for the Spanish system of innovation are different, depending on the way in which innovations are produced. If the Spanish subsidiary only plays a passive role in incorporating product or process innovations, the faster dynamism they present can have a much lower impact on our technological capabilities than the one derived from a local activity even though it is slower.

In spite of the basic similarities we have commented on, there are some by no means negligible differences between both collectives regarding their degree of innovativeness. This could be difficult to understand after knowing the similarities about technological resources. Nonetheless, although available data are not enough to make a final interpretations of these differences, We think they confirm the non-linear character of innovation.

Therefore we suggest three arguments to explain the differences we have pointed out.

1) The sectoral distribution of the firms which directly affects technological opportunities and their degree of appropriability.
2) The technological strategies adopted by firms that may belong to the same sector.[9]
3) The propensity to import. Because through imports some products or processes not available from inside the firm can be incorporated.

The second results indicator deals with technology exportation. In both samples data show a marginal role of this activity in DS

---

[9] In a previous work (Molero & Buesa, 1993) this aspect was confirmed for german subsidiaries. however there are no similar observations for dutch companies.

and GS. Less than 10% in both cases claim to export some technological inputs or services.

In explaining that behaviour we cannot use the argument of the low technological level of the firms, as can be the case for most national companies (Buesa & Molero, 1992; Sanchez & Vicens 1991). Rather we have to consider the link with the parent company and the role it assigns to Spanish affiliated companies. However, there are some results of GS to lead us to assert sometimes that their technological level is inferior compared to other firms of the same international group (Molero & Buesa, 1993). Moreover, the little exporting they do mostly consists of technical assistance, usually admitted as of lower level than licences or patents.

To finish this section we want to make some comments on the typology we made for delving deeper into the GS variety. It was possible because we had regular information from a substantial number of parent companies which not only complemented information coming from our questionnaires and interviews, but also help us in qualifying the answers of the subsidiaries (Molero & Buesa, 1993).

We took into account the following set of data:

First, the degree of internationalization of subsidiary production. We approached it through the company participation in the production of the group, complemented by considerations on the technological level of the company and the origin of the technology they use; see lines 1 to 4 of table 5.

Secondly, we used data on the company dynamism in incorporating new products and processes. As table 5 shows (*see* line 5), there is a sort of inverse relationship between the speed of innovation incorporation and the technological effort made by the subsidiary.

The third element refers to market positions, either domestic markets or exports (*see* lines 6 and 7 of Table 5). The outstanding relation arises between the rate of new incorporations and domestic market positions. The higher the first, the lower is the second.

Adding other complementary information, we reach a taxonomy in which three basic traits can be outlined.

One is the very particular case of subsidiaries having a Partial Technology Autonomy; any attempt at analysisng them as homo-

Table 5 Taxonomy of subsidiaries' technological behaviour

	Type of subsidiary				
	Passive adaptation (PA)	Active adaptation (AA)	Technological collaboration (TC)	Partial technology autonomy (PTA)	
				A	B
Technological level plant	Low	Average	High	Average	High
Source of technology	Parent	Mixed	Parent	Parent	Own
R & D	No	Poor	Average	No	High
Share group production	Low	Average	Average	Low	Very high
Rate of novelties incorporation	High	Average	Low	Low	Very high
Local market position	Low	Average	High	Average	High
Exporting propensity	Average	Average	Low	Average	High
Model sector	Automobile Auxiliary	Vehicle Engines	Electrical material Metal Products	Particular Cases	

A: Characteristics corresponding to the company as a whole.
B: Characteristics corresponding to the product(s) of exclusive responsibility
Source: Own elaboration

geneous totality is condemned to misunderstand their complex position.

A second basic trait is reflected in the Passive Adaptation type. They operate on the basis of an external flow which allows them to incorporate innovation rapidly. Nevertheless, the technological level and effort are low. Thus, in spite of the possibility of new incorporations, their market positions are modest in comparison to that of other subsidiaries.

Finally, the greater the technological effort and level, the higher is the participation in group activities and the stronger are the market shares.

IV. MNCS' TECHNOLOGICAL REGIMES AND DOMESTIC CONSEQUENCES

Having studied the basic features of their strategies, we are now going to analyze MNCS activity from the point of view of the internal organization of technology creation. It is a more qualitative approach based on the notion of "technological regime". This concept refers to a specific combination of particular knowledge bases, sources and degrees of technological opportunities, conditions of appropriability, and forms and degrees of technological advances" (Orsenigo, 1989).

The empirical source is a research into Madrid innovative firms, carried out in 1992 (Buesa & Molero, 1992). It dealt with 151 companies having different external signs of making technical innovation.[10] There are 27 of those firms whose control is in foreign hands; the rest are controlled by national persons or groups. So, we have made a systematic comparison between the two groups in order to establish whether they behave within the same pattern in relation to the following topics.

Sectoral distribution and size
Export orientation
Ways and means of acquiring technological inputs from other sources
Ways of creating own technological resources

[10] Among them, three very fundamental ones were: to do R&D programmes; to patent and to be included in some of the administration programmes for supporting firm's innovations. For more details see Buesa & Molero, 1992.

Product and process innovation incorporation
Technological level in relation to national or foreign competitors
Technology transfer to other firms
Forms of protecting technological knowledge
R&D activity, including intensity, types and organization

Before presenting the outstanding findings we want to highlight two general characteristics of them. First, the number of foreign firms is not enough to make a sectoral analysis. If sectorial distributions of national and foreign samples are not similar,[11] it is possible that some of the differences to be shown respond to distinct sectorial implantation.

On the other hand, in most aspects the corresponding behaviour presents a great similarity; thus, the contrasts we can establish are based on qualitative shades of a relatively similar pattern. We ought to keep in mind that the two samples are subgroups of a common population formed with firms whose basic characteristic is to be innovative agents.[12]

There are two other structural features which can influence global conduct. One is the size of the firms which shows a systematic advantage for foreign firms in comparison with the Spanish ones: in her group, firms of over 200 workers represent 32.8% of the total, while in the former it reaches 48.1%. On the contrary, small firms — below 50 employees — are 46.8% of the Spanish group and only 18.5% of the multinational one.

The second is the degree of external opening up. In the Spanish group, nearly one third (33.1%) do not export anything, while it falls to 11.1% in the foreign group. Firms with high propensity to export (exports to be more than 25% of sales) are more frequent within multinational subsidiaries — 37% — than in Spanish companies — 16.9%.[13]

Therefore, foreign firms are usually larger and export more and their presence is more frequent in branches such as Pharmacy,

---

[11] The χ^2 test allows us to accept the independence of the samples with 90% of confidence.

[12] It is important because there is a great deal of evidence showing foreign firms are substantially different from Spanish-owned ones if we consider all sorts of firms. See, among others, Buesa & Molero,1988 and Duran, 1990.

[13] For these two questions χ^2 values allow us to accept the independence of both distributions with 95% confidence.

Transport Material, Metallurgy and Chemicals.

Going into technological aspects, Table 6 shows subsidiaries have higher dependency on external sources for their technological development, above all as far as product technology is concerned. It is reflected in two different data: the lower number of exclusive own developments and the lower proportion of joint developments in which local firms have a predominant position over outside collaborators. The combination of both elements is included in the global autonomy index.

Tables 7 and 8 link the results of the sources and instruments the firms use in acquiring those technological inputs they do not produce by themselves.

Regarding the sources, the expected difference is the higher importance of group's firms in providing technology for MNCS' subsidiaries. Spanish firms are usually much less integrated in international or national groups, so this source has a quite minor significance.

On the contrary, MNCS subsidiaries work less frequently with Spanish engineering firms and other international companies operating in the same branch. As was highlighted in the previous section, it confirms the closed strategy follow by MNCS' in Spain

Table 6 Origin of the technology used by firms (in %)

	National control		Foreign control		Total	
	Technology of		Technology of		Technology of	
Origin	Product	Process	Product	Process	Product	Process
Not available	4.8	26.2	11.1	11.1	6.0	23.8
OD. Own development	53.2	37.9	37.9	44.4	50.3	39.1
EA. External acquisition	4.8	4.0	3.7	7.4	4.6	4.6
Both:						
OD>EA	24.2	15.3	18.5	14.8	23.2	15.2
OD = EA	6.5	10.5	3.7	3.7	6.0	9.3
OD<EA	6.5	5.6	25.9	18.5	9.9	7.9
ITA: Indicator Technological Autonomy	80.1	76.4	66.7	69.8	77.8	75.0

Source: Own elaboration
The Indicator of Technological Autonomy (ITA) is constructed with data of the firms for which the information is available. The values come from the following formula: ITA = OD + 0.75 (OD>EA) + 0.50 (OD = EA) + 0.25 (OD<EA) The values will rang between 100 (Maximum Autonomy) and O (Absolute dependency)

Table 7 Modalities of acquisition of external technology

	National	Control			Foreign	Control			Total			
	Spanish Agents		Foreign Agents		Spanish Agents		Foreign Agents		Spanish Agents		Foreign Agents	
Technology Acquisited	Firm	IE	Firm	IE	Firm	IE	Firm	IE	Firm	IE	Firm	IA
Clients or users	12.9	0.18	8.1	0.11	14.8	0.15	14.8	0.07	13.2	0.17	9.3	0.11
Suppliers of equipment	16.9	0.18	22.6	0.26	14.8	0.22	25.9	0.30	16.6	0.19	23.2	0.27
Other suppliers	4.0	0.02	7.3	0.06	11.1	0.11	18.5	0.00	5.3	0.04	9.3	0.05
Engineering firms	9.7	0.10	15.3	0.17	11.1	0.04	18.5	0.18	9.9	0.08	15.9	0.17
Other firms of the groups	7.3	0.11	6.5	0.08	14.8	0.22	55.6	0.96	8.6	0.13	15.2	0.24
Other firms of the sector	4.8	0.02	13.7	0.19	7.4	0.04	18.5	0.07	5.3	0.03	14.6	0.17

Source: Own elaboration
Firm: % of firms that are using this kind of modality
IE: Indicator of Evaluation elaborated by the following formula:

$$IA = (FP/100) * (1 + VI - NVI)$$

In which VI refers to the firms who are considering as Very Important the corresponding modality and NVI refers to the firms that are considering it as Not Very Important. So VI and NVI are expressing in decimals about the total of firms that are using each modality. The value will variate between a maximum of 2 (When all the firms are using a modality and appreciating it like very important) and a minimum of 0 (When none of de firms are using a modality or if they are using it but all the firms are appreciating it as not very important)

Table 8 Instruments used by the technology acquisition from other firms

	National	Control			Foreign	Control			Total			
	Spanish Agents		Foreign Agents		Spanish Agents		Foreign Agents		Spanish Agents		Foreign Agents	
Instruments	Firm	IE	Firm	IE	Firm	IE	Firm	IE	Firm	IE	Firm	IE
Patent license	1.6	0.00	14.5	0.19	7.4	0.07	37.0	0.44	2.6	0.01	18.5	0.24
License for other elements of industrial ownership	0.8	0.00	12.1	0.13	3.7	0.07	14.8	0.15	1.3	0.01	12.6	0.13
Technical assistance	6.5	0.05	13.7	0.11	7.4	0.15	18.5	0.22	6.6	0.07	14.6	0.13
Key turn plants	7.3	0.07	6.5	0.07	3.7	0.04	3.7	0.00	6.6	0.06	6.0	0.05
Capital goods	18.5	0.22	24.2	0.27	14.8	0.11	22.2	0.30	17.9	0.20	23.8	0.27
Software	12.1	0.14	23.4	0.27	3.7	0.07	11.1	0.11	10.6	0.13	21.2	0.24
Others	0.0	0.00	2.4	0.03	3.7	0.04	0.7	0.01	2.6	0.03	2.6	0.03

Source: Own elaboration
Firm: % of firms that are using the indicated type of instrument
IE: like in table 7

and their scant collaboration outside the group.

The analysis of the instruments through which the external technology is incorporated, brings us a picture of MNCS where the most interesting fact consists of a lower utilization of computer services (whether coming from Spanish and foreign firms), together with a higher utilization of disembodied technologies in the form of patents and technical assistance. In agreement with other studies, the pattern of the Spanish firms' purchase of technology confers much higher importance on mechanisms which embody technical knowledge, particularly capital goods acquisitions (Molero & Buesa, 1992).

Regarding the ways for companies to create their own technology, no noticeable difference is observed between the two groups. In both cases R&D and firm's experience occupy the first two places while design and production engineering are in second place, even though there is a slightly higher R&D activity in foreign subsidiaries. Much less importance have different forms of external collaborations either with private firms or with public institutions.

Afterward an in-depth study was made of several features of R&D organization to seek possible qualitative differences. No significant one was found related to aspects such as type of R&D (basic, applied, technical development, etc) or the external institutions with which the firms collaborate.[14] The main difference arises on asking about the period in which firms started to research. In fact, the average length of time doing R&D is higher in MNCS subsidiaries which, in turn, is related to an earlier moment of the firm's establishment or the firm's control.

Going into the analysis of some results indicators, Table 9 summarizes the available data on innovation introduction. The firms gave the percentage of sales corresponding either to products introduced in the last five years or to products manufactured with processes established in the same period.

From previous works (Buesa & Molero, 1992) we knew there are

[14] There is no contradiction between this assertion and the previous one when we said foreign subsidiaries collaborate less than Spanish firms. First of all, in the former section the question was about any external collaboration, not just R&D. Secondly, here it is said that, whatever the intensity of the collaboration is, the way they follow for its implementation is very similar. However we might mention a slightly higher R&D collaboration of subsidiaries with other group's firms.

Table 9 Effective introduction of innovations in the last 5 years

	National Control				Foreign Control				Total			
	Product Innovation		Process Innovation		Product Innovation		Process Innovation		Product Innovation		Process Innovation	
Introduction of Innovations (% of the sales)	IM	EX	IM	EX	IM	EX	IM	EX	IM	EX	IM	EX
None (0%)	4.0	12.1	4.8	8.9	3.7	11.1	3.7	7.4	4.0	11.9	4.6	8.6
Less than 25%	22.6	17.7	10.5	8.9	29.6	25.9	22.2	18.5	23.8	19.2	12.6	10.6
Between 25% and 50%	18.5	8.9	13.7	7.3	25.9	7.4	18.5	3.7	19.9	8.6	14.6	6.6
Between 51% and 75%	14.5	8.1	11.3	5.6	18.5	7.4	14.8	7.4	15.2	7.9	11.9	6.6
More than 75%	35.5	25.8	26.6	17.7	18.5	29.6	14.8	25.9	32.5	26.5	24.5	19.2
Not available	4.8	27.4	33.1	51.6	3.7	18.5	25.9	37.0	4.6	25.8	31.8	49.0
Innovative density*	52.5	46.7	56.6	48.3	38.5	45.5	40.0	52.9	50.0	46.4	53.4	49.3

Source: Own elaboration
IM: Internal Market
EX: Export
* % of the firms that are realizing more than 50% of their sales in the internal market or of their exports with new product or products ellaborated with new processes, counted on the total of the firms from which data are available.

important differences between firms regarding their domestic or external basic orientation. therefore, we introduced questions for measuring separately the weight of the innovation in relation to domestic sales and exportation.

As in other parts, the results do not distinguish perfectly between the two clusters. Nonetheless, there seems to be a slight trend of MNCS to be less active in renewing their production than innovative Spanish firms. The only probable exception has to do with international markets where Spanish branches of MNCS have a more rapid renewal of their products.

This finding can be affected by differences in sectorial allocation of the firms, even though we can not give its verification. Moreover, information from German subsidiaries, allows us to suggest that the higher external orientation of the multinational group is a result of being part of an international organization which, among other advantages, provides more internationally competitive products. The last argument can be additionally supported with other information of the research, which shows how foreign owned firms claim to have a better technological position compared to international competitors.

From the receiver economy it is of great interest to know whether the technology of the subsidiaries is widely spread among other local firms. The results of Table 10 suggest the conclusion

Table 10 Froms of transfer of technology to other firms (Percentage about the firms that are transferring technology)

Forms of transfer of technology	National control		Foreign control		Total	
	SF	FF	SF	FF	SF	FF
Patent license	5.6	7.3	0.0	14.8	4.6	8.6
License for other elements of industrial ownership	5.6	4.8	3.7	7.4	5.3	5.3
Technical assistance	23.4	22.6	7.4	14.8	20.5	21.2
Key turn plant	8.9	9.7	7.4	7.4	8.6	9.3
Capital goods	17.7	12.9	7.4	3.7	15.9	11.3
Software	23.4	12.9	3.7	7.4	19.9	11.9
Others	3.2	2.4	3.7	0.0	3.3	2.0

Source: Own elaboration
SF: Transfer of technology to Spanish Firms
FF: Transfer of technology to Foreign Firms

that MNCS' subsidiaries have a lower activity of technology transfer than innovative Spanish companies. Noteworthy is the scarce flow of technology to other Spanish firms, whatever the means of transfer we look at. In our opinion it confirms once again the relative isolation of MNCS' subsidiaries, which implies probably that diffusion effects are not proportional to the technological strength of those firms.

The last group of factors have to do with the appropriability and control of technological capabilities. Where their strategy is concerned regarding industrial property there is a slightly higher activity of foreign firms, particularly as far as international rights are concerned. That group has a double probability of patenting[15] in Europe and USA, compared to Spanish companies. The latter only present a very slightly higher probability of patenting in Spanish territory.

The former difference does not correspond to a less regular acquisition of technical knowledge because, in fact, Spanish innovative firms claim to have a similar regularity in obtaining that sort of knowledge.[16] Thus the explanation seems to lie in different possibilities and entrepreneurial strategies; MNCS have more resources and a longer experience in using legal methods to protect their technology, regardless of their capabilities.

Finally, we asked the firms to evaluate the importance of different methods of appropriating technical knowledge. As Table 11 shows we found the multinational group considers of greater importance patents and industrial secrets, in spite of both groups valuing regularity in innovation as the fundamental way to protect themselves from imitators.

V. CONCLUSIONS

Intermediate countries have particular characteristics which make the more extended theory not totally suitable to explain their role within the international pattern of technology creation and diffusion. Similarly, the strategies adopted by MNCS in these

---

[15] Defined as the percentage of firms with patents.

[16] 92,7% of the Spanish sample usually obtain regular new technical knowledge. In the foreign group the level is very similar, 85,2%.

Table 11 Valuation of the procedures of appropriation of the technological knowledge

	National control		Foreign control		Total	
Procedures	Firm	IE	Firm	IE	Firm	IE
Patents	50.0	0.41	63.0	0.63	52.3	0.45
Models of utility	42.0	0.24	44.5	0.26	42.4	0.25
Industrial secrets	58.1	0.51	70.4	0.59	60.3	0.52
Innovative regularity	82.3	1.36	81.5	1.30	82.1	1.35

Source: Own elaboration
Firm: % of the firms that are using each modality.
IE: Indicator of Evaluation (like the formula in table 7).

nations can differ substantially from the ones they are establishing in leading and less developed countries. We think Spain is a very appropriate example to study.

The evidence we have discussed is not enough to close a debate which is relatively new. Therefore we need to accumulate more empirical research and to debate critically their results and theoretical background if we truly want to know what our reality is.

Nevertheless, it is possible to establish some provisional conclusions in relation to economic analysis as well as to economic policy.

About analytical work, the first idea we should like to underline is that the intermediate situation is confirmed. Moreover the existence of "intermediate" cases implicitly confirms the uneven character of the internationalization of technological knowledge. In other words, the "globalization" thesis has to be used very carefully when considering countries not belonging to the core of the "world triad" (Patel, 1993; Dunning, 1994).

The second point concerns the need for a better knowledge of MNCS' activities as a requisite to evaluate correctly their contribution to the domestic system of innovation. Two central aspects arise for future investigations; the position occupied in relation to local firms and the relationships regarding environmental institutions.

A significant qualitative element in this respect is the length of time they have been operating in the country. The longer their stay is the better they appreciate the possibilities and limits of national firms and institution (Granstrand et al, 1993). To some extent, the similarity described between MNCS' subsidiaries and Spanish innovative firms show the adaptation of the former to local conditions. In further researches a way of advancing in this question is through case studies in a time perspective.

Finally we think most previous aspects can be incorporated to a methodology based on taxonomies as an intermediate possibility between general traditional models and empiricist positions. Regarding the first, it is important to overcome their lack of realism and the absence of valid political recommendations. The exaggerated empiricism is a kind of never-ending process of getting jobs for economists accumulating more and more data but obtaining only contradictory conclusions among different parameter estimations.

Remembering the two taxomonies used, the first – types of subsidiary – has been confirmed because the Dutch sample responded basically to the same patterns that the German ones did. Here one crucial question arises; if there are important differences in the international trajectory of German and Dutch MNCS (Patel & Pavitt, 1991), how can we explain their similar behaviour within the Spanish economy? In our opinion, it is a consequence of the lesser importance of the technological activity they develop in Spain. On the other hand, we have found a lot of similarities between our classification and other ones used in recent studies (Casson, 1991; Papanastassiou & Pearce, 1993; Taggart, 1993)

As far as Technological Regimes are concerned, there are some interesting differences we have underlined. However, it is very important to compare the behaviour of MNCS subsidiaries with the basic Regimes we identified (Buesa & Molero, 1992, 1993a). In doing so, we arrive at the conclusion that foreign group do not follow systematically any of those Regimes. In other words, although they present some peculiarities, they do not belong to a single group within the general collective, confirming their integration into the Spanish institutional framework.

Regarding political measures, the central idea is the necessity of modifying the classical set of instruments in promoting MNCS presence in this kind of country if we wish to get a better impact of their local activity (Cantwell, 1993a; Dunning, 1994). If in previous times, Spain and some other intermediate nations could base their attraction on some lower cost or protected markets, today they must be aware of the new factors MNCS are looking for.

Particularly if you seek the technologically dynamic part of MNCS, you have to have other stimuli different from public aids or low wages. One has to improve the R&D system, the educational organization (e.g universities and professional training), infrastructures, etc. This way you will receive more foreign investment producing higher spillovers and stronger integration with the national economy. In the same direction and in spite of its difficulty (Häkanson & Nobel, 1993; Papanastassiou & Pearce, 1993; Dunning, 1994), it is not possible to design Technological Policies which ignore the central part MNCS subsidiaries play in National Systems. Without forgetting national interests, today it is possible to think of a more active role of foreign subsidiaries in many national technological goals.

Countries like Spain offer some advantages for locating intermediate activities such as some applied research and technological developments. However, these advantages are limited by their deficiencies in technological infrastructures and skills. Moreover, other countries not very far from their level of development can compete with them if they make an effort in R&D resources. So the challenge is to act in another direction, by occupying a higher intermediate place on the basis of a superior technological development for which a better integration of MNCS is needed.

REFERENCES

Archibugi, D. & Michie, J. (1993) *The globalization of technology. Myths and realities.* Research Papers in Management Studies. Judge Institute of Management Studies. University of Cambridge. 1992/93. no 18.

Buesa, M. & Molero, J. (1988) *Estructura Industrial de España.* Fondo de Cultura Económica. Madrid.

Buesa, M. & Molero, J. (1992) *Patrones del cambio tecnológico y política industrial. Un estudio de las empresas innovadoras madrileñas.* Civitas. Madrid.

Buesa, M. & Molero, J. (1993). *Estrategias de las empresas de capital extranjero en España. El caso de las filiales de multinacionales Holandesas.* Instituto de Analisis Industrial y Financiero. Universidad Complutense. Madrid. Mimeo.

Buesa, M & Molero, J. (1993a). *Patrones de innovacion y estrategias tecnologicas en las empresas españolas.* In: Garcia Delgado, J.L. (ed). *España. Economía.* Espasa Calpe. Madrid.

Cantwell, J. (1989) *Technological Innovation and Multinational Corporations.* Oxford, Basil Blackwell.

Cantwell, J. (1991) "The International Agglomeration of R&D". In: Casson (1991).

Cantwell, J. (1993) *Multinational Corporations and Innovatory Activities: Towards a New, Evolutionary Approach.* Discussion Paper, no 172. University of Reading. Department of Economics.

Cantwell, J. (1993a) *The Internationalisation of Technological Activity in Historical Perspective.* Proceedings of the 19th Annual Conference of EIBA. Lisbon, December.

Cantwell, J. & Hodson, Ch. (1991) "Global R&D and UK Competitiveness". In: Casson (1991).

Casson, M. (1991) "International Comparative Advantage and the Location of R&D". In: Casson (ed). *Global Research Strategy and International Competitiveness.* Basil Blackwell. Oxford.

Chesnais, F. (1991) "La competitividad tecnologica como competitividad estructural". In F. Chesnais: *Competitividad Internacional y Gastos Militares.* Ediciones Ejercito. Madrid.

Circulo De Empresarios (1988) *Actitud y comportamiento de las grandes empresas españolas ante la innovación. Madrid.*

Dosi, G. et al.(1988): Technical Change and Economic Theory. Pinter, London.

Dunning, J. (1994): "Multinational enterprises and the globalization of innovatory capacity". *Research Policy*, 23.

Duran, J.J. (1990): *Estrategia y evaluacion de inversiones directas en el exterior.* Instituto Español de Comercio Exterior. Madrid.

Freeman, Ch. & Perez, C. (1988) "Structural crisis of adjustment, business cycles and investment behaviour". In: G. Dosi et al. (1988).

Freeman, Ch. (ed) (1990) *The economics of innovation.* Aldershot, Edward Elgar. London.

Granstrand, O; Häkanson, L and Sjölander, S. (1993): "Internationalization of R&D. A survey of some recent research". *Research Policy*, 22.

Häkanson, L. (1991): "Locational determinants of foreign R&D in Swedish multinationals". *Paper 91/4.* Institute of International Business. School of Economics. Stockholm.

Häkanson, L & Nobel, R. (1993) "Determinants of Foreign R&D in Swedish Multinationals". *Research Policy*, 22.

Howells, S. (1990) "The location and organization of research and development: new horizons". *Research Policy*, 19.

INE. (1993): *Estadistica sobre las actividades de investigacion científica y desarrollo tecnológico (I + D). 1990. Instituto Nacional de Estadística. Madrid.*

Malerba, F. & Orsenigo, L. (1990) "Technological regimes and patterns of innovation: a theoretical and empirical investigation of Italian case". In: A. Heertje & M. Perlman (eds): *Evolving technology and market structure.* Ann Arbor. Michigan University Press.

Molero, J. (1983) "Foreign Technology in the Spanish Economy: an Analysis of the Recent Evolution". *Research Policy.* 5.

Molero, J. (1992) "La internacionalizacion de la Industria Española y el Cambio tecnológico". *Cuadernos de Relaciones Laborales*, no 1.

Molero, J. & Buesa, M. (1993) "Multinational companies and technological change: Basic traits and taxonomy of the behaviour of German industrial companies in Spain". *Research Policy*, 22.

Muñoz, J., Roldan, S. & Serrano, A. (1978): *La internacionalización del capital en España. Edicusa. Madrid.*

OECD (1992) *Technology and the Economy. The key relationship.* Paris.
Orsenigo, L. (1989) *The Emergence of Biotechnology.* Pinter. London.
Papanastassiou, M & Pearce, R. (1993) *Global innovation strategies of MNCS and European Integration: the role of regional R&D facilities.* Proceedings of the 19th Annual Conference of EIBA. Lisbon, December, 1993.
Pavitt, K. (1984) "Sectoral patterns of technical change: towards a taxonomy and theory". *Research Policy*, 6.
Patel, P. (1993) *Localised Production of Technology for Global Markets.* S.P.R.U. University of Sussex. Mimeo.
Patel, P. & Pavitt, K. (1991) "Europe's technological performance". In: Ch. Freeman, M. Sharp and W. Walker (Eds.): *Global Competition and the Environment in the 1990's.* Printer. London.
Patel, P. & Pavitt, K. (1991a) "Large firms in the production of the world's technology: an important case of 'non-globalisation' ". *Journal of International Business Studies*, vol. 1. First trimester.
Pearce, R. D. (1990) *The internationalization of research and development.* MacMillan. London.
Pearce, R. D. & Singh, S. (1991) "The Overseas Laboratory". In: Casson (1991).
Pearce, R. D. & Satwinder, S. (1992) *Globalising Research and Development.* MacMillan. London.
Sanchez, P. & Vicens, J. (1991) "Exporting Technology. Recent developments in the export of technology by Spanish companies". *Science and Public Policy*, vol. 18, no 5. October.
Taggart, J.H. (1993) *Strategy Conflict in the MNE: Parent and Subsidiary.* Paper presented to the 19th Annual Conference of EIBA. Lisbon, December.
Von Boehmer, A. (1991) "Global R&D activities of U.S. multinational corporations: some empirical results". In: D. Kocaoglu & K. Niwa (Eds.): *Technology Management.* Portland.
Warrant, F. (1991): *Deploiement mondial de la R&D industrielle: facteur et garant de la globalisation de la technologie et de l'economie?* FAST. Bruselas.
Wortman, M. (1991): Country study of the Federal Republic of Germany. Commission of the European Communities. Monitor/Fast. Vol. 17. Prospective Dossier, no 2. "Globalization of Economy and technology".

The TNCs' Changing Investment Strategies in the Latin American Manufacturing Sector

Daniel Chudnovsky[1]

I. INTRODUCTION

Following early attempts in Chile and Mexico, other Latin American economies have started the 1990s in the middle of stabilization-cum-structural adjustment programmes which, among other purposes, aim at transforming the traditional import substitution industrialization (ISI) process into an outward oriented growth process, through privatization and the opening of the economies to international trade, foreign direct investment (FDI) and technology.

Partly as a result of these programmes, inflation has been reduced (except in Brazil), external debt has been renegotiated, growth has been resumed (though in per capita terms it is still very low) and external financial flows (including capital repatriation) and imports have boomed in most countries.

While the low interest rates in the United States and the recession in other industrialized countries have played a significant role in increasing the flow of external capital to the region, trade liberalization facilitated the sharp growth of imports (from

[1] Director of Centro de Investigaciones para la Transformación (CENIT), Buenos Aires. This paper has been partly based on two previous pieces (Chudnovsky, 1991 and 1993).

$US 94 in 1990 to $US 148 billion in 1993). Even with the moderate growth experienced in exports,[2] the large current account deficit of the region was more than compensated for with the great inflow of external capital.

Within this new macroeconomic context, whereas domestic investment shows signs of some recovery, FDI to Latin America has sharply increased since the mid 1980s and especially in the 1990s (Table 1).

Despite the shortcomings of the aggregate figures on FDI flows, it is important to discuss the available data briefly before entering into the main topic of this paper.

To put recent FDI flows to Latin America in perspective, it is important to bear in mind the unparalleled growth of world FDI flows since 1985 have mostly taken place in industrialized countries, whose share as destination increased from 75 in 1980–84 to 83% in 1988–89. This unprecedented growth in FDI may be explained not only by the recovery of the world economy. The significant growth in Japanese FDI, the emergence of new outward investors among developed and Asian developing countries, the rise in the number of cross-border mergers and takeovers, the deregulation of many services and the 1992 programme to integrate the European Community are the main factors behind this trend (UNCTC, 1991a).

However, due to the poor economic conditions in the United States and to some extent in Western Europe, a slowdown in the growth of inflows was already visible in 1990 and there was a significant decline in FDI inflows in industrialized countries in 1991.

FDI flows to East, South and South-East Asia have also grown fast during 1985–90 and hence their share as a destination market has not decreased. In fact, due to continued growth and the decline registered in developed countries the share of this region in world inflows has sharply increased in 1991.

The growth in FDI to these developing countries was due not only to the good performance of these economies but also to the increasing flow of investments by Japanese TNCs and firms. The buoyant import growth that started in Japan since the yen

[2] Merchandise exports grew from U$S 121 to 133 billion between 1991 and 1993 and external capital flows increased from U$S 21 in 1990 to 62 billion in 1992. In 1993 such flows were estimated in U$S 54.6 billion (CEPAL, 1993).

revaluation has pushed Japanese firms to establish subsidiaries in Asian developing countries to be able to export not only to the United States (as was the traditional case) but also back to Japan (UNCTAD, 1990).

Despite the clear trend in the 1980s towards liberalizing most FDI regimes that several Latin American countries established in the 1970s (UNCTC, 1988), the share of Latin America and the Caribbean in total world inflows sharply declined from 14.8 to 4.1 % over the periods 1980–84 and 1985–89. In 1990–91 that share went up to 6.6%, due to the growing inflows in 1991.

As can be observed in table 1, a sharp increase in the absolute amounts of FDI is visible in 1987–89 and especially in 1990–1991. In this connection, and bearing in mind that the data are based on balance of payments information, a number of points can be made.

First, whereas a recovery in FDI flows in 1987–89 as compared with 1983–86 is visible in most large and medium size countries (with the exception of Colombia), this is not the case when the comparison between 1987–89 and 1980–82 is made. While countries like Mexico, Argentina and Colombia had already recovered in 1987–89 the flows of the early 1980s, in Chile and Venezuela this only happened in the early 1990s. Inflows to the largest host country, Brazil, did not recover and in fact sharply decreased in 1991.

Second, a significant part of the inflows was due to debt equity swaps that gained momentum mostly in 1987 and 1988. In the case of Argentina, Brazil, Chile and Mexico, 45% of FDI flows in 1985–89 were made through debt equity conversions (calculated on the basis of the figures of UNCTC 1991b).

This method of attracting FDI seems to be very expensive because it is a subsidy to investments that were probably going to be made anyway, may create macroeconomic problems (e.g. inflation) and, what is more, redistributes important assets rather than bringing new funds into the importing country.

Finally, in countries like Argentina, Venezuela and Mexico, FDI inflows have largely been channeled to the privatization of State firms, often through debt equity swaps. Probably half of FDI inflows in 1991 were due to privatization schemes (BID, 1992). Although foreign partners usually bring new managerial and technological inputs to modernize the privatized firms, without specific investigations the net financial and economic benefits of

Table 1 Inflows of foreign direct investment

	Annual average inflows (Millions of dollars)		Shares #	
	1980–84	1985–86	1980–84 %	1985–86 %
All Countries	49710.1	65070.4	100.0	100.0
Developed Countries	37185.1	51089.1	74.8	78.5
Developing Countries	12507.2	13965.9	25.2	21.5
South & SE Asia	4655.7	5656.2	9.4	8.7
Latin America	7371.9	5514.2	14.8	8.5
Tax Havens*	529.0	1554.8	7.2	28.2
L.A. exc. Tax Havens	6842.9	3959.4	92.8	71.8
Argentina	580.7	746.5	7.9	13.5
Bolivia	51.3	10.0	0.7	0.2
Brazil	2447.0	834.0	33.2	15.1
Chile	332.3	115.0	4.5	2.1
Colombia	262.7	848.5	3.6	15.4
Costa Rica	50.4	65.5	0.7	1.2
Dominican Republic	57.0	43.1	0.8	0.8
El Salvador	-0.3	18.3	0.0	0.3
Ecuador	56.7	66.0	0.8	1.2
Grenada	0.6	4.6	0.0	0.1
Guatemala	105.0	65.3	1.4	1.2
Guyana	1.1	-3.6	0.0	-0.1
Haiti	9.5	4.9	0.1	0.1
Honduras	5.3	28.8	0.1	0.5
Jamaica	0.1	-6.8	0.0	-0.1
Mexico	2215.3	1007.0	30.1	18.3
Paraguay	33.4	0.7	0.5	0.0
Peru	66.7	11.5	0.9	0.2
Trin. & Tobago	215.4	-6.7	2.9	-0.1
Uruguay	112.9	18.8	1.5	0.3
Venezuela	165.3	42.0	2.2	0.8
Virgin Islands	0.5	6.4	0.0	0.1

Table 1 (continued)

	Annual average inflows (Millions of dollars)		Shares #	
	1987–89	1990–91	1987–89 %	1990–91 %
All Countries	61722.5	174341.4	100.0	100.0
Developed Countries	133915.6	14009.2	82.8	80.3
Developing Countries	127794.3	33321.3	17.2	19.1
South & SE Asia	13811.6	18197.4	8.5	10.4
Latin America	10264.9	11591.4	6.3	6.6
Tax Havens*	3251.8	823.2	31.7	7.1
L.A. exc. Tax Havens	7013.1	10768.3	68.3	92.9
Argentina	718.7	2223.5	7.0	19.2
Bolivia	1.2	39.6	0.0	0.3
Brazil	1820.3	1692.5	17.7	14.6
Chile	185.0	412.5	1.8	3.6
Colombia	366.0	460.5	3.6	4.0
Costa Rica	101.3	152.2	1.0	1.3
Dominican Republic	101.7	138.9	1.0	1.2
El Salvador	16.1	13.5	0.2	0.1
Ecuador	78.3	83.5	0.8	0.7
Grenada	11.9	12.0	0.1	0.1
Guatemala	185.4	69.2	1.8	0.6
Guyana	1.3	8.0	0.0	0.1
Haiti	8.1	10.9	0.1	0.1
Honduras	46.0	44.1	0.4	0.4
Jamaica	32.8	132.5	0.3	1.1
Mexico	2959.0	3697.0	28.8	31.9
Paraguay	8.8	74.2	0.1	0'
Peru	39.0	17.0	0.4	
Trin.& Tobago	81.6	139.3	0.8	01.2
Uruguay	67.7	44.0	0.7	0.4
Venezuela	107.7	1182.5	1.0	10.2
Virgin Islands	81.9	18.0	0.8	0.2

Share of all countries for regions, and share of L.A. inflows for countries and Tax Havens
* Bahamas, Bermuda, Cayman Island, Netherlands Antilles, Panama
SOURCE: Calculations on UNCTC estimates on IMF Balance of Payments tape, retrieved on 16 October 1992

these operations cannot be assessed.

Whereas the FDI role in privatized enterprises is a new phenomenon that is beyond the scope of this paper, our purpose here is to discuss the changing strategies of foreign manufacturing firms in view of the new conditions that they are facing. In this connection, the main issue we would like to shed light on is to what extent foreign owned firms operating in the manufacturing sector of the main Latin American countries have been contributing to increase the competitiveness of such countries, through efficiency seeking and eventually through resource enhancing investments. And to what extent may such investments lead to a deeper integration into the international production networks dominated by the transnational corporations (TNCs) (UNCTAD, 1993)?.

To examine the emerging evidence on these firms' strategies in the 1980s and early 1990s it is important to bear in mind the role played by TNCs in the ISI and in the exports generated by this process in the 1970s and 1980s. This is discussed in section 2. The poor performance of Latin American economies in the 1980s -as discussed in section 3 — is also a key aspect to be taken into account in an approach to the current situation.

The available evidence on the rationalized investments undertaken by foreign firms in Mexico, Brazil and Argentina, their rationale and their limitations is discussed in section 4. Some concluding remarks are made in the final section.

2. THE ROLE OF TNCS IN THE ISI

The industrialization process that gained momentum since World War II has transformed the manufacturing sector into the most rapidly growing area for TNCs activities in Latin America. TNCs from the United States and some European countries have participated in the industrialization process of a number of Latin American countries since the late 1950s.

As a result of this process in the late 1970s and early 1980s, foreign firms had a share in the manufacturing production that varied between one fourth and one third in the main Latin American countries (UNCTC, 1988, table X.1).

Although the main motivation for TNCs to participate in the ISI in the 1950s and 1960s was to take advantage of the growing and protected domestic market, several affiliates of TNCs started to export a few years later to compensate for excess capacity, in response to export incentives and other changes introduced in the trade and foreign exchange regime (Fritsch and Franco, 1991). At the same time, it has also been pointed out by Teitel and Toumi (1987) that the ISI in countries with a significant domestic market was a preamble to the export phase, in the sense that it made possible a learning process by which the production of skilled intensive goods became more competitive.

These skill-intensive goods and technological services have sometimes been exported by domestic firms as subcontractors of TNCs specializing in engineering goods or services (Sapir, 1989). In standardized products like auto parts, buses, tractors and construction and mining machinery that have been manufactured in Brazil (and to a lesser extent in Argentina) by affiliates of TNCs since the 1950s, such companies have also been playing the role of technology intermediaries, creating assets that have been useful in generating exports (Chudnovsky, 1989). While the share of manufactured exports accounted for by the foreign affiliates of host countries is normally about the same as their share of local production (table X.1 of UNCTC, 1988), their export propensities appear to be no higher than those of domestic enterprises from the same industry (Vaitsos, 1978). However, since their import propensities were generally higher than their domestic equivalents (Newfarmer, 1985, ch. 2) their direct contribution to the trade balance has been generally negative (Lahera, 1985),[3] except in countries with trade balancing requirements (e.g. in Brazil).

Regarding Brazil, whereas in the classical ISI period, FDI was not only motivated by the large domestic market but also by the protection given by the trade policy and the liberal treatment to foreign capital, in the late 1960s and 1970s government policies towards export promotion and ownership requirements shaped the market orientation and forms in which TNCs participated in Brazilian industrialization (Evans, 1979; Fritsch and Franco, 1991).

The export promotion policies from the mid 1960s, the specific

[3] Since no attempt has been made in these studies to properly assess the balance of payments effects of TNCs activities taking into account not only the capital account but also assuming different counterfactual situations, the information collected on direct imports and exports by TNCs only gives an indication of the most visible effect of their operations on trade flows.

incentives coupled with export performance requirements biased towards TNC affiliates (especially in the automobile industry), the increased sophistication of the production processes and product adaptations taking place in rationalized investments made by the subsidiaries and the marketing channels of the TNCs were the main factors explaining the important share of TNCs in the Brazilian growing exports of manufactures (Fritsch and Franco, 1991).

Besides the significant participation of State firms in some key branches, the Brazilian government encouraged the formation of joint ventures to strengthen the position of local capital and maximize gains from technology transfer. The petrochemical industry was a key example, followed later on by joint ventures in other branches, like some segments of the computer industry.

Most of the issues that are discussed in the literature on TNCs and industrialization refer to the advanced industrialization process in the 1960s and 1970s where TNCs were important actors in some of the emerging key industries. While welcoming the assets brought by the TNCs, their impact on the balance of payments, on the industrial structure and on technological development and upon domestic competitors, suppliers and customers (*see* Chudnovsky 1993 for a survey of the relevant literature) were at issue for most Latin American countries.

3. THE DIFFICULT 1980S

The performance of Latin American exports in the 1980s was one of the few relatively positive economic indicators in what has been referred to as a "lost decade" to illustrate the magnitude of the setback suffered in terms of development (ECLAC, 1990).

However, the share of Latin American exports in world merchandise trade, after reaching 5.9% in 1984 decreased to 3.9% in 1990. Despite the fact that manufacturers increased their share in the value of Latin American exports from 14.7 to 33.7% between 1980 and 1988, the share of most Latin American countries (with the exception of Brazil and Mexico) in world exports of manufactures was lower in 1988 than in 1980 (UNCTAD, 1991).[4]

[4] It is interesting to point out that despite the Chilean export boom, her share in

Furthermore, whereas Latin America did rather well in exports of resource based goods and in some cases of low wage processes, few advances have been made in high tech product exports.

Export growth of manufactures was not only due to the recessive conditions in domestic markets that led to excess capacity. It was also a result of the continuous process of devaluation of domestic currencies, reduced costs of labour and depredation of natural resources. High exchange rates and extremely low wages gave international competitiveness to a number of branches that were built in the import substitution era and that due to the new conditions in domestic markets had substantial idle capacity.

What is more important is that the growth in exports was not based on capital accumulation, improved technologies and corresponding productivity gains and hence is hardly sustainable (Kell and Marchese, 1991). This is the sort of competitiveness that was labelled as "spurious" (ECLAC, 1990).

Manufacturing output was not only smaller than before the crisis but also more concentrated and with significant sectoral differences. Manufacturing branches producing intermediate and consumer goods may have increased their participation in the reduced output, while engineering branches' share declined. In other words, branches based on low wages and natural resources and/or producing industrial commodities on the basis of subsidized fixed assets have increased their relative share, at the expense of branches based on skilled labor.

In contrast with the crisis faced by developing countries in Latin America, a number of countries in East and South Asia managed to perform well in the 1980s. In the case of the Asian NICs and some ASEAN countries, a process of manufactured export-led growth continued in the 1980s, especially after the recovery in world demand since 1983. The sharp expansion of exports from these countries was accompanied by continued increases in investment and by stronger domestic consumption. The growth in exports and in investment induced buoyant import growth.

The fiscal crisis and the slowdown in economic growth and productive investment have had serious repercussions on the

---

world manufactures exports actually decreased. Furthermore, the share of Chilean total exports in world exports was lower in 1987 (0.22) than in 1974 (0.31). Despite the export diversification achieved by Chile, most exports are resource based commodities, with little value added and concentrated in relatively few markets (Ominami & Madrid, 1989).

resources available for education and for R & D.

In this connection, the contrast between Latin America and East Asian NIEs regarding science and technology indicators is sharp. Resources allocated to R & D on GDP in Latin America (0.5%) were only a third of the proportion that the Asian newly industrialized economies devoted to this activity. Although the stock of engineers and scientists was similar in both Latin America and East Asian NIEs (11.5 per thousand of economically active inhabitants), the flow of college graduates per thousand inhabitants was much lower (15.6 vis a vis 47.8) (Peres Nuñez, 1992).

The fall and stagnation in productive investment has been well reflected in the reduction of gross domestic investment in GDP from 26.5% in 1980–82 to 20% in 1987–89 on average for all Latin American countries. Furthermore, from the relatively high figures in the early 1980s, capital goods imports by developing America sharply decreased in current dollars in 1983. Since 1984 such imports started to grow again and only in 1989 were able to slightly surpass the 1981 level (in nominal dollars). However, capital goods imports by developing America increased at a much lower growth rate than similar imports in developing Asia.

The serious crisis faced by Latin America in the 1980s has not affected the competitiveness of all enterprises in the same way and not all firms have reacted to it in the same manner.

Although Latin American manufacturing sectors were never homogeneous, it seems that the new conditions have increased the structural heterogeneity of enterprises regarding branches, size, ownership, market orientation and technology. The growing heterogeneity is, to some extent, a consequence of the different strategies followed by domestic and foreign firms.

4. COMPANY STRATEGIES DURING THE CRISIS AND IN THE EARLY 1990s

Within a global picture of low productive investment and higher technological gaps vis-a-vis industrialized countries important differences can be perceived. Productivity levels, technological and organizational efforts, reliance on imported technologies and modernity of the physical and technological stock (including the incorporation of microelectronics-based machinery and equipment) are widely different not only between branches but also inside branches – and apparently regardless of size and ownership of the firms.

Regarding ownership patterns it is important to bear in mind that nationally owned firms, and especially those belonging to the large private groups, have increased their importance in the economic life of the region. These groups, which in some cases originated in the 19th century, have quickly grown in recent years and participated in extractive and agricultural activities and in manufacturing and services (mainly financial).

Domestic firms operating in Argentina, especially those belonging to the large groups have increased their global participation, in contrast to what happened with foreign firms (Basualdo, 1987). This situation is not peculiar to Argentina. In countries like Chile, Brazil, Mexico and Venezuela, the large domestic groups have probably also increased their economic significance in recent years, at the expense of foreign affiliates in some cases, and in other instances, at the expense of the state and independent domestic firms.

Although these groups have very diversified activities, with a growth path highly influenced by the need to augment the value of their financial assets, in some exceptional cases they have well equipped factories with qualified personnel making high value added goods not only for the internal market but also for export. At the same time, these groups have had joint ventures or technological agreements with partners from industrialized countries to strengthen their productive and marketing skills and to obtain relatively modern product and process technologies (Basualdo & Fuchs, 1989).

The participation of foreign affiliates in the manufacturing sector is probably lower than in the mid 1970s,[5] although it is very significant in the production of some key branches and in exports, as clearly indicated by the high share of foreign firms in the manufactured exports of Mexico and Brazil (Fritsch and Franco, 1991; Peres Nuñez, 1990; Unger, 1990).

Furthermore, TNCs have started to reorientate their strategies

[5] In the Argentine case, for instance, the global participation of foreign firms in industrial production was reduced from 30.4% in 1973 to 26.8% in 1984 (Azpiazu, 1992). However, this global reduction did not mean that all foreign firms have followed a defensive strategy or even left the country. Many firms especially those with diversified activities have been active in the country.

to take into account the new conditions imposed by the crisis and the structural adjustment programmes in progress.

A recent study of 63 TNCs affiliates operating in Mexico indicates that the firms had made efficiency investments to modify the product mix, reduce costs, improve quality and seek new export markets during the period of crisis after 1982. However, most exports derived from such measures are concentrated in the automotive sector (UNCTC, 1992; Peres Nuñez, 1990).

The transformation of the Mexican automotive industry into the main exporter of manufactured products, completely reversing the traditional trade deficit of the sector, was a result of the changing international environment, especially the force of Japanese competition, the introduction of new technologies and the sectoral policies followed by the Mexican government in the late 1970s and early 1980s.

Export expansion was based on the rationalized investments made since 1978 by TNCs to produce engines. An increase in exports was required to protect or increase domestic market share in Mexico, which at the time of the 1977 government decree was booming. Furthermore all producers needed additional engine capacity as they restructured their global operations.

Although the 1983 automotive decree attempted to rationalize the industry and improve its trade balance in the midst of the crisis, only a small number of cars were exported in the late 1980s and mostly from Ford's new Hermosillo plant. The engine plants built in the late 1970s still generated the lion's share of sectoral exports (Shapiro, 1993).

Furthermore, although the export performance of Mexican based firms provides some evidence of the competitiveness achieved by such firms in making finished vehicles in Mexico (even if exports are made at manipulated transfer prices), it is important to point out that existing producers have enjoyed trade protection against foreign competition. It is not clear how existing firms would be able to face import competition, if imports of finished vehicles were liberalized.

A combination of fiscal and trade incentives, slowdown in domestic demand and global strategies of the TNCs led to a significant growth of Brazilian automotive exports in the 1980s. Most of those exports were accounted for by finished vehicles, though engines and auto parts were also exported.

Despite the significant growth in exports and the incorporation of some advanced production technologies, Brazilian automobile industry has serious competitive problems. As thoroughly studied by Womack, Jones and Roos (1990) in an MIT international survey on the subject, Brazilian plants (all owned by TNCs) lag far behind world average practice, regarding productivity (48 hours per vehicle in comparison with 16 hours in Japan), quality (even in vehicles made for export to the United States), level of automation and product age (11.4 years, the oldest of the sample). Brazilian plants are also less productive than those in other LDCs notably Mexico and in East Asia. However, in some plants, elements of lean production[6] have already been introduced, though without changing the basic manufacturing approach followed in mass production.

The Mexican and Brazilian experiences in integrating automobile production into the global competitive framework in which the main TNCs are operating is a significant development. Whereas the dramatic reversal of the trade balance has reduced the traditional concern over the negative impact of the industry upon the balance of trade (though not necessarily on the balance of payments) other important questions remain at issue. The more reduced local content of Mexican-based production, the near disappearance of domestic manufacturers of vehicles in both cases, the relatively poor productivity and quality performance of most plants and the unknown impact of the new plants on the development of domestic technological capabilities are important issues that, although not easy to quantify, should be taken into account in any assessment of the developmental impact of these efficiency seeking investments.

Turning to other sectors in which TNCs are also important in Brazil, in a research based on a sample of 55 TNC affiliates operating in that country, it was found that the companies have taken many rationalization measures to deal with the new conditions in 1990 and 1991. Jointly with the introduction of total quality control techniques and better managerial and administra-

---

[6] Lean production(or toyotism) is "lean" because 'it uses less of everything compared with mass production — half the human effort in the factory, half the manufacturing space, half the investment in tools, half the engineering hours to develop a new product in half the time. Also, it requires keeping far less than half the needed inventory on site, results in many fewer defects, and produces a greater and ever growing variety of products" (Womack, Jones and Roos, 1990, p.13)

tive schemes, the firms have sharply reduced the employment of technical and production personnel. Furthermore, a clear trend towards lower vertical integration, specializing the product mix and abandoning the manufacturing of high-tech goods was detected (Bielschowsky, 1992).

On the basis of interviews held in Brazil in early 1993 with 104 firms of which 41 were foreign owned, a more accurate picture of the microeconomic adjustment taking place since the late 1980s is available.

Despite the significant changes taking place on the trade front in Brazil and the fact that exports account on average for a quarter of total sales in the surveyed firms, the recession in the domestic market has been the major determinant of their current strategies of change.

Both domestic and foreign firms in Brazil have been active, reducing production costs through a variety of rationalization measures. Such measures include not only operative and administrative personnel lay offs but also a more efficient use of inputs and eliminating bottlenecks, improving quality and the whole production process through introduction of industrial automation and organizational techniques, etc.

However, these efficiency seeking activities have been made without significant investments in tangible assets and while scaling down expenditures for intangible assets like training, R & D, engineering and marketing. In this way, the rationalization process so far has not implied any resource enhancement activity (Bielschowsky, 1993).

Trade liberalization and privatization in a context of reduced inflation and high growth like that experienced by Argentina since 1991 have strongly modified the conditions in which foreign firms are doing business in the country.

Whereas many subsidiaries of TNCs have continued their domestic market orientation and have tried to defend their market share through rationalization measures, in the case of the automobile and autoparts industry a restructuring process is under way.

Subsidiaries have generally taken advantage of the recent trade liberalization to complement their products with imported goods. In a survey of 61 leading foreign firms it was found that their total imports increased from $US 1.2 to 1.9 billion between 1991 and 1992. Nearly 40% of the value of such imports was final goods for commercialization. Furthermore, firms have generally reduced the local content of their production (Kosacoff & Bezchinsky, 1993).

To be able to compete with imported goods entering into the country with low tariffs and an overvalued peso, the firms have not only relied on imports from their parent companies and affiliates. They have also taken a variety of rationalization measures to increase the efficiency of their manufacturing processes, mainly through organizational techniques and the incorporation of some machinery and equipment. However, since only 3% of the value of the mentioned imports in 1992 were capital goods it seems that relatively little investment in physical assets has been taking place.

Similarly to Mexico, within the current trade liberalization programme the companies operating in the automotive sector in Argentina have been protected from imported cars from other sources through quotas and high tariffs. Furthermore, in exchange for an export commitment to Brazil and other destinations and an efficiency investment plan, they themselves are allowed to import finished vehicles from their parent companies paying a preferential custom duty.

Although the existing vehicle firms (of which the two leading ones are majority owned by domestic entrepreneurs that operate under license from Fiat, Peugeot and Renault), have started to make the planned investments in view of the booming domestic market since 1991, so far actual exports are far lower than those originally committed.

Current rationalized investments in the automotive sector were encouraged by negotiations initiated in 1987 that led to a sectoral trade agreement with Brazil which came into force in 1991. In view of this possibility Ford and Volkswagen created in 1987 a joint venture, Autolatina, whose goal is to rationalize and integrate its Argentinian and Brazilian operations. A wholly owned subsidiary was set up in Argentina (under a debt equity conversion scheme) to manufacture gear boxes to export to Brazil and Germany. The local associate of Fiat in Argentina has also specialized part of its engine production to export to Brazil.

In addition to this managed trade experiment, the only TNCs that continue exporting most of their output in the new conditions are those based on natural resources. Most of the remaining TNCs and many foreign newcomers that have taken over domestic enterprises in the last few years have generally geared their investments to the buoyant domestic market. In this way, so far the globalization process in the Argentine case is significant only on the import side.

5. CONCLUDING REMARKS

The available evidence clearly indicates that the subsidiaries of TNCs operating in the manufacturing sector of the large Latin American countries have made significant efficiency seeking investments to be able to cope with the crisis first and then with trade liberalization. With these investments foreign firms have apparently been able to keep their market share vis-a-vis imported goods in the domestic markets. In this way, it appears that the goods produced by them, though with a lower local content, are probably more competitive than those made in the past during the ISI period. However, these efficiency investments have generally been made while reducing skilled employment and without too much fixed investment. Neither the linkages to the domestic economy nor the exports generated by such investments seem to be very significant.

Although the more technologically advanced export activities undertaken by TNCS' in Latin America have to be carefully assessed in terms of their domestic impact, it seems that traditional concerns about TNCs' impact on the balance of trade (and perhaps on the balance of payments) have receded in Mexico and Brazil though not in Argentina. Still, little is known about the impact of these export activities on prices and quality of the goods sold in the domestic markets and more generally on the creation of dynamic comparative advantages (i.e. spillover effects on domestic subcontractors, research institutes, employment and training of more skilled personnel, etc).

On the basis of the scanty evidence available, it seems that so far the kind of resource enhancing investments that would allow these countries to participate with high value added exports in integrated international production have been mostly limited to the Mexican automotive sector and scattered examples in Brazil and Argentina.

While the cautious attitude observed so far may change as time passes and the TNCs become more convinced about the prospects of the host countries with regard to becoming sites for resource enhancing investments, an appropriate though difficult to design policy package, like those in place in some Asian industrializing countries (Lim and Fong, 1991) may accelerate such decisions (see Chudnovsky, 1991).

In this connection, from acknowledging the fact that tariff and non-tariff protection in the activities where TNCs have channeled their market seeking investments were at the root of most of the social costs derived from their presence in the ISI, it does not follow -as is generally assumed by orthodox economists- that a mere change in trade policies will necessarily incorporate existing and new affiliates from TNCs into their international networks with high value added products.

Depending on how trade liberalization and other policies are implemented and what stage of economic development the host country is at, TNCs may continue with resource based or internal market seeking investments and/or may move into resource enhancing investments that may increase the social benefits of their presence.

It is very important to bear in mind that in the Mexican case the improved efficiency and the growing exports by TNC affiliates were not only consequences of the real devaluation of the exchange rate and access to imported parts and components in view of the trade liberalization measures. Sectoral programmes in the automotive and computer industries by which protection from foreign competition in the domestic market was granted in return for certain performance requirements, especially regarding exports have also been crucial incentives for such moves. Nonetheless, in other cases like pharmaceuticals, neither the macroeconomic situation nor the sectoral programme led to similar results in terms of export expansion (UNCTC, 1992).

Fostering TNC exports in the technologically more complex industries is certainly important to facilitate economies of scale and specialization, create spillovers and compensate for the high import content of some of these activities. However, as the Brazilian experience in the automobile industry in the 1980s clearly suggests, higher exports may not be enough for achieving greater competitiveness. Therefore, while keeping exports as the main target for sectoral policies, other variables should be incorporated like training, investment in fixed assets and development of local suppliers.

It may be also important to introduce more competition and eventually allow newcomers in the domestic market to increase the social benefits of the presence of TNCs in skill and capital intensive activities. This may be achieved both by reducing the prices and increasing the quality of the goods and services produced through more efficient manufacturing and organizational techniques.

If, at the same time, the host country makes a deliberate effort to foster indigenous technical and managerial capabilities in the activities related to the branches in question by relying on efficient restructuring policies, FDI-competitiveness and trade linkages can be better exploited. To rely on different forms of TNC involvement is not a substitute for encouraging indigenous efforts in the task of building up technological and managerial capabilities that seem indispensable to the promotion of efficient industrial development.

REFERENCES

Azpiazu D. (1992) "Las Empresas Transnacionales en una economía en transición: la experiencia argentina en los años 80' Cepal, Santiago de Chile, (mimeo).

Basualdo E.(1987) "Características de la desindustrialización argentina: alternativas de industrialización", CEDAL-Flacso, Buenos Aires (mimeo).

Basualdo E. & Fuchs M.(1989) "Nuevas formas de inversión de las empresas extranjeras en la industria argentina", CEPAL, Buenos Aires.

BID, (1992) Progreso Economico y Social en América Latina. Informe 1992, Washington DC.

Bielschowsky R. (1992) "Transnational corporations and the manufacturing sector in Brazil" (mimeo) CEPAL, Santiago de Chile.

Bielschowsky R. (1993) "Adjusting for survival: domestic and foreign manufacturing firms in Brazil in the early 1990s" (mimeo) CEPAL, Santiago de Chile.

CEPAL (1993) Balance preliminar de la economía de América Latina y el Caribe, Santiago de Chile, Naciones Unidas.

Chudnovsky D. (1989) "South South Trade in Capital Goods: The Experiences of Argentina and Brazil" in Vivianne Ventura-Dias (ed) South South Trade. Trends, Issues and Obstacles to Its Growth New York, Praeger.

Chudnovsky D. (1991) "Beyond Macroeconomic Stability in Latin America. The need for integrated trade and innovation policies" CENIT, Buenos Aires.

Chudnovsky D. (1993) "Introduction" to Daniel Chudnovsky (ed) TNCs and Industrialization, United Nations Library on Transnational Corporations, London, Routledge.

ECLAC (1990), Changing Production Patterns with Social Equity, Santiago de Chile, United Nations.

Evans P. (1979) Dependent Development: The Alliance of Multinational, State and Local Capital in Brazil, Princeton: Princeton University Press.

Fritsch W. & Franco G. (1991) Foreign Direct Investment in Brazil. Its Impact

on Industrial Restructuring OECD Development Centre, Paris.
Kell G. and Marchese S. (1991) "Developing countries' exports of textiles and metals: the question of sustainability of recent growth" UNCTAD Review October.
Kosacoff B. & Bezchinsky G. (1993) "De la sustitución de importaciones a la globalización. Las empresas transnacionales en la industria argentina" en Bernardo.
Kosacoff El desafío de la competitividad. La industria argentina en transformación CEPAL/Alianza Editorial, Buenos Aires.
Lahera E. (1985) "Las empresas transnacionales y el comercio internacional de América Latina" Revista de la Cepal Marzo.
Lim L. and Fong Pang Eng (1991) Foreign Direct Investment and Industrialization in Malaysia, Singapore, Taiwan and Thailand, OECD Development Centre, Paris.
Newfarmer R. (1985) (ed) Profits, Progress and Poverty. Case Studies of International Industries in Latin America, University of Notre Dame Press, Notre Dame, Indiana.
Ominami C. & Madrid R. (1989) La Inserción de Chile en los Mercados Internacionales, Dos Mundos, Santiago de Chile.
Peres Nuñez W. (1990) Foreign direct investment and industrial development in Mexico, OECD Development Centre, Paris.
Peres Nuñez W.(1992) "Latin America's experience with technology policies. Current situation and prospects" (mimeo).
Sapir A. (1989) "Trade among developing countries in investment-related technological services" in Viviane Ventura Dias (ed) South-South Trade. Trends, Issues, and Obstacles to its Growth. New York, Praeger.
Shapiro H.(1993) "Automobiles: From Import Substitution to Export Promotion in Brazil and Mexico" in David Yoffe (ed) Beyond Free Trade. Firms, governments, and global competition Harvard Business School Press, Boston, Mass.
Teitel S. y Toumi F. (1987) "De la sustitución de importaciones a las exportaciones: la experiencia de las exportaciones de manufacturas de Argentina y Brasil" Desarrollo Económico, Buenos Aires, abril-junio.
UNCTAD (1990) Trade and Development Report Geneva.
UNCTAD (1991) "Transfer and development of technology in a changing world environment" (TD/B/C.6/153) Geneva.
UNCTAD (1993) World Investment Report 1993. Transnational Corporations and Integrated International Production, United Nations, New York.
UNCTC (1988) Transnational Corporations in World Development' Trends and Prospects, United Nations, New York.
UNCTC (1991a) World Investment Report 1991. The Triad in foreign direct investment United Nations, New York.
UNCTC (1991b) "Transnational banks and debt-equity conversion" New York
UNCTC (1992) "Foreign Direct Investment and Industrial Restructuring in Mexico" Current Studies No. 18, United Nations, New York.
Unger K. (1990), Las exportaciones mexicanas ante la reestructuración industrial internacional. La evidencia de las industrias química y automotriz México DF., Fondo de Cultura Econémica.
Vaitsos C. (1978) "Crisis in Regional Economic Cooperation (Integration) among

Developing Countries: A Survey' World Development June.
Womack J., Jones D. & Roos D. (1990) The machine that changed the world. New York, Macmillan.

Author Index

F = Footnote and T = Table

www.ingramcontent.com/pod-product-compliance
Ingram Content Group UK Ltd.
Pitfield, Milton Keynes, MK11 3LW, UK
UKHW020400010325
455677UK00021B/553

9 781138 983779